Care at the End of Life

Jeff Round
Editor

Care at the End of Life

An Economic Perspective

 **Adis**

Editor
Jeff Round
Lecturer in Health Economics
School of Social and Community Medicine
University of Bristol
Bristol
UK

ISBN 978-3-319-28266-4   ISBN 978-3-319-28267-1   (eBook)
DOI 10.1007/978-3-319-28267-1

Library of Congress Control Number: 2016933266

Springer Cham Heidelberg New York Dordrecht London

Printed on acid-free paper

Adis is a brand of Springer
Springer International Publishing AG Switzerland is part of Springer Science+Business Media (www.springer.com)

Preface

In the summer of 2010, I joined the Marie Curie Palliative Care Research Unit at University College London, then under the directorship of Dr Louise Jones. My role was to support the work of the unit as the in-house health economist. Before I started in the post, I expected that I would be doing many of the things a health economist does on a day-to-day basis when working in a clinical research setting – conducting economic evaluations of clinical trials or building decision models to investigate the cost-effectiveness of interventions. And though I did do these things, I quickly learned that there was a lot that economists didn't yet know about end of life care.

We still know very little about how much is being spent on end of life care or whether it is being spent to good effect. There is disagreement in the field about how best to measure outcomes for patients. There is no consensus on how (or even if) to include in evaluations costs and benefits not just for the patient but also of those close to them. There are also important questions to be answered about whether end of life care should be considered a special case, deserving of greater resources than other clinical areas. We must also ask whether the statistical and other methodological tools we have available are sufficient to answer our research questions, or do they need further development? The list goes on. In the years since I started working in the field, things have started to change. While it remains a minority interest, end of life and palliative care is increasingly attracting the attention of economists who are presented with a field of interesting, challenging and important questions.

To answer these questions is not simply an esoteric exercise, of interest merely to academics but few others. The way these questions are answered is fundamental in determining how resources are allocated across different patient groups. At the risk of hyperbole, in extremis the way these questions are answered can sometimes mean the difference between life and death for patients. Economists and others responsible for such decision-making have a duty to do so in an open and transparent fashion. I hope that readers will find something valuable in this book to guide them when faced with such questions. The chapters that follow are presented according to three broad themes, though many of the essays could fit comfortably in more than one of the themes.

The first theme addresses questions of methodology – what are we doing now, and how can we do things better in future? In Chap. 2 Johnston asks if the methods of economic evaluation are fit for purpose when considering end of life populations, while in Chap. 3 Hunter provides guidance on how to design and evaluate complex interventions, a common study type in this population. In Chap. 4 Bardsley provides an illustration of how we can best use evidence to inform policy and practice when randomised or other forms of clinical trial are not possible. Chapter 5 sees Flynn and colleagues present a novel method for preference elicitation at the end of life, and in Chap. 6 Baio and Leurent discuss the problems of dealing with missing data, with particular reference to studies involving patients at the end of life.

The second theme focuses on whether we need different tools for measuring outcomes and whether different decision rules should apply if the patient group is considered end of life. First there are two chapters on the measurement of outcomes for people at the end of life. Coast and colleagues make the case for the capabilities approach to outcome measurement in Chap. 7, while Sampson (Chap. 8) presents a challenge to the foundations on which current outcome measures and capability instruments are based. These might be read alongside my own thoughts, published elsewhere [1], to give an overview of the debate in this area. And irrespective of how we measure outcomes, we need to consider how to allocate those resources. In Chap. 9 McCabe et al. consider whether it is appropriate to give additional resources to patients at the end of life, while Deogaonkar et al. (Chap. 10) present the results of an empirical study examining societal preferences for resource allocation at the end of life.

This question is continued into the final section, on end of life care and society. Here Shah (Chap. 11) considers the broader evidence for societal preferences for differential allocation of resources to those at the end of life. In Chap. 12 Hulme et al. consider the economic impacts to those who provide informal care to people at the end of life. Attention then turns to children, where Stevens and Round (Chap. 13) discuss how best to measure outcomes when dealing with children with life-limiting and terminal illnesses. And finally, Round and Llewelyn (Chap. 14) offer thoughts on patient choice at the end of life – how do choice-driven health and social policy, as well as societal views of illness and autonomy, influence the care available to people at the end of life?

There are of course many questions that are not addressed in this volume – the actual cost of caring for people at the end of life, the ways in which care is produced in different settings, the systems and structures that determine what care is available to whom and so on. That is unavoidable – no single volume can cover everything. However, those questions that are considered here are among the most important facing economists and other researchers working in end of life care today – how should we conduct research in an often vulnerable population, is there something unique about the end of life population that requires different ways of thinking about the way we allocate resources and how does the care we give at the end of life relate to and influence the rest of society? My hope is that the answers and debate presented in this book inspire much more of the same and that more economists are encouraged to take an interest in this fascinating and vitally important clinical area.

Bristol, UK   Jeff Round
February, 2016

Reference

1. Round J (2012) Is a QALY still a QALY at the end of life? Journal of Health Economics 31(3): 521–552

Acknowledgements

There are a great many people responsible for the existence of this book. First and foremost, without the chapter authors there is no book, and so my greatest thanks go out to each of them. I hope readers will agree with me that the chapters they have provided are interesting, informative and challenging. I could not have asked for more. I would also like to thank the editorial and production teams at Springer for allowing me to publish the book in the first place and for their support (and patience) in taking the book from a germ of an idea to a reality. Though not directly involved with this book, the charity Marie Curie are also very deserving of a thank you for the support they have provided to me over the years. They were one of the first organisations to recognise the contribution health economists can make to improving care for people at the end of life. They have also provided funding for my PhD fees and never asked for anything other than academically robust and honest research in return. And finally I would like to thank Dr Louise Jones, whose support over the years with my work in this area has been invaluable. Her enthusiasm and encouragement have been vital to any achievements of mine in this field.

Contents

Part I Introduction

1 **Care of People When They Face Death and Dying:
Definitions, International Context and the
Development of Research** 3
Louise Jones

**Part II Methodological Challenges in Researching Patients
at the End of Life**

2 **The Application of Economic Evaluation Techniques to Studies
of Palliative and End-of-Life Care** 19
Bridget M. Johnston

3 **The Role of the Health Economist in the Evaluation
and Development of Complex Interventions in End-of-Life Care** 31
Rachael Maree Hunter

4 **Retrospective Analyses of End-of-Life Care
Using Large Data Sets** 47
Martin Bardsley

5 **Preference Elicitation at the End of Life** 63
Terry N. Flynn, Charlie Corke, and Elisabeth Huynh

6 **An Introduction to Handling Missing Data in Health
Economic Evaluations** 73
Gianluca Baio and Baptiste Leurent

Part III Measuring and Valuing Outcomes

7 **Measuring and Valuing Outcomes for Care
   at the End of Life: The Capability Approach**.   89
   Joanna Coast, Cara Bailey, Alastair Canaway, and Philip Kinghorn

8 **Identifying Objects of Value at the End of Life**   103
   Christopher J. Sampson

9 **Life at a Premium: Considering an End-of-Life Premium
   in Value-Based Reimbursement**.   123
   Christopher McCabe, Mike Paulden, James O'Mahony,
   Richard Edlin, and Anthony Culyer

10 **Eliciting Societal Views on the Value of Life-Extending
    Treatments Using Q Methodology**.   141
    Rohan Deogaonkar, Rachel Baker, Helen Mason,
    Neil McHugh, and Marissa Collins

Part IV End of Life Care and Society

11 **Does Society Place Special Value on End of Life Treatments?**   155
    Koonal Shah

12 **What About Informal Carers and Families?**   167
    Claire Hulme, Fiona Carmichael, and David Meads

13 **Measuring and Valuing Health-Related Quality of Life
    in Children with Terminal and Life-Limiting Illness**   177
    Katherine Stevens and Jeff Round

14 **Living Up to a Good Death: Complexities and Constraints
    in End of Life Choices**.   193
    Jeff Round and Henry Llewellyn

About the Editor

Jeff Round is a health economist in the School of Social and Community Medicine at the University of Bristol. From 2010, when he first joined the Marie Curie Palliative Care Research Unit at University College London, his primary research interests have been in the economics of end of life and palliative care. He has published on a range of topics relating to the economics of end of life care, including the costs of caring for people at the end of life, economic evaluations of complex interventions and the most appropriate methods for the measurement and valuation of outcomes. He is also interested in the role of informal caregivers at the end of life, which is the focus of his PhD research. His work in this area is focused on the impact of caregiving on the economic and labour market outcomes of caregivers as well as on their health and wellbeing.

Part I
Introduction

Chapter 1
Care of People When They Face Death and Dying: Definitions, International Context and the Development of Research

Louise Jones

1.1 Introduction

Consider for a moment how you might feel if you learned that you had a life-threatening illness and that, despite the best treatments being available, you were going to die as a result. It could happen.

There is no them and us where illness is concerned: we all have the potential to suffer and inevitably we all will die. We may be young; we may be old; we may have reached any stage of physiological or personal development. We may have family; we may feel alone. Death is inescapable; it is the only experience certain to be faced by all people of every background, of every faith, of every disposition across the globe. It will, unavoidably, happen to us all.

If you were told that you were dying, you might experience a wide range of emotions. Apart from feeling unwell, you might be afraid, sad and concerned for those you love. At any age, you might dread the idea of losing not only your strength but also a sense of control over your life and your future. You might wonder what will happen as the illness gets worse, as you experience death itself, and ponder whether there is anything further to experience in an afterlife. What might be of most importance to you in such circumstances? Immediate responses could reasonably include a desire for effective treatments, good medical and nursing care and support from family, friends and professionals.

It is human and humane to hope that, when ill health takes over, good healthcare will be available for every person. What exactly do we mean by good healthcare? We must start with an accurate diagnosis and an acceptable and affordable treatment plan. If we are lucky, this will be accompanied by care that is considerate of our wishes and feelings, that is compassionate and that takes account of the experiences

L. Jones
Marie Curie Palliative Care Research Department, UCL Division of Psychiatry,
University College London, London W1T 7NF, UK
e-mail: caroline.jones@ucl.ac.uk

© Springer International Publishing Switzerland 2016   3
J. Round (ed.), *Care at the End of Life: An Economic Perspective*,
DOI 10.1007/978-3-319-28267-1_1

of those who are close to us. We might hope to be helped to make sense of what is happening to us, to find meaning in how our diagnosis affects us both internally and externally. For those in whom illness is progressive and advanced, we might hope to face the approach of death in a manner that is appropriate to both who we are and who we have now become. We might hope to have reconciled any personal conflicts and to be able to leave a legacy to those left behind that enhances rather than diminishes their ability to lead fulfilling lives.

These are lofty aims indeed, but it is through reflections such as these that initiatives to understand and improve 'end-of-life care' have developed.

1.1.1   Confusing Terminology: 'End-of-Life', 'Palliative', 'Supportive' and 'Terminal' Care

For the purposes of health and social care planning in the UK, a consensus has been reached by a number of national organisations that a useful definition of 'end-of-life care' is care that 'helps all those with advanced, progressive, incurable illness to live as well as possible until they die. It enables the supportive and palliative care needs of both patient and family to be identified and met throughout the last phase of life and into bereavement. It includes management of pain and other symptoms and provision of psychological, social, spiritual and practical support' [1]. This definition incorporates both the term 'palliative' care, which is widely used internationally, and the term 'supportive' care; it also includes care in the last days and hours of life which is often referred to as 'terminal care'.

Care for any patient is said to be 'palliative' when the cure of their condition is no longer likely; with the knowledge that death is an unavoidable outcome, the focus of care shifts from the pursuit of recovery to the management of the condition and the needs of the patient and those close to them. Close attention is paid not only to the medical state of the patient (in particular, effective control of, e.g. pain, nausea and vomiting or shortness of breath) but also to addressing any psychological or spiritual distress and needs for help with practical, financial and family issues arising from the illness. The precise timing of when this occurs varies widely between patients, according to the extent of the disease and the nature of the diagnosis. It may happen many months in advance of death or when death is very close.

The World Health Organisation (WHO) states that 'palliative care' aims to prevent and relieve suffering through 'early identification and impeccable assessment and treatment of pain and other problems, physical, psychosocial and spiritual' [2]. Palliative care uses an interdisciplinary approach [3], drawing on the skills of doctors, nurses, social workers, chaplains, physiotherapists, and experts in psychological and complementary therapies. Palliative care does not hasten or postpone death. Rather it attempts to enable the patient and those close to them to maintain the best possible quality of life up until the point of death. This may include using a 'supportive care' approach to encourage people to achieve as much as they can both physically and emotionally whilst keeping their dependence on health and social care providers to a minimum [4].

As illness progresses and health deteriorates, a point is reached at which irreversible physical changes have taken place, and death within a short period has become inevitable. The patient has now entered the dying phase and 'terminal care' is needed. Detailed attention to pain and symptoms such as agitation and difficulty in breathing is required, as well as spiritual support for the patient and those close to them. Family members and close friends may remain in contact with the professional team after the death and thus be helped in adjusting to their bereavement.

Palliative care appropriate for children and their families is described by the WHO as 'the active total care of the child's body, mind and spirit. It begins when life-threatening or life-limiting illness is diagnosed and continues regardless of whether or not a child receives treatment directed at the disease' [5]. Using a broad multidisciplinary approach, care includes the family and makes use of the community resources that are available; it can be implemented successfully even if resources are limited, and can be provided in tertiary care facilities, in community health centres and in children's homes. Little work has been done to investigate quality of life in child populations. Stevens and Round (Chap. 13) provide an overview of what is available and how it might be relevant when working in end-of-life care research.

1.1.2 Timing and Transitions in Care

The point at which end-of-life care becomes appropriate is the subject of much debate (see Coast et al., Chap. 7). The main problem is the difficulty in identifying in real time when the end stage of an illness has begun. In practice, many people only receive palliative care when active curative treatment ceases and standard therapies have failed. This point of transition may be very difficult to recognise and negotiate for patients, families and professionals who are involved in their care. It can also be difficult to detect when the patient has progressed to the terminal phase and is about to die. Accurate prognostication remains elusive, and international efforts continue to establish prognostic tools that have reasonable accuracy in helping clinicians to predict how much longer a person who is gravely ill may survive [6].

In the UK, using guidance from the General Medical Council, a consensus has been reached that people are considered to be approaching the 'end of life' when they are likely to die within the next 12 months. This includes people whose death is imminent (expected within a few hours or days) and those with (a) advanced, progressive, incurable conditions; (b) general frailty and co-existing conditions that mean they are expected to die within 12 months; (c) existing conditions if they are at risk of dying from a sudden acute crisis in their condition; and (d) life-threatening acute conditions caused by sudden catastrophic events. In addition, for some people the appropriate start for end-of-life care might be at the time of diagnosis of a condition that usually carries a poor prognosis, for example, motor neurone disease or advanced liver disease [7].

In some countries there is a trend for the early introduction of a more holistic or 'palliative' approach to care, in parallel to optimal medical or surgical treatment of the main condition. Indeed there is some evidence that those people receiving palliative care alongside active therapies in cancer have better prognostic outcomes [8]. In children, a wide range of congenital and acquired conditions are life-threatening and life-limiting [9], and palliative care tends to be offered from the point of diagnosis, alongside other treatments. Many parents wish for active attempts at curative treatment for their child to persist right up until the dying phase whilst also accepting palliative care [10]. Similar attitudes towards their own care may also be seen amongst adults, and it is important to respect individual coping styles in the face of life-limiting and life-threatening illness.

1.1.3   Who Delivers End-of-Life Care?

Historically, 'palliative care' as a specialty developed mainly from the desire of clinicians working in the hospice movement to offer a pain-free and peaceful death to those affected by terminal cancer. However, it is now increasingly appreciated that good end-of-life care, including symptom control and holistic support of patients and families, is applicable not only to those with advanced cancer but also to all those with advanced progressive conditions, such as end-stage heart failure [11], renal failure [12], dementia [13] and other neurological disorders [14].

End-of-life care may be offered in all settings directly to patients and families either by teams who have received specialist training or by other professionals who are specialists in their own fields but are guided by palliative care experts. The provision of a specialist in end-of-life care to join and integrate fully with clinical teams in all specialties may not be necessary. It may also not be a realistic aim because of the sheer numbers of patients involved and the relative lack of clinicians who specialise in end-of-life care. A more practicable model is the use of specialists in an advisory capacity to train and support professionals in other specialties (e.g. nephrology, cardiology, hepatology) on general principles of good end-of-life care whilst being available to provide specialist advice themselves for complex cases. This style of working can be implemented with the co-operation of other clinical teams in hospitals or in the community (at home or in care homes). An example of this is the increasingly considered option of a maximum conservative management approach to end-stage renal disease in which supportive care is optimised by nephrologists with input from palliative care specialists [15]. In both developed and developing countries, a substantial proportion of end-of-life care is provided by independent hospice services [16]. In the UK, many hospices are funded by the voluntary sector. In the USA, Medicare and private insurance plans fund hospice care often in dedicated buildings that may or may not be run by profit-making organisations [17]. Dedicated hospice facilities are usually reserved for the specialist management of people with complex end-of-life needs or for those in whom death is imminent, and demand for this kind of care may grow as the population ages.

1.1.4 Care Worldwide

In the developed world, most people have access to healthcare provided by either the state or their own investment or a mixture of the two. Diagnostic skills and effective treatments for many diseases have improved. As a consequence, death has come to be regarded as an unacceptable outcome to be avoided, rather than as a natural end point to be embraced. Social care needs are often addressed by a combination of support from family, friends and what is provided by the state (Chap. 12). In the less developed world, for complex cultural, economic and political reasons, good health and good care when illness supervenes remain not fully achievable for many people. As a result, care is often provided within family structures, and people are more accustomed to the sight of the sick and the dying.

An overarching guide for caring for people at the end of life across the world has been set out by the WHO, and data on care needs and provision can be found in a recent report prepared with the Worldwide Palliative Care Alliance [18]. A four-pillar public health model is recommended comprising (i) appropriate government policies (e.g. a national health system, essential medicines and education), (ii) adequate drug availability, (iii) the education of health professionals and (iv) the implementation of palliative care at all levels of healthcare provision. The WHO recognises that morphine is an essential medicine for the treatment of pain and that it is safe, effective, inexpensive and easy to administer in settings where resources are scarce [19]. However data from the Global Access to Pain Relief Initiative [20] indicate that more than 2.9 million people worldwide die each year in moderate or severe pain without access to adequate pain treatment. The Global Opioid Policy Initiative [21] recognises that in some countries pain relief is restricted by a lack of opioid analgesics. Following a successful project to evaluate the availability and accessibility of opioids and the regulatory barriers that exist in Europe, the European Society for Medical Oncology (ESMO) and the European Association for Palliative Care (EAPC) are expanding their research to areas where data are scarce, in particular Africa, Asia, the Middle East, Latin America and the Caribbean. This work involves collaboration with the Union for International Cancer Control, the Pain and Policy Studies Group of the University of Wisconsin and the WHO, together with a consortium of 17 international oncology and palliative care societies. The results are awaited.

1.2 Challenges in End-of-Life Care Research

Research in end-of-life care is a relatively new discipline and has developed gradually since the growth of the hospice movement in the 1970s and the recognition of palliative care as a medical specialty in the late 1980s. End-of-life care is provided clinically by practitioners such as doctors, nurses, social workers, chaplains and therapists working together to address issues such as the control of pain and other symptoms, caring, quality of life and the practical and existential issues surrounding death and bereavement. As a consequence, research in the field has attracted a number of thinkers from across medicine, nursing, social science, sociology, philosophy, theology and beyond. Through the coming together of interested people from this wide range of disciplines, a community of academics has developed to lead thinking in this area. The trail was blazed internationally by colleagues in North America, with the first International Congress on Palliative Care being held in Canada in 1976, and the European Association for Palliative Care, which held its first international congress in Paris in 1990. The first national UK Palliative Care Congress was held in 1995.

Early research was largely qualitative, based on observation and interviews. Studies were small, data collection and analysis initially lacked sophistication, and many simply anecdotal case reports appeared. A large volume of literature described the needs of the population, but little research was undertaken to attempt to devise and test ways in which to address and meet these needs. Crucially, many of the issues that had to be tackled were complex and required imaginative research designs to unpick them. In addition, there remained key clinical questions that required a robust evidence base and might have been answered best using quantitative (rather than qualitative) data, obtained through randomised controlled trials or a mixed methods approach, including what we now refer to as health services research. At first, research focussed on the needs of people with advanced cancer, as this was the population amongst which palliative care was first developed and for which it was provided. Whilst this area remains important, research has now developed to consider the needs of those with other advanced, progressive, life-limiting illnesses (in particular dementia and end-stage organ failure), including those found in children.

The challenges in conducting high-quality research in end-of-life care should not be thought insurmountable. Many are very similar to those encountered in mental health and primary care studies. All seek to understand vulnerable populations who may be difficult to identify and contact, are based in the community and have complex and deteriorating health and social care needs. These populations require complex pharmacological management and also present issues of capacity and informed consent.

In the formative days of the specialty, issues around costs of care and economics were considered by only a few researchers or service providers. Some palliative care specialists may have been reluctant to accept that care in such a sensitive and fundamental area should be subject to pragmatism and the consideration of money. We are now more aware that it is important to understand not only the cost-effectiveness of different treatments but also the costs of care to health and social care providers, to families and other informal carers and to wider society. Difficult decisions must be made on how finite resources are allocated, and there are many competing interests that must be balanced (see Johnston, Chap. 2). Such issues touch on the fundamental values of a society and how its members think about the sick, the vulnerable and those who are dying.

1.2.1 Complexity and Interventions to Improve Care

People who are approaching death and their families often have complex clinical and social care needs. Specialist end-of-life care aims to manage this complexity and the issues associated with it. Some solutions may be simple, but in general a number of simple measures may be needed, and these, working separately or together, comprise a 'complex intervention' [22, 23]. It may not always be clear how each component operates; it may be difficult to know which component is active and which other components are needed for this activity to produce results (see Hunter, Chap. 3). 'Active' components may be thought of as those that can be linked specifically to the likely effects of an intervention on resulting outcomes and without which the intervention would be ineffective [24].

Recognising the importance to many specialties of understanding complex health and social care interventions, in 2000 the UK Medical Research Council brought together experts from a range of academic disciplines to consider methods to develop and test such interventions. Their initial publication described four linear phases, similar to those that might be understood in the introduction of a relatively simple pharmacological treatment to market, starting with theoretical modelling and ending with large-scale marketing and surveillance [22]. However, for complex interventions concerning the delivery of care at a number of levels, often in the community, such a linear model may be too simplistic.

The experts reconvened and in 2008 published more sophisticated guidance [23]. This allowed a more flexible approach, dovetailing the theoretical underpinning stages and qualitative data with iterative processes. They also recommended including sociological and behavioural theory and realist rather than positivist approaches where needed. They suggested that feasibility and acceptability phases could be longer and that there might be much to be learned from naturalistic experiments. More imaginative trial designs were also suggested, such as cluster randomisation and the use of wait-list controls and stepped-wedge approaches. The experts also stated that collecting qualitative data to understand the experience of receiving interventions that are tested using quantitative methods might provide valuable information, especially at the feasibility stage.

To apply these principles and develop them further and specifically for research in end-of-life care, building on the MRC recommendations [23], the MORECare study [25] sought to develop evidence-based guidance on the best methods for the design and conduct of palliative care research. They conducted systematic literature reviews and convened expert groups, using consensus methods to identify challenges. The work has led to the publication of the MORECare guidance statement, which describes 36 best practice solutions for methods in end-of-life care research, for use alongside existing statements for reporting studies. Topics covered include participation and recruitment, ethics, attrition, integration of mixed methods, complex outcomes and economic evaluation.

1.2.2   Qualitative and Quantitative Research

Qualitative and quantitative methods, used individually or in combination in mixed methods work, are both valuable in addressing research questions of relevance to end-of-life care. Qualitative research is descriptive, inductive and configurative. It enables the understanding of the personal perspective, and rigorous and sophisticated methods of analysis are now widely used. It illuminates areas that would otherwise have remained unknown, draws out concepts that might have been thought of as unimportant and shows the richness and diversity of the human experience and condition (see Flynn et al., Chap. 5). Brought together from a number of sources, it allows us to understand the commonalities and differences in experiences of illness. Methods might include interview techniques to collect narratives and allow patients to tell their own stories of illness and observation of real-life situations (comparable to the methodology of anthropologists), asking patients and families to keep reflective diaries, to take photographs or to communicate through social media to enhance our means of collecting rich and diverse data.

By contrast, quantitative methods are hypothesis driven; they are unavoidably reductive and use a summative approach and standardised measures to assess outcomes. They may use longitudinal or cross-sectional data (for an example, see Bardsley, Chap. 4), and they have the capacity to assess causes and related effects, thereby paving the way for the testing of possible solutions to problems. Empirical data can be collected through the use of cohort studies or trials. High-quality experimental evidence is derived from data generated by randomised controlled trials of treatments or complex interventions to improve care. The robustness of the evidence is based on the rationale that randomisation is the best method of minimising bias as it takes account of all variables, both the known and the unknown, that might affect the outcome of a particular intervention. Trials test whether an intervention works in the population that enters that trial. If large numbers are used, this increases the robustness of the results. Data using similar outcome measures from several trials attempting to test the same intervention can be combined in meta-analyses to test further the strength of the findings.

There are particular challenges in conducting trials with populations who are vulnerable and who have complex needs. These are well described in a paper from an Australian expert group [26] that discusses the appropriate selection of trial design and the consideration of ethical issues in undertaking research with people who are vulnerable as a consequence of severe illness. Technical issues include the choice of appropriate follow-up data collection times and possible or even likely loss to follow-up due to attrition from failing health or death (Baio and Leurent address missing data in end-of-life research in Chap. 6). Outcome measures should be kept short, meaningful and easy to complete and might include the use of validated observational scales and carer-rated proxy measures. It is common that multiple outcomes are assessed, often using different measures across studies; however, this heterogeneity hampers the extent to which meta-analyses are possible. There are also issues in the transfer of data across populations that differ according to diagnosis or age;

particular caution is needed in extrapolating outcomes relevant in adult populations to those for children [27]. In general, sample sizes may be too small, and large-scale multisite studies are recommended to enhance the robustness of results.

1.2.3 Database Work

Interest in the conduct of epidemiological studies using publicly available data is growing. In the UK, the government has supported the establishment of a National End of Life Care Intelligence Network [28]. This uses public health research techniques to explore, through national healthcare databases, such questions as the prevalence of different types of cancer and other advanced progressive illnesses, mortality statistics, the reporting of causes of death, hospital admission figures and consultation and prescription rates in primary care settings. There have also been attempts to meet the challenge of incorporating national data on provision and use of social care [29]. Such work requires the exploration of analytic techniques that take account of the complexity of circumstances surrounding care towards the end of life. There are also methodological challenges that arise when working with large databases, and much can be learned from experts in epidemiology and public health research.

1.2.4 Combining Qualitative and Quantitative Data

The use of mixed methods in research brings together what we learn from the qualitative perspective about the patient experience with quantitative data derived from trials or cohort studies. This combined approach provides opportunities to increase our understanding of how or why, as well as whether, a treatment or intervention does or does not work. Both the MRC and MORECare guidelines encourage the use of qualitative evidence to give greater depth to quantitative findings. Hearing about the patient's experience of a new approach to care may enhance our understanding of the hard data collected in a trial and inform our understanding of why some interventions work in practice and some do not. Indeed, it is becoming recognised that it may be helpful to incorporate knowledge from behavioural science and sociology literature in the early development and theoretical modelling phases of intervention development. Intervention design may also be informed by using qualitative data on patients' views to guide decisions on which components to include and which to leave out; there is some evidence that interventions designed in this way might be more likely to be effective [30]. Such increased knowledge is likely to be useful in appreciating and interpreting data on costs of interventions in healthcare and in identifying which components of interventions might provide best value for money. Such economic benefits may offset the increase in costs of carrying out mixed methods research which may involve more lengthy processes and larger investigating teams with experts in both qualitative and quantitative methods.

Winning the funding for research in open competition relies on the quality of the research methods being high and the skill mix of the research team being appropriate to answer the questions posed in a manner that is robust and meaningful. Cross-disciplinary input is very valuable and there is much to be gained from experts in palliative care seeking collaborators with specific methodological expertise in fields such as behavioural science, sociology, anthropology, statistics and health economics to join them in the planning and conduct of research. Nowadays, researchers are also encouraged to listen to the public voice and include patient representatives on study teams throughout the research process. Strong support for such patient and public involvement is shown, for example, by the UK INVOLVE initiative [31]. Public opinion now has some influence on the themes for research prioritised by funders, for example, some agencies work with the James Lind Alliance to garner views and develop broad research questions [32, 33]. Participation of patients and the public in these ways increases our understanding of what might be important to any of us when we become ill and thus the areas of concern in which a research budget might be best put to use.

1.2.5   Quality of Life in People Who Face Deteriorating Health

The determination of what it is that constitutes 'quality of life' is central to research in health economics. Health-related quality of life is a key outcome that economists consider in their evaluations of care and treatments. The use of standardised outcome measures enables comparisons to be made across treatments, across diseases and across populations. The most commonly used units of assessment are quality-adjusted life-years (QALYs), usually derived from the EQ5D scale [34] completed by patients who rate the state of their health at a fixed point in time. This measure relies on the central precept that improved health is possible. In those who face illness where the prognosis is poor and the outcome of death in the near future is very likely, their health is deteriorating rather than improving; they may also have a limited time left to live. It may thus be necessary to consider new ways of assessing quality of life in those who face advanced progressive illnesses (again, see Coast et al., Chap. 7). Effective analysis of these issues may be aided by the collection of qualitative data to elicit the views of patients and families on what is important to people when they are well, or are unwell and expecting recovery, or are unwell and facing end-stage disease and approaching death.

1.2.6   Quality of Life and Capacity

With those who are relatively well, even in their illness, it is easy to discuss and explore those areas of life that might be said to enhance its quality. But there are some situations in which people may temporarily or permanently lose their ability to communicate. In both children and adults, there are a number of different scenarios that may occur: capacity may not yet be present (neonates and children), or it may be fluctuant (drugs, brain tumours), deteriorating (progressive neurological diseases), reversible (delirium, infection) or irreversibly lost (dementia). Towards the end of life, capacity may fluctuate, and it may be irreversibly lost in the hours immediately before death [35].

When mental capacity is lacking, it may not be appropriate to focus on subjective aspects of quality of life that rely on health and an ability to function and can be reported by patients themselves. Of more importance may be objective considerations such as the processes of care and how care may be delivered and received; these may be assessed by observation or by asking proxies to complete assessments on the patient's behalf. Care should take into account any knowledge of preferences expressed before capacity was compromised, and attempts should be made to ensure careful assessment and management of symptoms including effective pain control, attention to spiritual needs and involvement of family and close friends in decisions affecting the care of the patient [35].

1.2.7 Health Economics and End-of-Life Care

In this book, we focus on health economic issues that arise during the last phases of life, when palliative, supportive and terminal care are needed. As the population ages, more people worldwide are living with and dying from advanced progressive illnesses. Careful thought must be given to the appropriate use of resources for their health and social care (see McCabe et al., Chap. 9; Deogaonkar et al., Chap. 10; and Shah, Chap. 11 for discussions on understanding societal views towards end-of-life care).

It is important to bear in mind the views, circumstances and available resources of the societies in which care is being undertaken and in which illness and death are being experienced by both patients and those who are close to them. How much a society is able and prepared to spend on those who are sick and face approaching death may differ; views will vary across (and within) continents and countries and between faith and value systems. Not all societies at all times will have the scope to consider human suffering from illness in the same ways.

In the following chapters, we shall explore in depth the conceptual challenges for health economics by thinking about the complex issues raised by life-threatening illnesses, death and dying. We shall consider the methodological challenges of conducting robust and meaningful health economic research. We shall learn about cost-effectiveness and cost utility, as well as considering issues of equity and the allocation of resources that in healthcare are likely to be insufficient to always meet the demand meaningfully.

Reflecting on the concepts and problems that we have explored in this chapter, it is reasonable to assert that the value of meaningful, considered and well-delivered care at the end of life should be measured in the reduction of physical, psychological and existential suffering for those who face life-threatening illness and their families, as well as in better outcomes and experiences in bereavement for those who are left behind.

References

1. Commissioning End of Life Care: initial action of commissioners (2011) Collaborative publication from the National Council for Palliative Care (NCPC), Dying Matters, NHS National End of Life Care Programme, Public Health England National End of Life Care Intelligence Network. This publication is available as a web-based resource and also as a download from the NCPC and National End of Life Care Programme websites: www.ncpc.org.uk. www.endoflifecareforadults.nhs.uk
2. World Health Organisation (2015) http://www.who.int/cancer/palliative/definition/en/. Accessed 20 July 2015
3. European Association for Palliative Care (2010) http://www.eapcnet.eu/Corporate/AbouttheEAPC/Definitionandaims.aspx. Accessed 20 July 2015
4. UK National Council for Palliative Care (NCPC). http://www.ncpc.org.uk/palliative-care-explained. Accessed 20 July 2015
5. World Health Organisation (2015) Definition palliative care for children. http://www.who.int/cancer/palliative/definition/en/. Accessed 20 July 2015
6. Gwilliam B, Keeley V, Todd C, Gittens M, Roberts C, Kelly L, Barclay S, Stone P (2011) Improving prognostication in advanced cancer: development of the Prognosis in Palliative care Study (PIPS) predictor models. BMJ 25;343:d4920. doi: 10.1136/bmj.d4920
7. Treatment and care towards the end of life: good practice in decision making. General Medical Council. Published 20 May 2010 http://www.gmc-uk.org/End_of_life.pdf_32486688.pdf
8. Greer JA, Jackson VA, Meier DE, Temel JS (2013) Early integration of palliative care services with standard oncology care for patients with advanced cancer. CA Cancer J Clin 63(5):349–363. doi:10.3322/caac.21192, Epub 2013 Jul 15. Review
9. Hain R, Devins M (2011) Directory of life-limiting conditions. Cardiff. http://www.together-forshortlives.org.uk/assets/0000/7089/Directory_of_LLC_v1.3.pdf
10. Bluebond-Langner M, Belasco JB, Goldman A, Belasco C (2007) Understanding parents' approaches to care and treatment of children with cancer when standard therapy has failed. J Clin Oncol 25(17):2414–2419
11. Browne S, Macdonald S, May CR, Macleod U, Mair FS (2014) Patient, carer and professional perspectives on barriers and facilitators to quality care in advanced heart failure. PLoS One 9(3):e93288. doi:10.1371/journal.pone.0093288. eCollection 2014
12. Kane PM, Vinen K, Murtagh FE (2013) Palliative care for advanced renal disease: a summary of the evidence and future direction. Palliat Med 27(9):817–821. doi:10.1177/0269216313491796, Epub 2013 Jun 13
13. Hendriks SA, Smalbrugge M, Hertogh CM, van der Steen JT (2014) Dying with dementia: symptoms, treatment, and quality of life in the last week of life. J Pain Symptom Manage 47(4):710–720. doi:10.1016/j.jpainsymman.2013.05.015, Epub 2013 Jul 31
14. Boersma I, Mivasaki J, Kutner J, Kluger B (2014) Palliative care and neurology: time for a paradigm shift. Neurology. doi:10.1212/WNL.0000000000000674. Epub 2 July 2014.
15. Carson RC, Juszczak M, Davenport A, Burns A (2009) Is maximum conservative management an equivalent treatment option to dialysis for elderly patients with significant comorbid disease? Clin J Am Soc Nephrol 4(10):1611–1619
16. Wright M, Wood J, Lynch T, Clark D (2008) Mapping levels of palliative care development: a global view. J Pain Symptom Manage 35:469–485

17. Candy B, Holman A, Leurent B, Davis S, Jones L (2011) Hospice care delivered at home, in nursing homes and in dedicated hospice facilities: a systematic review of quantitative and qualitative evidence. Int J Nurs Stud 48(1):121–133. doi:10.1016/j.ijnurstu.2010.08.003, Epub 2010 Sep 16

18. Global Atlas of Palliative Care (2014) Worldwide Palliative Care Alliance and World Health Organisation. http://www.who.int/nmh/Global_Atlas_of_Palliative_Care.pdf

19. World Health Organisation (2004) In: Davies E, Higginson IJ (eds) The solid facts palliative care. http://www.euro.who.int/document/E82931.pdf. Archived by WebCite® at http://www.webcitation.org/5o4n0gQIJ

20. Global Access to Pain Relief Initiative (http://www.uicc.org/programmes/gapri) part of the Union for International Cancer Control

21. Cherny NI, Cleary J, Scholten W, Radbruch L, Torode J (2013) The Global Opioid Policy Initiative (GOPI) project to evaluate the availability and accessibility of opioids for the management of cancer pain in Africa, Asia, Latin America and the Caribbean, and the Middle East: introduction and methodology. Ann Oncol 24(Suppl 11):xi7–xi13

22. MRC (2000) A framework for the development and evaluation of RCTs for complex interventions to improve health. Medical Research Council, London, p 18

23. MRC (2008) Developing and evaluating complex interventions: new guidance Medical Research Council. http://www.mrc.ac.uk/documents/pdf/complex-interventions-guidance/

24. McCleary N, Duncan EM, Stewart F, Francis JJ (2013) Active ingredients are reported more often for pharmacologic than non-pharmacologic interventions: an illustrative review of reporting practices in titles and abstracts. Trials 14:146. doi:10.1186/1745-6215-14-146

25. The MORECare study. http://www.kcl.ac.uk/lsm/research/divisions/cicelysaunders/research/studies/morecare.aspx

26. Shelby-James TM, Hardy J, Agar M, Yates P, Mitchell G, Sanderson C, Luckett T, Abernethy AP, Currow DC (2012) Designing and conducting randomized controlled trials in palliative care: a summary of discussions from the 2010 clinical research forum of the Australian Palliative Care Clinical Studies Collaborative. Palliat Med 26(8):1042–1047. doi:10.1177/0269216311417036, Epub 2011 Aug 15

27. Bluebond-Langner M, Beecham E, Candy B, Langner R, Jones L (2013) Preferred place of death for children and young people with life-limiting and life-threatening conditions: a systematic review of the literature and recommendations for future inquiry and policy. Palliat Med 27(8):705–713. doi:10.1177/0269216313483186, Epub 2013 Apr 23. Review

28. Public Health England: the National End of Life Care Intelligence Network. http://www.endoflifecare-intelligence.org.uk/home

29. Bardsley M, Billings J, Dixon J, Georghiou T, Lewis GH, Steventon A (2011) Predicting who will use intensive social care: case finding tools based on linked health and social care data. Age Ageing 40(2):265–270. doi:10.1093/ageing/afq181, Epub 2011 Jan 20

30. Candy B, King M, Jones L, Oliver S (2011) Using qualitative synthesis to explore heterogeneity of complex interventions. BMC Med Res Methodol 11:124. doi:10.1186/1471-2288-11-124

31. NHS National Institute for Health Research INVOLVE initiative. http://www.invo.org.uk/

32. The James Lind Alliance. http://www.lindalliance.org/

33. The palliative and end of life care priority setting partnership final report (2015). http://www.palliativecarepsp.org.uk/wp-content/uploads/2015/01/PeolcPSP_Final_Report.pdf

34. http://www.euroqol.org/about-eq-5d.html

35. Round J, Sampson EL, Jones L (2014) A framework for understanding quality of life in individuals without capacity. Qual Life Res 23(2):477–484. doi:10.1007/s11136-013-0500-z, Epub 2013 Aug 22

Part II
Methodological Challenges in
Researching Patients at the End of Life

Chapter 2
The Application of Economic Evaluation Techniques to Studies of Palliative and End-of-Life Care

Bridget M. Johnston

2.1 Background

Healthcare systems throughout the world are facing enormous difficulties arising from the growing costs associated with shifting demographics, increasing consumer expectations and technological advances. Policy makers face a considerable dilemma – how best to respond to limitless demand for finite resources. In order to maximise health outcomes subject to their budget constraint, policy makers cannot base decisions exclusively upon evidence that the intervention or programme will work; they also require evidence that the intervention is the most efficient use of available resources and provides value for money. Economic evaluation has become an important tool for this purpose because it facilitates the description and comparison of the benefits and costs of competing uses of resources within a common framework [1]. Despite increased emphasis on establishing value for money, the evidence base for the cost-effectiveness of palliative and end-of-life care interventions remains small [2, 3].

Interventions at the end of life are often complex and by their very nature will give rise to difficulties in identifying, measuring and valuing inputs and consequences for the purpose of conducting economic evaluations. In the first instance, many palliative care services are highly tailored to meet each patient's needs and preferences, making it difficult to specify what they will or should contain [4]. Services are also targeted towards highly heterogeneous patient groups, with a range of illnesses and care needs. Because patients receiving the interventions are living with an advanced illness, many will die during the study period (see Baio and Leurent on missing data, Chap. 6). Additionally, services may be delivered across a

B.M. Johnston
Centre for Health Policy and Management, Trinity College Dublin,
Dublin, Ireland
e-mail: BJOHNST@tcd.ie

© Springer International Publishing Switzerland 2016

J. Round (ed.), *Care at the End of Life: An Economic Perspective*,
DOI 10.1007/978-3-319-28267-1_2

number of care settings, and organisation can be significantly influenced by location, cultural norms and the history of service provision. As a result, it can be difficult for researchers evaluating palliative or end-of-life care to design robust studies that account for issues such as patient capacity to consent or participate and gatekeeping by healthcare professionals or patients' family and friends and allow for comparison between control and intervention groups.

Economic evaluation of palliative care services remains limited due to a number of challenges related to capturing accurate information about all relevant activities and costs, in addition to identifying, measuring and valuing outcomes. Against the backdrop of increased competition for limited resources, however, methods must be developed which overcome these difficulties and accurately measure the cost-effectiveness of these interventions. Evidence from economic evaluations would not only make it possible to evaluate the value for money of palliative care relative to other healthcare activities but also whether the service models currently funded are the most efficient use of resources. Otherwise, there is a risk that these interventions could lose out on funding when competing with services for which there is better evidence about cost-effectiveness.

This chapter will provide a brief introduction to the use of health economics in palliative and end-of-life care, focusing primarily on the challenges in conducting economic evaluations in the area and the alternative approaches and strategies proposed by various researchers to address these difficulties.

2.2   Study Design

Palliative care services have been expanding worldwide with the objective of providing a model of care that addresses the physical, emotional and spiritual needs of patients at the end of life and the wellbeing of their family and caregivers. In addition, the principles of palliative care are now recognised as being useful throughout the course of any life-limiting illness and not only for patients who are not responding to curative treatments [5]. However, there is limited evidence available to aid in the development of clinical guidelines, service provision and treatments in palliative care.

Although researchers have recommended that it is feasible to conduct methodological robust clinical trials for palliative care interventions [6], funding is poor [7] and has been hindered by a lack of consensus about research guidelines. While efforts have been made to develop good practice solutions for evaluation studies [8], it remains difficult to carry out randomised controlled trials (RCTs) in end-of-life and palliative care owing to a number of methodological and ethical issues [8, 9]:

- Services are personalised and vary between patients, making it difficult to standardise the design and delivery of care.
- Frail or cognitively impaired patients may lack the capacity to consent.
- Relevant outcomes can be difficult to capture when patients lack capacity.
- An overprotective culture can result in gatekeeping by healthcare professionals.
- Clinicians may have ethical concerns about enrolling patients in studies where they may not receive a comprehensive range of services.
- Varying levels of willingness to prioritise research amongst healthcare professionals.
- Patients are living with advanced illness and often die before the study is completed.

These challenges are not exclusive to RCTs and are often cited as being barriers to all types of research with this patient cohort. Consequently, the potential for many forms of high-quality clinical research may be constrained by poor recruitment, bias, high attrition and insufficient sample size.

Identifying and avoiding bias in studies is crucial as this reduces the potential for errors in estimating the effect of the intervention. Two significant sources of bias in palliative care research are selection bias and confounding [10]. Selection bias arises when proper randomisation of the sample has not been achieved [11]. This may be the result of factors such as high attrition amongst participants; a tendency for healthier patients to be agreeable to participate in research; eligibility criteria limiting the number of potential participants; or self-selection, i.e. the decision about access to an intervention may be correlated in some way with characteristics of patients, caregivers or clinicians. Confounding occurs when the outcome of interest is correlated with the factors that influence selection into the intervention group, making it difficult to determine whether a direct cause-effect relationship exists between the outcomes observed and the intervention. Potentially cofounding variables in palliative care research include relatively straightforward factors such as age or gender, in additional to those factors which are not as readily observed or measured such as symptom burden, individual preferences for aggressive interventions at the end of life and care setting [10, 12].

So what can be done to facilitate the design of robust research and collection of the relevant data required for conducting an economic evaluation? Guidance for evaluating complex interventions offers a number of suggestions for addressing some of the methodological difficulties researchers may encounter when attempting to measure their impact. Although RCTs are often regarded as the 'gold standard' for assessing the impact of an intervention, alternative experimental design (Box 2.1) and adopting a nonrandomised approach are both appropriate and acceptable strategies in many instances [13] (for an example of this, see Bardsley, Chap. 4, in this volume).

Box 2.1: Study Design Alternatives

Individually randomised trials – Individuals are randomly allocated to receive either an experimental treatment or an alternative such as usual care, placebo or placed on a waiting list.

Cluster randomised trials – Groups of individuals such as a community, medical practice or hospital are randomly allocated an experimental intervention. This approach may prevent contamination of the control group, therefore reducing the risk of biased estimates of effect size. However, cluster trials tend to have much larger sample sizes than individually randomised trials and are vulnerable to recruitment bias [14].

Stepped wedge designs – Randomisation is achieved through the phasing of implementation of the experimental intervention. This type of design may address ethical concerns about patients not receiving an intervention that appears to be effective.

Preference trials – When patients have very strong preferences, it may be appropriate for intervention allocation to be determined by those preferences or for patients to be randomised before the consent process begins. Taking preferences into account can reduce the likelihood of recruitment or adherence issues arising from patients not being allocated the treatment they prefer.

Propensity scoring – Allows for estimation of treatment effect when randomisation is not possible through the pairing of treatment and control units with similar values on the propensity score. This reduces the impact of selection bias in the estimation of a treatment effect.

N-of-1 trials – Randomised trials in individual patients developed to determine the most appropriate treatment choice. Such approaches attempt to address variability in individual responses to treatments rather than extrapolating trial results across large populations.

Adapted from Craig et al. [13]

There is another pertinent issue to consider in both the development of and reporting about studies that examine the effects of palliative care interventions. Crucially, studies need to report on comparisons between clearly defined new models of care and existing standards for delivering care [15]. It should be clear exactly *what* is being compared with *what*. While robust study design is an important consideration when approaching economic evaluation, it is only one element, and careful attention must be provided to fully capturing the inputs to and consequences of the intervention being delivered.

Clinicians also play a key role in supporting research into palliative care interventions; however, there can be barriers to their participation that will need to be adequately addressed during the design and implementation and of any study. For example, they may have ethical concerns about involving people with advanced

Table 2.1 Types of economic evaluation

Is there a comparison of two or more alternatives?	Are both costs and benefits analysed?		
	No: partial evaluations		Yes
No	**Examines only outcomes**	**Examines only costs**	Cost and outcome evaluation of a single treatment
	Outcome description	Cost description	
Yes	Effectiveness or efficacy analysis	Cost analysis	**Full economic evaluation**
			Cost-minimisation analysis
			Cost-effectiveness analysis
			Cost-benefit analysis
			Cost-utility analysis

Adapted from Drummond et al. [19]

illness and their caregivers in research if they believe that the process is either burdensome or of questionable benefit to the individual [16]. Further to this, clinicians may also question the appropriateness of enrolling patients with limited life expectancy in RCTs if it could result in restricted access to services that may be of benefit to them [15]. Concerns have also been raised about 'gatekeeping' by clinical staff which can prevent researchers from accessing potential study participants [17, 18]. However, assuming that patients or caregivers should not be offered the opportunity to participate in research simply because of the nature of their illness may not be ethical, even if the intention is to protect patients from perceived distress [8]. In order to reduce the potential for gatekeeping, researchers need to develop approaches to recruitment and data collection that address potential sources of concern for clinical staff while emphasising recent findings demonstrating that participating in research can be a positive experience for patients and their caregivers [16].

2.3 Methods of Economic Evaluation and Their Application to Palliative or End-of-Life Care Interventions

A number of different approaches to economic evaluation are utilised in healthcare, each with different characteristics. Partial evaluations only consider some elements of costs or outcomes and, therefore, do not allow for comparison across treatments. Full evaluations consider both costs and outcomes and compare these across alternative interventions [19] (Table 2.1).

There are four types of full economic evaluation: cost-minimisation analysis, cost-effectiveness analysis, cost-benefit analysis and cost-utility analysis. Each technique measures the consequences of healthcare interventions differently; therefore, the choice of which approach to take will be influenced by the purpose of the analysis and the availability of suitable data [20] (see Box 2.2).

Box 2.2: Definitions of Full Economic Evaluation

Cost-minimisation: comparison between two or more alternatives that are assumed to provide identical health outcomes in order to identify the option that has the lowest costs.

Cost-effectiveness: comparison of costs of alternative treatments relative to the amount of change in a common effect. The effect can be measured using many different types of units including change in pain scores, life years gained or costs per case prevented. These evaluations do not allow for comparison between interventions that have different outcomes because a common metric is not used.

Cost-utility: measurement of the costs of an intervention and valuing of its outcomes in a metric that captures its impact on survival and quality of life.

Cost-benefit: the costs and benefits of an intervention are valued in monetary terms.

Adapted from Gray et al. [20]

The application of economic evaluation techniques to palliative interventions is limited and has been slow to develop. As a result, evidence about the cost-effectiveness of palliative care relative to other interventions is scant, with only one study [21] meeting these criteria identified in a recent systematic review [3]. This analysis examined the difference in costs and outcomes in a randomised trial of a palliative care intervention for patients with multiple sclerosis and their caregivers. Outcomes for patients were measured on the Palliative Outcome Scale (POS-8), while caregiver burden was measured using the Zarit Carer Burden Inventory (ZBI). Other examples of full economic evaluations include a cost-benefit analysis undertaken by Iskedjian et al. that compared individuals' willingness to pay for treatment with methylnaltrexone along with usual care relative to usual care alone for the treatment of opioid-induced constipation [22] and a study by Round et al. of rehabilitation services for those living with cancer [4].

2.4 Costs of Providing Care at the End of Life

Identifying and valuing inputs to care is not a straightforward process when evaluating palliative care interventions, and there are a number of difficulties in collecting all of the relevant data necessary to estimate costs for the purpose of economic evaluation. For instance, it is generally not possible to be certain exactly when a person has entered the end-of-life phase. It may be difficult to determine how best to include costs for treatments that could be simultaneously curative and palliative in intent [15]. In addition, palliative care is personalised and provided by multidisciplinary teams, making it difficult to identify and define the activities of palliative care professionals [23]. In many cases, there are also significant inputs to care provided by family or friends that can be challenging to accurately capture and value. Without accurate information about all the relevant costs, patterns in variation cannot be identified, and it is difficult to ensure that resources are being allocated to the most efficient interventions.

A further consideration when calculating costs is which ones should be included in the analysis. This will ultimately depend on the perspective chosen. The two main alternative perspectives are the payer and societal. The payer perspective considers only the costs involved, potential cost savings and changes in health status for the targeted population which are directly relevant to the organisation implementing of funding the intervention (usually the health service), while the societal perspective considers all costs, regardless of who it is that incurs them. This could include out-of-pocket costs incurred by the patient; the opportunity costs for family and friends who provide informal care; costs for providing social care services (if not directly funded by the health service); and productivity losses incurred by employers.

The difficulty with only considering the payer's perspective is that it effectively assumes, perhaps erroneously, that there are no costs for non-payers. Moreover, there appears to be inconsistencies in the methodology given that benefits to service users are included but their potential costs are not considered. However, pragmatically this perspective may be a sensible choice if the non-payer costs are relatively small and the effort to assess them is high.

The majority of palliative care evaluations have adopted a payer perspective, leaving the role of informal care and costs incurred by patients and informal caregivers and their impact on formal costs unexplored [3], yet it is clear that in addition to the inputs provided by formal care, palliative care patients often receive significant support in the community from family and informal caregivers [24] and social care services. While out-of-pocket expenditure for direct costs such as transportation, modifications to the home, medications and insurance payments are easier to measure and record, there are a number of factors which can make it challenging to estimate indirect costs experienced by informal caregivers, e.g. how to measure time spent caregiving, what value to place on opportunity costs incurred by caregivers who are not in formal employment and how best to assess the influence of caring externalities on the marginal value of time spent caring [25]. This is a complex process that may only result in capturing costs that are small or are similar between the options being compared. This must be balanced against the risk that not taking the costs of providing social care services or those incurred by patients and families into consideration may result in preference being given to interventions or models of care where a larger proportion of costs are covered by patients and informal caregivers or social care services.

Care at the end of life is known to account for a significant proportion of healthcare resources [26]. Estimates from the United States indicate that approximately 25 % of healthcare expenditure is directed towards individuals in their last year of life [27]. Eighty percent of the Federal Medicare programme expenditures are for patients during their final year of life, with half of that spending being linked to patients during their last 2 months of life [26]. Overall, Medicare costs for people who die are almost three times higher (276 %) than the costs of care for people of the same age who are alive [28]. In the United Kingdom, approximately 20 % of hospital bed days are utilised for end-of-life care [26]. Given the concern about rising healthcare expenditure, growing interest in the costs of providing care at the end of life may be linked to the perception that these can be contained by reducing unnecessary, aggressive and expensive treatments. Although the evidence is limited, evaluation of the economic impact of palliative care interventions suggests that these services play a role in reducing costs at the end of life [3].

2.5   Measuring Outcomes

Knowing the costs of providing an intervention only tells part of the story. In order to understand whether or not an intervention is worth paying for, policy makers need to also have evidence about the impact of the intervention on individuals. To this effect, outcome measurement serves three very important purposes. In the first instance, it guides healthcare resource allocation by allowing for comparison of costs and outcomes across different interventions, aids in measuring the quality of service provision to inform the management of service delivery and provides evidence about the impact of treatments on individuals [29]. There are a number of criteria that an outcome measure should meet if it is to be used to generate information about cost-effectiveness [30]:

- Established reliability and validity in the patient population
- Captures clinically relevant information
- Sensitive to important changes over time
- Can be integrated into clinical routines
- Easy to administer and interpret
- Suitable for use across various care settings

However, measuring outcomes in the context of palliative and end-of-life care present a number of obstacles. Firstly, it may be ethically inappropriate to attempt to capture this information directly from patients who are frail or cognitively impaired [8]. Clinicians may need to rely on information provided by proxies, but this approach is not without its own difficulties. It is also unclear how the consequences should be measured for interventions that are simultaneously palliative and curative in nature [15]. Another factor to consider is how to attribute improvements in a patient's quality of life to palliative care services when multiple services have been utilised [2]. There may also be barriers in the clinical setting to collecting outcomes data. In addition, there is not a clear date when the benefits of accessing palliative care begin, as there can be benefit in knowing that support and symptom control at the end of life will be accessible if needed. Given the holistic approach to care emphasised in palliative care, the potential benefits to caregivers may also need to be measured in order to capture all of the outcomes derived from an intervention [9].

2.5.1   The QALY Debate

The tool most commonly used in cost-utility analysis is the quality-adjusted life year (QALY), which combines information about the impact of an intervention on mortality and quality of life into one common metric. The appeal in using the QALY framework is that it facilitates comparison of the cost-effectiveness of virtually all types of healthcare interventions [19]. Policy makers can then choose how best to use this information to set funding priorities. While they may have a number of other objectives to consider when such as addressing health inequalities, political goals and supporting innovation, if the main objective is to maximise health outcomes, then priority may be given to those interventions that have the lowest cost-per-QALY.

Although the use of QALYs has become the accepted standard for conducting economic evaluations, there are a number of practical and theoretical reasons this approach is not always acceptable. The use of QALYs and how appropriate they are for measuring outcomes in cost-utility analyses of palliative and end-of-life care has been heavily debated in the literature [15, 29, 31–33]. While the benefits of palliative care can be measured in QALYs, there are a number of reasons why these interventions do not produce high QALY gains:

- Their objective is not to extend life, but to improve quality of life for the time remaining. Even when substantial improvements in quality of life are achieved, these are often short-lived.
- The QALY framework is patient centric and does not take into account the externalities of palliative care interventions for family members or informal caregivers.
- QALYs are concerned entirely with health; however, there is evidence to suggest that patients nearing the end of their life value attributes of care that would not be captured in an evaluative framework that focuses on health [34].
- Spiritual and psychosocial wellbeing are domains of palliative care that are not included in QALY scores [2].

Each of these factors may contribute to palliative care interventions having a higher cost-per-QALY than other healthcare activities. Cost-utility estimations of palliative care in patients with pancreatic cancer [35] confirm that prolonged survival is a key factor to increasing cost-effectiveness within the QALY framework. Therefore, a policy of QALY maximisation will result in priority being given to funding healthcare interventions for individuals with longer life expectancy. Hughes (2005) describes this anomaly as being palliative care's 'QALY problem' [31].

Additional concerns about the QALY framework in palliative care have been raised in the literature. Economic evaluation is underpinned by the assumption that individuals seek to maximise utility; however, this is not supported by recent research [36], which revealed evidence of near lexicographic preferences with respect to end-of-life care. Research conducted by McNamee and Seymour found that patients had distinct preferences for process of care and that incorporating these process values within the QALY framework rather than the standard approach of using preferences for health outcomes could alter the ranking of interventions [37]. Normand highlights that the use of QALYs may be questionable because the approach extends from the assumption that time is additive, with each segment equally weighted [15, 29]. Round argues however, that if additional value is given to time at the end of life, then an equity weight should be applied to these segments of time in order to estimate QALYs. There are practical difficulties that need to be resolved before weighting could be incorporated into economic evaluation of healthcare interventions [33].

2.5.2 Alternative Tools and Approaches

Alternative approaches to the standard QALY framework have been explored by a number of researchers. Normand [29] has proposed the Palliative Care Yardstick (PalY) as a means for incorporating dimensions of palliative care that are not considered when calculating QALYs, such as caregiver externalities. Sutton and Coast (2013) have developed an alternative framework for measuring outcomes for economic evaluation of end-of-life care [34]. Although Round [33] suggests that the QALY problem 'is largely a case of special pleading', Sutton and Coast's findings appear to support the argument that the existing framework fails to take many of the benefits of palliative care interventions into account.

Hughes [31] suggests that the most appropriate response to palliative care's QALY problem is for the evaluative framework to reject the assumption that the impact of a period of time in a person's life can only be measured in proportion to their overall length of life. It follows then that the pathway to death may have a more substantial effect on the overall value of a person's life than the QALY framework allows for. Therefore, it may be more useful to develop methods that focus on measurement of longitudinal experiences and collect evidence about preferences between various trajectories [15].

The use of discrete choice experiments (DCEs) has been shown to be a useful tool for eliciting user preferences for end-of-life care [36]. Knowing which attributes of care packages patients value most can provide valuable information for policy makers about how services would best be delivered and would help ensure that resources allocated towards palliative care are spent efficiently. Formal attempts to elicit preferences for palliative care services have been limited to specific services (such as day hospice and inpatient hospital care) and provide only limited understanding of the ways in which preferences vary with different needs and circumstances. Recent work has also demonstrated that there are difficulties in collecting information about preferences from service users through the DCE framework (REF: IARE paper in draft). While it is important to have the appropriate tools, it is also vital that there is a clear understanding of what the most useful approaches are and the feasibility of conducting DCEs across various care settings and with different service user groups. Further research is also required to determine how best to incorporate DCEs into a framework for economic evaluation, which could facilitate comparison between palliative care interventions and other healthcare activities [38].

The debate over how best to measure and value outcomes is ongoing. Part II of this volume focuses specifically on this and includes contributions from Coast, Round, McCabe, Shah, Baker and Flynn.

2.6 Conclusion

The evidence base for the cost and effectiveness of palliative care interventions is limited and needs to be strengthened. In order for this to happen, tools must be developed that help demonstrate the cost-effectiveness of palliative care services relative to other healthcare interventions. While opinions differ as to how this can be achieved, increasing competition for resources means that the challenges in applying economic evaluation techniques to palliative care services will need to be overcome before it will be possible to accurately compare these services with other healthcare activities.

However, if it is generally accepted that all people should have access to high-quality end-of-life care, then it is important to ensure that resources allocated to end-of-life care are spent efficiently. To this end, knowing which attributes of palliative care packages patients and caregivers value could provide useful information for policy makers about how services could be best delivered to maximise value for money until such time that more robust data about the cost-effectiveness of these interventions becomes available.

References

1. Morris S, Devlin N, Parkin D (2007) Economic analysis in health care. Wiley, Chichester
2. Murtagh FEM et al (2013) Capturing activity, costs, and outcomes: the challenges to be overcome for successful economic evaluation in palliative care. Prog Palliat Care 0:1–4
3. Smith S, Brick A, O'Hara S, Normand C (2013) Evidence on the cost and cost-effectiveness of palliative care: a literature review. Palliat Med. doi:10.1177/0269216313493466
4. Round J, Leurent B, Jones L (2014) A cost-utility analysis of a rehabilitation service for people living with and beyond cancer. BMC Health Serv Res 14:1–11
5. Sepúlveda C, Marlin A, Yoshida T, Ullrich A (2002) Palliative care: the World Health Organization's global perspective. J Pain Symptom 24:91–96
6. Raftery JP et al (1996) A randomized controlled trial of the cost-effectiveness of a district co-ordinating service for terminally ill cancer patients. Palliat Med 10:151–161
7. Sleeman KE, Gomes B, Higginson IJ (2012) Research into end-of-life cancer care—investment is needed. Lancet 379:519
8. Higginson IJ et al (2013) Evaluating complex interventions in end of life care: the MORECare statement on good practice generated by a synthesis of transparent expert consultations and systematic reviews. BMC Med 11:111
9. Zimmerman C, Riechelmann R, Krzyzanowska M (2008) CLINICIAN' S CORNER effectiveness of specialized palliative care. JAMA 299:1698–1709
10. Starks H, Diehr P, Curtis JR (2009) The challenge of selection bias and confounding in palliative care research. J Palliat Med 12:181–187
11. Pannucci CJ, Wilkins EG (2010) Identifying and avoiding bias in research. Plast Reconstr Surg 126:619–625
12. Addington-Hall JM, Bruera E, Higginson IJ, Payne S (2007) Research methods in palliative care. Oxford University Press, Oxford
13. Craig P, Dieppe P, Macintyre S, Michie S (2008) Developing and evaluating complex interventions: new guidance. http://eprints.ucl.ac.uk/103060/
14. Torgerson DJ (2001) Contamination in trials: is cluster randomisation the answer? BMJ (Clin Res Ed) 322:355–357
15. Normand C (2012) Setting priorities in and for end-of-life care: challenges in the application of economic evaluation. Health Econ Policy Law 7:431–439
16. Gysels M et al (2013) MORECare research methods guidance development: recommendations for ethical issues in palliative and end-of-life care research. Palliat Med 27:908–917
17. White C, Hardy J (2008) Gatekeeping from palliative care research trials. Prog Palliat Care 16:167–171
18. Stone PC et al (2013) Factors affecting recruitment to an observational multicentre palliative care study. BMJ Supportive and Palliative Care 3(3):1–6. doi:10.1136/bmjspcare-2012-000396

19. Drummond MF, Sculpher MJ, Torrance GW, O'Brien BJ, Stoddart GL (2005) Methods for the economic evaluation of health care programmes. Oxford University Press, Oxford
20. Gray AM, Clarke PM, Wolstenholme JL, Wordsworth S (2011) Applied methods of cost-effectiveness analysis in health care. Oxford Press, Oxford. p 313
21. Higginson IJ et al (2009) Is short-term palliative care cost-effective in multiple sclerosis? A randomized phase II trial. J Pain Symptom Manage 38:816–826
22. Iskedjian M et al (2011) Methylnaltrexone in the treatment of opioid-induced constipation in cancer patients receiving palliative care: willingness-to-pay and cost-benefit analysis. J Pain Symptom Manage 41:104–115
23. Higginson IJ, Hearn J, Myers K, Naysmith A (2000) Palliative day care: what do services do? Palliative Day Care Project Group. Palliat Med 14:277–286
24. Gomes B, Harding R, Foley KM, Higginson IJ (2009) Optimal approaches to the health economics of palliative care: report of an international think tank. J Pain Symptom Manage 38:4–10
25. McDaid D (2001) Estimating the costs of informal care for people with Alzheimer's disease: methodological and practical challenges. Int J Geriatr Psychiatry 16:400–405
26. Hatziandreu E, Archontakis F, Daly A (2008) The potential cost savings of greater use of home-and hospice-based end of life care in England. http://oai.dtic.mil/oai/oai?verb=getReco rd&metadataPrefix=html&identifier=ADA496672
27. Riley GF, Lubitz JD (2010) Long-term trends in medicare payments in the last year of life. Health Serv Res 45:565–576
28. Davis MP et al (2005) The financial benefits of acute inpatient palliative medicine: an inter-institutional comparative analysis by all patient refined-diagnosis related group and case mix index. J Support Oncol 3:313–316
29. Normand C (2009) Measuring outcomes in palliative care: limitations of QALYs and the road to PalYs. J Pain Symptom Manage 38:27–31
30. Fitzpatrick R, Davey C, Buxton MJ, Jones DR (1998) Evaluating patient-based outcome measures for use in clinical trials. Health Technology Assessment 2(14):i–iv;1–74. http://www.ncbi.nlm.nih.gov/pubmed/9812244
31. Hughes J (2005) Palliative care and the QALY problem. Health Care Anal: HCA: J Health Philos Policy 13:289–301
32. Coast J et al (2008) Investigating Choice Experiments for Preferences of Older People (ICEPOP): evaluative spaces in health economics. J Health Serv Res Policy 13(Suppl 3):31–37
33. Round J (2012) Is a QALY still a QALY at the end of life? J Health Econ 31:521–527
34. Sutton EJ, Coast J (2013) Development of a supportive care measure for economic evaluation of end-of-life care using qualitative methods. Palliat Med. doi:10.1177/0269216313489368
35. Ljungman D, Hyltander A, Lundholm K (2013) Cost-utility estimations of palliative care in patients with pancreatic adenocarcinoma: a retrospective analysis. World J Surg. doi:10.1007/s00268-013-2003-z
36. Douglas H-R, Normand CE, Higginson IJ, Goodwin DM (2005) A new approach to eliciting patients' preferences for palliative day care: the choice experiment method. J Pain Symptom Manage 29:435–445
37. McNamee P, Seymour J (2008) Incorporation of process preferences within the QALY framework: a study of alternative methods. Med Dec Making: Int J Soc Med Decis Making 28:443–452
38. de Bekker-Grob E, Ryan M, Gerard K (2012) Discrete choice experiments in health economics: a review of the literature. Health Econ 172:145–172

Chapter 3
The Role of the Health Economist in the Evaluation and Development of Complex Interventions in End-of-Life Care

Rachael Maree Hunter

3.1 Introduction

3.1.1 What Are Complex Interventions?

Complex interventions are interventions or new healthcare technologies with many interacting components. Although most clinical trials could arguably be characterised as complex, the key distinguishing feature of complex interventions is that they involve the evaluation of multiple, potentially interacting components of an intervention, some of which may be challenging to measure or to systematically control. This is in contrast to trials of pharmaceutical products where the aim typically is to establish the physiological effectiveness of a particular drug while holding as many other factors as possible constant. Another important distinction is that in pharmaceutical trials, the recipient of treatment is generally the patient, while in complex interventions, the recipient is sometimes the patient, but it can also be the patient's clinical professional, the hospital they attend or a government body such as a local authority. A simple example of a complex intervention is a behavioural intervention, such as training, given to the clinical professional with the aim of improving the quality of patient care. When evaluating the intervention, researchers will need to consider a range of factors beyond the intervention itself that may influence its effectiveness. These may include the variability between clinicians, the casemix (complexity) of their patients and that the patient and clinician exist in organisations with potentially different political, physical and social environments.

The challenge for evaluating complex interventions is then to design an evaluation that accounts for these different, interacting levels of care and their related social,

R.M. Hunter
Research Department of Primary Care and Population Health, Priment Clinical Trials Unit, University College London (UCL), London, UK
e-mail: r.hunter@ucl.ac.uk

© Springer International Publishing Switzerland 2016   31
J. Round (ed.), *Care at the End of Life: An Economic Perspective*,
DOI 10.1007/978-3-319-28267-1_3

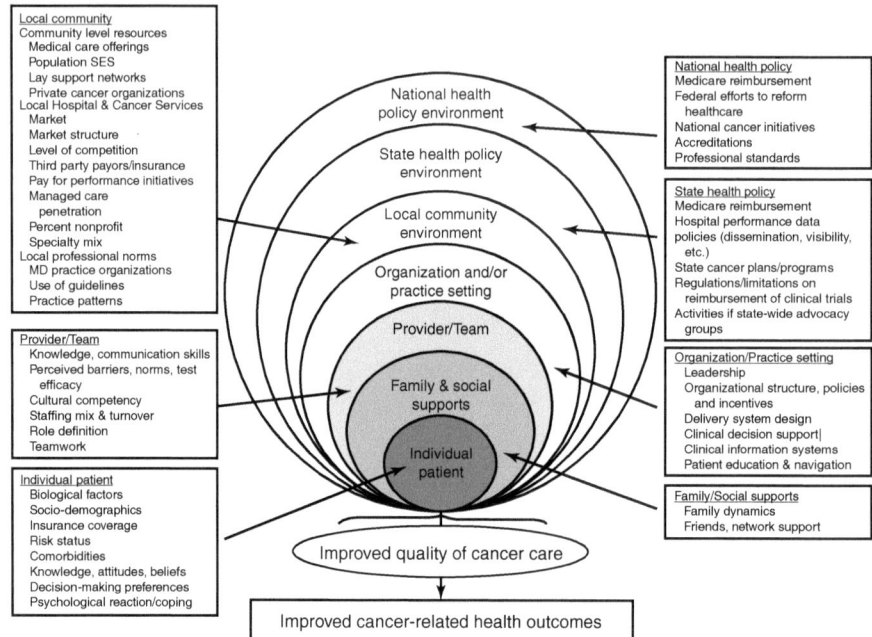

Fig. 3.1 Multilevel influences of care

environmental and individual factors so that one can tease out if the intervention is effective. Taplin et al. [1, 2] highlighted the importance of thinking of this complexity through consideration of the different levels of care in cancer care and developed an ecological diagram to help demonstrate this (Fig. 3.1). Although the diagram was developed in the United States (US) and for cancer care, the various levels are relevant to any complex intervention and to healthcare systems in most countries. In the example above, the researcher wants to know whether the training intervention is effective in improving the quality of patient care. To assist with the process the United Kingdom's (UK) Medical Research Council (MRC) provides the guidance document "Developing and evaluating complex interventions" [3], which updates guidance published in 2000 [4]. Further updates to the guidance have also provided additional advice on how to conduct process evaluations, generally a subsidiary study of an evaluation that focuses on implementation, impact and contextual factors [5]. This chapter will draw heavily on the recent 2006 MRC guidance [3], but with the aim of providing additional information for health economists involved in evaluating complex interventions in end-of-life care.

3.1.2   Complex Interventions and End-of-Life Care

Care at the end of life covers a range of disease areas and care settings. Care for many needs to be coordinated across a number of settings and providers including care in the home, hospitals, social care, supported living, care homes and hospices.

Many of the clinical professionals that are involved with care at the end of life are also "generalist" such as GPs and primary care nurses, so that end-of-life care may form only part of their workload and is not their area of expertise. For the families and unpaid carers of people at the end of life who may have found themselves in a caring role, they may not have the skills or resources they need to adequately care for the person. Given that at the end of life a person may no longer be able to independently care for themselves, complex interventions interacting with different care settings and professionals represent a common way of improving patient care at the end of life. Interventions commonly include activities like training, auditing or performance monitoring and can have objectives such as increasing compliance with evidence-based care, increasing skills or knowledge or improving the way that clinical professionals interact with each other across care settings or organisations.

The evaluation of the Lewisham Case Management Scheme is one good example of evaluating a complex intervention in end-of-life care, in this case, intensive case management of dementia patients being cared for by specialist mental health services [6]. As the intervention was at the level of the service and not the patient, patients could not be randomly allocated to intervention or control – either a patient was referred to a service that had intensive case management or they were referred to a team that did not have case management. The nature of the intervention (intensive case management) was also such that it was not possible to blind clinical staff or patients to which group they were in. Instead the research team used a quasi-experimental design to evaluate the effectiveness of case management in one community mental health team for the elderly (CMHTE) to no intensive case management in a second, matched CMHTE. Case managers in the intervention group then worked with the patient, the patient's carers and multiple health and social care organisations with the aim of preventing patients from entering long term care. A major impact of this model was relief for carers [6].

Evaluating end-of-life care has another feature that differentiates it from the model of pharmaceutical-phased drug trials and moves it into the realm of complex interventions: this is that the outcome of interest may have moved away from treatment efficacy. Instead outcomes such as quality of life, quality of care, dignity, compassion, pain reduction and evidence-based care are sometimes more important. Parkinson's disease, a neurodegenerative disease where patients' symptoms progressively worsen and as yet has no cure, is an example of a disease area where although new expensive pharmaceutical treatments are being developed, the emphasis is on symptom relief and quality of life. As a result it is important to get right which costs and outcomes are measured when evaluating a new treatment [7].

Physical, psychological and cognitive decline may also introduce additional complexities when evaluating interventions including obtaining informed consent from patients and measuring patient-reported outcomes. The outcomes to measure are featured heavily within the complex interventions' development and evaluation framework, and although outcomes have been discussed elsewhere [8, 9], they will be discussed here specifically in regard to how they fit within the evaluation of complex interventions (see Sect. 3.2.2 in this chapter).

Although the structure for the development and evaluation of complex interventions presents an ideal framework for service evaluation, design and improvement in end-of-life care, it is not always utilised. The NICE clinical guidelines (CG) for palliative care for cancer and CG for dementia recommended three tools in managing end-of-life care, all of which were complex interventions: the Gold Standards Framework (see www.goldstandardsframework.nhs.uk/) [10], the Liverpool Care Pathway (LCP) for the dying patient (now no longer practised [11]) and the Preferred Place of Care Plan (see www.cancerlancashire.org.uk/ppc.html). However, these have limited evidence of effectiveness, having not been systematically evaluated. This created particular concern with the LCP, which has since been stopped following a review of the evidence [11]. A randomised control trial (RCT) evaluating the Gold Standards Framework has now been completed and is awaiting publication.

3.1.3 Economic Evaluations and End-of-Life Care

Economic evaluations of complex interventions at the end of life occur even more infrequently, with a meta-synthesis of development and evaluation end-of-life care interventions carried out in 2010, finding limited evidence of economic evaluations of end-of-life care looking beyond cost implications [12]. Economic evaluations though play an important role in end-of-life care. A report by the English National Audit Office looking at the cost of two causes of death, cancer and organ failure, found the total cost of providing care in the last year of life to be £1.8 billion and £553 million respectively. A 10 % variation in the daily cost of care across these two conditions represents a yearly change of costs of £122 million [13]. Given that the number of cancer deaths alone in England in Wales is projected to increase from 7.6 million in 2008 to 11.5 million in 2030 [12], the total cost of end-of-life care is likely to account for an increasing percentage of the health and social care budget. How those at the end of life are cared for is sometimes referred to as the "litmus test of society" – how we care for those in need is a reflection of society's values as a whole. The role health economists can play in this economically challenging situation is to provide evidence towards how limited resources can be spent in a way that maximises the benefit to patients and society.

3.2 The Cycle of Complex Intervention Development and Evaluation

Regardless of the location where the intervention occurs or who is the intended recipient complex interventions involve a cycle of development and evaluation, with each stage feeding into each other (Fig. 3.2). The following sections will discuss each stage in the cycle and the role of the health economist and address considerations specific to economic evaluations of end-of-life care complex interventions.

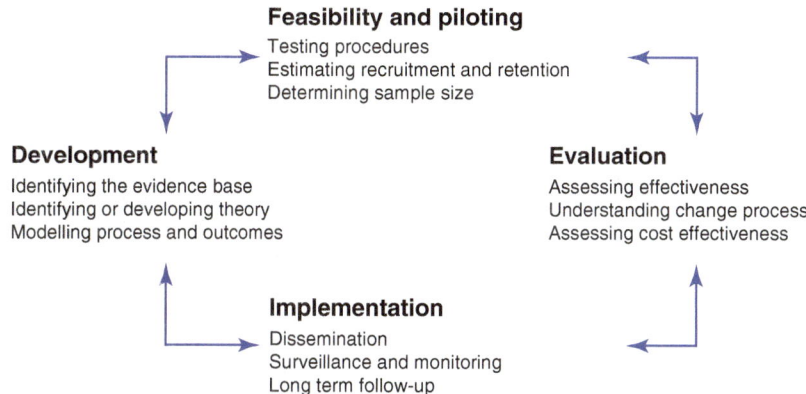

Fig. 3.2 Cycle of development and evaluation for complex interventions

3.2.1   Intervention Development

Although intervention development is generally the first step, within the complex intervention framework, it is an iterative process, with feedback from the other stages in the cycle feeding back into redeveloping and improving the intervention.

The health economist generally has limited involvement at this stage, but in some instances can be an important contributor. They can play a role in synthesising the current evidence on costs and outcomes for the area of work, modelling the current care pathway and estimating what impact the new intervention might have on costs and consequences. The work of the health economist might help identify if an intervention is unlikely to ever be cost-effective at an early stage and identify ways to address this, as was the case for an intervention to reduce falls-related injuries in older people. The early economic analysis identified that at the predicted level of effectiveness for the trial the intervention had a 40 % chance of being cost-effective at a willingness to pay threshold of £30,000 per quality adjusted life year gained (QALY). The analysis found that the algorithm for identifying at risk patients needed to be amended and improved to increase the probability that the intervention is cost-effective [14].

A more forward-thinking area health economists can also be involved with is *extra value of perfect information* (EVPI) analysis. This combines information on what is currently known about a given research area, where the gaps in knowledge are or where there is uncertainty and what the size of the clinical problem is. Using this information EVPI can provide an estimation of how much money should be invested into research in a particular area. *Extra value of partial perfect information* (EVPPI) goes further and identifies which specific parameters are most uncertain and potentially have the greatest impact on costs and effectiveness, and hence should receive additional attention in the research design. This methodology presents an innovative way to think about prioritising research funding, and research has identified how it could be used within the current health research funding framework in England [15]. However, its use has been limited in informing research priorities. More information about research methods for economic evaluation and EVPI/EVPPI can be found in Briggs [16].

3.2.2 Feasibility of Trial

A feasibility trial in the evaluation and development of complex interventions cycle is similar to a phase II trial in drug trials. The intervention has been developed, but the aim of the feasibility trial is to assess if it can be evaluated in a scientifically rigorous way. Feasibility trials of complex interventions are sometimes overlooked, but are a very important component of the intervention development and evaluation cycle. They provide information to researchers about what the main evaluation should look like or if changes to the intervention and/or trial design should be made before embarking on a full confirmatory trial. A well-designed feasibility trial assists researchers to easily proceed into a full evaluation if all the signs point to what should happen next or in some instances provides the necessary information to redesign the intervention or trial so as to increase the likelihood that it will be successful next time. Table 3.1 provides a summary of the objectives of a feasibility trial and the role that the health economist plays in each objective. Some of the questions that the health economist needs to think about will overlap with questions for the trial as a whole so it is important the health economist works closely with all members of the team.

The role of the health economist in a feasibility trial is to focus on objective [2] below, outcome measurement. They might also help with providing an estimation of "cost per dose", in particular for trials looking at the benefits of additional therapy sessions or what impact improving or reducing the number of patients involved in the intervention may have on costs. It may be helpful at this stage for the health economist to provide information on the fixed and variable costs of the intervention and what the marginal cost per patient is (see texts such as Drummond et al. [17] for further detail).

In end-of-life care, there will be specific issues to address regarding what the most suitable patient-reported outcome measure for use in an economic evaluation might be. What cost data should be collected and how best to ensure the right information is collected to inform policy makers and commissioners is also important. The reality is that even though an intervention may not have been fully evaluated yet, it might already be being implemented in services. As a result, it can sometimes be up to the health economist to provide initial signals of the financially viability and sustainability of the intervention. Similar to how a well-designed feasibility trial will inform the next steps for trial design, a well-designed economic evaluation at this stage will ensure that the right information is collected as part of the final evaluation. Missing data is a particular issue in end-of-life trials, particularly in relation to healthcare resource use [18]. As a result, the methods for collecting healthcare resource data may need careful consideration. Feasibility trials present the

Table 3.1 Objectives of a feasibility trial and questions for the trial and health economics to answer

Feasibility trial objective	Questions for the trial to answer	Questions for the health economics to answer
(1) Recruitment to the trial	Can sites be recruited to the trial, for example, GP practices or care homes?	Are sites able to provide data on health and social care resource use? How much information is a reasonable amount to ask sites or patients to provide without overburdening them? If informal carers are to be involved, how will they be identified and contacted?
	Will patients consent to be part of the trial?	
(2) Outcome measures and missing data	What should the primary outcome in the trial be? What are its statistical properties?	What health and social carer resource use data is required?
	Will patients complete questionnaires?	Is cost and resource use information for a societal cost perspective required?
	How much missing data is there?	Does information need to be collected from informal carers on costs and consequences?
		What should the outcome in the denominator of the incremental cost-effectiveness ratio (ICER) be?
		How much missing data is there?
(3) Retention in a trial	Will patients, carers and/or clinicians engage with or do the intervention?	What are the cost implications of patients, carers and/or clinicians not engaging with the intervention? What impact does engagement with the intervention have on the average cost per patient of the intervention?
	Will the relevant parties provide the data needed for follow-up?	Can the data required by collected at follow-up?
(4) Acceptability of the intervention	Do patients, carers and/or clinicians find the intervention acceptable? This can sometimes be answered by [3]. Retention, but sometimes a specific qualitative component, is included to answer this question	Similar to [3], does patients' willingness to engage with the intervention have an impact on costs or effectiveness? This issue is particularly important where screening for a disease is part of the intervention. Invasive tests may have better diagnostic properties, but patients may be less willing to consent to an invasive test, making it a less effective intervention
(5) Fidelity to the intervention	Can the intervention be delivered in a consistent way in line with the protocol?	Are there any cost implications to local variation in how the intervention is delivered?

ideal situation for piloting data collection methods and may also provide information on where most of the costs are and hence where to focus efforts in the main trial.

Health economists can address this by thinking through some of the following questions:

1. Who are the main stakeholders in the implementation, funding and ongoing delivery of the intervention? Who will be the main audience for this evaluation? This can help to address questions about what cost perspective to use and what outcomes to collect.

2. What resources are available to collect health and social care cost data as part of the feasibility trail? Whether to use patient-/carer-completed questionnaires, clinical staff-completed questionnaires or medical records to collect details of health and social care resource use can sometimes be determined if there are administrative resources available for the different methods. Although medical records in some instances can provide a relatively reliable record of health and social care resource use, it can be an expensive and time-consuming way to collect the data, and data that is missing by omission is not always informative: is the data missing because the healthcare event did not occur or because nobody recorded that it occurred? Primary care data in particular can sometimes be incomplete for acute care attendances [19]. Social care data can sometimes be particularly challenging to obtain from electronic records and may be a combination of state-financed and out-of-pocket costs. As a result, data may need to be collected directly from patients and/or carers. There are limited resources available on costing social care packages, and costs can vary significantly between providers. Researchers may need to engage with local government, providers or other commissioners to obtain social care resource unit costs. Patient-/carer-completed questionnaires can present a cheaper option, but can have more missing data, particularly if whole questionnaires are missing. Consideration also needs to be made as to the cognitive ability of patients who may struggle to complete questionnaires or patient diaries. The reliability of self-reporting of health and social care use can vary by age [20] and mental health [21]. Questionnaire completion may also require administrative resources to chase patients or carers for responses. Researcher interviews, where researchers interview patients, carers or clinical staff about resource use, present an alternative option but have significant cost and logistical implications, particularly in multisite interventions. These can be more effective for certain disease areas not just for collecting resource use but also quality of life data. Patients with Parkinson's disease have less missing items on the Short-Form 36 (SF-36) if it is collected by interview rather than postal completion [7].

3. Are unpaid carers affected by the intervention? Accounting for the cost and quality of life for unpaid carers presents a particular methodological challenge for health economists evaluating interventions at the end of life [22]. Informal care from families and friends can account for 80 % of the cost of end-of-life care across a range of disease areas [18]. Informal care may also represent a potential substitute good in that if healthcare costs increase, intervention delivery may

have shifted away from informal care, or conversely a decrease in healthcare use may be because the burden on informal care has increased [10]. This was the effect seen in the Lewisham Case Management Evaluation, where as healthcare expenditure increased, the impact on carers decreased [10]. As a result, a healthcare intervention that appears cost saving from a health and social care cost perspective, due to decreased resources for patients, may have huge societal cost implications if the cost savings have been made at the expense of informal carers. In a study looking at the cost of dementia care, the median time spent by informal carers assisting the person with dementia was 7 h a day. 40 % of carers (mostly sons or daughters of the person with dementia) had to cut down or give up on work to care for the person. As a result, informal care provided at the home had an equivalent total cost to society as a patient living in a care home [22]. The effect of a disease on work can also be important, particularly in diseases such as Parkinson's disease that can affect working age adults, with 29 % of adults with Parkinson's needing to take early retirement because of the disease [7]. How to collect this data and value it is an important area to address at the feasibility stage.

4. What data is needed to cost the intervention? Intervention costs may not be straightforward for complex interventions and can vary widely. As the recipient of the intervention is sometimes the clinical professional or organisation, trials of complex interventions are generally multisite or multi-therapist. Previous guidelines have suggested that to ensure consistency between sites and therapists, complex intervention trial protocols need to be highly detailed in their description of what needs to be delivered with intensive processes to assess fidelity and compliance with the protocol which are also generally incorporated into the trial [4]. The more recent guidance though has softened this requirement, suggesting that some interventions may be more effective if they are able to vary to take into local variations. The degree of variation allowed and whether this itself should be intentionally addressed is dependent on the aim of the evaluation [3, 5]. A large amount of information is likely to be collected on clinical practitioners' attendance of training session and how often patients use an intervention as part of routine trial data collection. It may be though that questionnaires need to be given to clinical staff delivering the intervention to determine the cost implications. Overburdened health and social care staff may not always be receptive to additional questionnaires, and hence routine data should be used where possible, particularly data collected as part of contractual obligations on the provider, or other methods identified such as taking a sample of intervention sessions. Another challenge is in making sure the control group gets equal data collection (if featured in the trial design at this stage).

In summary, the aim of an economic evaluation alongside a feasibility trial is to determine what information should be collected for the economic evaluation alongside a full evaluation and the best way to collect that data. Descriptive statistics should be reported on data completeness, but caution should be exercised when reporting mean costs and confidence intervals as feasibility trials tend to have small patient numbers, and hence results may be misleading. The analysis may provide some early signals of how likely it is that the intervention will be cost-effective and where the focus of cost data collection needs to be in a full trial. Estimates from feasibility trials can also be incorporated into the process of developing a decision analytic model, as discussed above in *Intervention Development*. Used alongside EVPI and EVPPI, data from a feasibility trial can provide additional information on what inputs in the model would warrant additional time and focus in a full trial.

3.2.3 Evaluation

Although much is made of the final, confirmatory randomised control trial in drug trials, in the life cycle of complex interventions, evaluation is only one iterative stage, though an important – and potentially expensive – one.

If a successful feasibility trial has been conducted, involving a health economist at an early stage in the design, then the role of a health economist in evaluation is generally straightforward: what has been learned in the feasibility trial can now be put into practice to inform a well-conducted and rigorous economic evaluation that answers the relevant research question and provides the necessary information to stakeholders. This is not always the case though, and if a health economist's first involvement with a complex intervention is at the evaluation stage, they will need to ask themselves the feasibility trial questions set out above.

What might be new at this stage is the introduction of a control group, as these are not always included in a feasibility trial. In complex interventions, the control group is not usually "no treatment" as ethically the patient will still require some care. Instead usual care is the standard control condition, and a key challenge for evaluating complex interventions is defining what is the current standard of care. For example, in some psychological therapy trials, what is known as an "active control" or "non-active therapy" might be used in addition to standard care. Here, the patient does not receive the novel therapy as prescribed, but will spend time with a therapist not trained in the new methodology. This can help determine whether any observed effect of treatment is not a result of just person-to-person interaction alone [23]. These trials may fall within the category of *explanatory trials*, where the aim is to establish mechanisms for change, rather than *pragmatic trials* that aim so see how the intervention would function in real life. The challenge here for a health economist is that they are most interested in the results of a pragmatic trial; how to account for the costs and effectiveness of a control group that would not exist in practice presents a challenge.

As it is unethical to disallow patient access to standard treatments available to them as part of routine care, some health and social care services accessible to patients in the control group may be similar to the intervention being trialled. Assessing the effectiveness of a new intervention can prove more challenging when routine care is already of high quality. For example, assertive outreach for patients with serious mental illness has been found to be beneficial in countries such as the United States and Australia. Yet in randomised control trials (RCTs) conducted in the United Kingdom, the intervention does not appear to provide any additional benefit compared to routine care. It has been hypothesised that this is because the quality of state-funded health and social care is higher in the United Kingdom than in the United States. The multifaceted nature of complex interventions makes it hard to distinguish the precise reasons why trials in the United Kingdom have been unable to replicate the findings of United States and Australian trials. Meta-analysis of trial data has suggested that inpatient mental healthcare use and to a lesser extent compliance with the recommended structure of assertive outreach may be better explanations for why this difference occurs [24].

3.2.4 Other Trials Designs

Whereas in the evaluation of pharmaceutical products randomised controlled trials (RCTs) with an active treatment arm and a placebo arm are considered the gold standard for reducing bias, in complex interventions, patient-level RCTs may not always be possible. In the evaluation of a new policy, the implementation of the change will be based on political will, available funding and the ways in which the policy is delivered. For example, some policies that must be implemented across a wide geographical area are not suitable for RCTs, as there is no level at which an area can be randomised to provide a robust answer to the research question. As a result, researchers may need to use a range of methods to evaluate the effectiveness of the intervention. For health economists, this might be best facilitated by a difference-in-difference approach using observational data, as was the case in the evaluation of stroke care reconfiguration [25]. This study compared the implementation of stroke care reconfiguration in two cities in England. Hospital Episode Statistics (HES), routinely collected hospital statistics for the National Health Service (NHS) in England, were obtained before, during and after the implementation of the new stroke model of care for inpatient stays where the primary diagnosis was stroke. Regression analysis and the difference-in-difference approach were used to evaluate if there was a significant reduction in hospital length of stay or mortality in the two cities after implementation of the new stroke model compared to the rest of England. The use of retrospective analysis of large data sets is also covered elsewhere in this volume (Chap. 4).

Observational data can be a preferred way to evaluate interventions for a variety of reasons:

1. The costs of large RCTs can sometimes be prohibitive. Sometimes the information needed to make a decision about implementing an intervention can be more cost-effectively obtained from observational data.
2. If researchers are interested in evaluating the effectiveness of an intervention on rare events, a very large sample size is required. Routinely collected observational data generally contain greater patient numbers and hence more rare events than would be possible in a trial.

3. An RCT is not possible because of the nature of the intervention. This is usually the case for interventions that occur at an organisational, regional or national level, for example, performance requirements such as quality outcomes framework (QOFs) and financial reimbursement for general practitioners for good performance.
4. Trials do not always reflect real-life costs, patients and practices. Firstly, they are heavily protocolised, so that standards of care are equal across treatment arms and provide a standard of care that would not normally be observed in every day care. Secondly, not all patients that are approached to take part in research consent to take part. As a result, the characteristics of patients that agree to take part in research may be different to the patient group that will eventually receive treatment.

A number of techniques exist for trying to estimate causality in the absence of randomised experiments. Econometricians will be familiar with potential analytical tools. In addition to the difference-in-difference method described above, other techniques include instrumental variables and regression discontinuity designs. Angrist and Pischke [26] provide an accessible overview of these techniques to the interested reader.

Patient-level randomisation, as would occur in a gold-standard RCT, may not be possible when evaluating complex interventions. This may be due to issues of (a) contamination, where a practitioner given training on improving the quality of care for patients is unlikely to be able to forget that training for control patients, or (b) for practical reasons, where specific sites are randomised to receive an intervention, and hence all patients in that site then receive the intervention. This is particularly the case for ward-based interventions, such as improving the quality of care on a ward or in a care home. In this the site is then randomised to different groups in what is called a *cluster randomised control trial* with each ward, hospital, care home or hospice representing a cluster. The Gold Standards Framework was evaluated as a cluster randomised control trial, where care homes were randomised to different levels of facilitation in implementing the framework. The trial is now complete with results to be published soon. Clustering and randomisation can also occur at the level of the clinical practitioner due to individual differences between clinicians in the quality and effectiveness of the care they provide as well as contamination if they have been trained in a particular therapy. In this case, allowance for clustering should be included in the economic evaluation. Bootstrapping, resampling of costs and consequences from patients in different clusters, is considered methodologically rigorous enough to address the issue of clustering, and care should be taken if another analytical method is chosen [27].

Randomisation at the level of site also may not be possible for some interventions as not all sites randomised to the intervention may be able to identify the resources required to implement the intervention at the right time. Also, if equipoise of the effectiveness of the intervention tips towards the intervention being more effective than current practice, it might not be ethical to withhold the intervention from the control group. In these cases, a step-wedge design is sometimes used, where the intervention is introduced into all sites but in a phased way. Data is collected at all sites at different follow-up points regardless of whether the intervention has yet been implemented. In this way, sites can act as their own control, but a variable for the confounding effect of calendar time is included. This can present methodological challenges for analysis in terms of what is considered the comparator, sample size estimation and handling duration of follow-up. These issues have been covered elsewhere in the statistical literature [28]. What has not been addressed though is the impact this has on economic evaluations and how to handle this, as there are no known published economic evaluations alongside a step-wedge trial.

3.2.5 Implementation

Implementation is probably one of the most important parts of the evaluation and development of complex interventions and should be considered at all stages in the process. At the very beginning of intervention, development researchers need to ask themselves "can this intervention be implemented in a real-world health or social care setting?" If the answer is "no", there is a big question mark over the value of the research being carried out.

Health economists play an important role in informing the feasibility and acceptability of implementation. Although economic evaluations in drug trials aim to answer the question "is the new technology cost-effective?" in complex interventions, health economists should also engage with commissioners and providers early on to explore the real financial impact of an intervention and consider use of other techniques for reporting results such as budget impact analysis. It is recommended that when they design the economic evaluation, they should do so with information on what would be most informative for policy makers, commissioners and providers and should engage early on to make sure they are measuring the right things in the trials.

How much an intervention costs to implement is an important consideration when undertaking an evaluation, and one that is sometimes not accounted for, even in economic evaluations [12]. It does present challenges though. Although the cost of training and additional equipment might be easy to estimate, how to estimate the cost of changes to practice or policy might be more challenging. For interventions which require improved quality of medical records or monitoring of patient outcomes, changes to IT systems might be required, and reporting and recording of patient information may take additional time. Valuing the opportunity cost of these changes to practice, given that this time could be spent doing other tasks directly associated with patient care, it is not always straightforward.

3.3 Conclusion

Complex interventions are particularly relevant in the evaluation of interventions to improve the quality of end-of-life care. Of particular note are interventions that improve the quality of care for patients, such as the Gold Standards Framework, where the recipients of the intervention are practitioners who then pass on the benefits to patients. These, and other complex interventions, can present methodological challenges in their design, analysis and interpretation. To provide a framework for addressing these challenges, the MRC has published guidance on evaluating complex interventions which sets out four iterative stages in the cycle of development and evaluation of complex interventions. Health economists have a role to play in all stages in the cycle. At the development stage, decision analytic models can provide initial signals as to if the intervention is likely to be cost-effective. Coupled with EVPI and EVPPI, models can provide information on what variables should be the focus of future research. If health economists are involved at the feasibility stage of the cycle, they can provide input into relevant outcomes and data collection, information which is important when moving on to a full trial.

As financial challenges continue to play an ever greater role in health and social care planning and delivery, health economists will be called on even more frequently to provide important information on best use of limited resource. For example, health economists can provide valuable information to relevant stakeholders about the financial implications of implementing new interventions, weighed up alongside benefits. Health economists will increasingly be called on to provide input into the analysis of large observational data sets as a potentially efficient way to evaluate complex interventions. This will also be the case for initiatives that do not fit neatly into an RCT design, such as the implementation of policy initiatives into large geographical areas. Analysis plans for economic evaluations will require novel methodological considerations as trial designs adapt and change to respond to calls for more efficient ways to evaluate complex interventions.

References

1. Taplin SH, Clauser S, Rodgers AB, Breslau E, Rayson D (2010) Interfaces across the cancer continuum offer opportunities to improve the process of care. J Natl Cancer Inst Monogr 2010(40):104–110, Epub 2010/04/14
2. Taplin SH, Anhang Price R, Edwards HM, Foster MK, Breslau ES, Chollette V et al (2012) Introduction: understanding and influencing multilevel factors across the cancer care continuum. J Natl Cancer Inst Monogr 2012(44):2–10, Epub 2012/05/25
3. Craig P, Dieppe P, Macintyre S, Michie S, Nazareth I, Petticrew M (2008) Developing and evaluating complex interventions: the new Medical Research Council guidance. BMJ 337:a1655
4. Campbell M, Fitzpatrick R, Haines A, Kinmonth AL, Sandercock P, Spiegelhalter D et al (2000) Framework for design and evaluation of complex interventions to improve health. BMJ 321(7262):694–696
5. Moore GF, Audrey S, Barker M, Bond L, Bonell C, Hardeman W et al (2015) Process evaluation of complex interventions: Medical Research Council guidance. BMJ 350:h1258
6. Challis D, von Abendorff R, Brown P, Chesterman J, Hughes J (2002) Care management, dementia care and specialist mental health services: an evaluation. Int J Geriatr Psychiatry 17(4):315–325, Epub 2002/05/08
7. Rubenstein LM, DeLeo A, Chrischilles EA (2001) Economic and health-related quality of life considerations of new therapies in Parkinson's disease. PharmacoEconomics 19(7):729–752, Epub 2001/09/11

8. Round J (2012) Is a QALY still a QALY at the end of life? J Health Econ 31(3):521–527, Epub 2012/05/18
9. Round J, Sampson EL, Jones L (2014) A framework for understanding quality of life in individuals without capacity. Qual Life Res Int J Qual Life Asp Treat Care Rehab 23(2):477–484, Epub 2013/08/27
10. Thomas K (2003) Caring for the dying at home. Companions on a journey. Radcliffe Medical Press, Oxford
11. Neuberger J (2013) More care, less pathway. A review of the Liverpool Care Pathway. Department of Health. https://www.gov.uk/government/publications/review-of-liverpool-care-pathway-for-dying-patients
12. Evans CJ, Harding R, Higginson IJ (2013) 'Best practice' in developing and evaluating palliative and end-of-life care services: a meta-synthesis of research methods for the MORECare project. Palliat Med 27(10):885–898, Epub 2013/01/17
13. Hatziandreu E, Archontakis F, Daly A (2008) In: Office NA (ed) The potential cost savings of greater use of home- and hospice- based end of life care in England. RAND, Cambridge, UK
14. Eldridge S, Spencer A, Cryer C, Parsons S, Underwood M, Feder G (2005) Why modelling an complex intervention is an important precursor to trial design: lessons from studying an intervention to reduce falls-related injuries in older people. J Health Serv Res Policy 10(3):133–142, Epub 2005/08/02
15. Tappenden P, Chilcott JB, Eggington S, Oakley J, McCabe C (2004) Methods for expected value of information analysis in complex health economic models: developments on the health economics of interferon-beta and glatiramer acetate for multiple sclerosis. Health Technol Assess 8(27):iii, 1–78. Epub 2004/06/25
16. Briggs A, Sculpher M, Claxton K (2006) Decision modelling of health economic evaluation. Oxford University Press, Oxford
17. Drummond MF, Sculpher MJ, Torrence GW, O'Brien BJ, Stoddart GL (2005) Methods for the economic evaluation of health care programmes, 3rd edn. Oxford University Press, Oxford
18. McCrone P (2009) Capturing the costs of end-of-life care: comparisons of multiple sclerosis, Parkinson's disease, and dementia. J Pain Symptom Manag 38(1):62–67, Epub 2009/07/21
19. Patel A, Rendu A, Moran P, Leese M, Mann A, Knapp M (2005) A comparison of two methods of collecting economic data in primary care. Fam Pract 22(3):323–327, Epub 2005/04/13
20. Wallihan DB, Stump TE, Callahan CM (1999) Accuracy of self-reported health services use and patterns of care among urban older adults. Med Care 37(7):662–670, Epub 1999/07/29
21. Rozario PA, Morrow-Howell N, Proctor E (2004) Comparing the congruency of self-report and provider records of depressed elders' service use by provider type. Med Care 42(10):952–959, Epub 2004/09/21
22. Gage H, Cheynel J, Williams P, Mitchell K, Stinton C, Katz J et al (2015) Service utilisation and family support of people with dementia: a cohort study in England. Int J Geriatr Psychiatry 30(2):166–177
23. Chambless DL, Hollon SD (1998) Defining empirically supported therapies. J Consult Clin Psychol 66(1):7–18, Epub 1998/03/07
24. Burns T, Knapp M, Catty J, Healey A, Henderson J, Watt H et al (2001) Home treatment for mental health problems: a systematic review. Health Technol Assess 5(15):1–139, Epub 2001/09/05
25. Morris S, Hunter RM, Ramsay AI, Boaden R, McKevitt C, Perry C et al (2014) Impact of centralising acute stroke services in English metropolitan areas on mortality and length of hospital stay: difference-in-differences analysis. BMJ 349:g4757, Epub 2014/08/08
26. Angrist JD, Pischke J-S (2014) Mastering 'metrics: the path from cause to effect. Princeton University Press, Princeton
27. Gomes M, Ng ES, Grieve R, Nixon R, Carpenter J, Thompson SG (2012) Developing appropriate methods for cost-effectiveness analysis of cluster randomized trials. Med Decis Making Int J Soc Med Decis Making 32(2):350–361, Epub 2011/10/22
28. Hemming K, Haines TP, Chilton PJ, Girling AJ, Lilford RJ (2015) The stepped wedge cluster randomised trial: rationale, design, analysis, and reporting. BMJ 350:h391, Epub 2015/02/11

Chapter 4
Retrospective Analyses of End-of-Life Care Using Large Data Sets

Martin Bardsley

4.1 Introduction

Over the past decade, end-of-life care has become an important element in health policy in many countries. As a result there is now a keen interest amongst those funding and providing health care to understand more about what models of care deliver in terms of both the quality of services and the effective use of resources – whether publicly funded or private.

There are some key policy issues that have helped raise the profile of end-of-life care. Firstly, end-of-life care is thought to be costly – though as various recent studies have found the exact costs involved are not precise [1–3]. The NAO report estimated that the annual cost of end-of-life care for people with cancer was around £1.8 billion. They concluded that a shift to palliative care resulting in 20 % fewer emergency admissions and five fewer bed days per person would save £171 million per year.

Moreover it is predicted that the annual number of deaths will increase by 17 % between 2012 and 2030, with a growing proportion of deaths being amongst the very elderly [4]. With a sustained period of flat or falling healthcare expenditure seemingly likely, the growth in inpatient hospital care that would be required to cope with the rising number of deaths (based on current patterns of where people die) would seem implausible. This highlights the growing need for effective home- or community-based end-of-life care services. Surveys consistently suggest that the majority of people would prefer to die or be cared for at the end of life at home [5–8]. However, in England and Wales, 54 % of people died in the hospital in 2010, with only 21 % of deaths taking place at home [9]. Although the proportion of home deaths rose from 2004 to 2010, with the increase particularly seen in people with cancer [10], the

M. Bardsley
Nuffield Trust, New Cavendish Street, London, UK
e-mail: martin.bardsley@nuffieldtrust.org.uk

© Springer International Publishing Switzerland 2016
J. Round (ed.), *Care at the End of Life: An Economic Perspective*,
DOI 10.1007/978-3-319-28267-1_4

proportion of people who die at home in England and Wales has been found to be significantly lower than in some other developed countries [11–13].

4.2   Developing Information About End-of-Life Care

Now more than ever, there is a need for good-quality evidence and analysis that informs commissioning and policy decisions. However there has been a shortage of basic information about service delivered at the end of life [3, 14], and studies of effectiveness and cost-effectiveness face particular challenges [15, 16].

For many aspects of healthcare, the randomised controlled trial is held up as the best way to obtain evidence of the value of an intervention. However as other chapters describe (see Jones, Chap. 1 and Johnston, Chap. 2), the application of prospective randomisation methods at the end of life is particularly difficult. Aside from the logistical and ethical difficulties of recruitment and organising intervention at the end of life, there are also the limitations that derive from all RCTs, namely, the generalisability to everyday practice. Even with a pragmatic design without restrictive inclusion criteria [17], the trial may exclude certain patient subgroups or models of provisions that are of key interest to decision-making [18–20].

However it is clear that other forms of evidence are valid and in some cases the use of observation studies is the only one that is feasible [21]. Prospective trials can also be more also difficult to undertake where we want to look at established programmes of care or where new interventions are coming into place, but pilot programmes have not been designed from the outset with evaluation in mind. In these instances, it is important to be able to use methods that allow programmes to be evaluated retrospectively.

4.3   Retrospective Approaches Using Existing Data Sets

As an alternative to prospective studies, there is a growing interest in developing evaluative approaches that are retrospective and that draw on existing data sets. In particular by using information from death registration or activity of health and social care providers, it is possible to build up some profiles of care delivered [22]. For example in England, websites developed by the Public Health team in the South West demonstrate how this intelligence can be marshalled to develop local profiles (see http://www.endoflifecare-intelligence.org.uk/home). These forms of readily accessible data are useful for local service planning and have been used to understand, for example, the variation between areas in the proportion of people dying at home versus hospital.

Though these analyses do provide valuable intelligence, they also have some limitations when evaluating a particular service.

(a) When data are in aggregated form, it can be difficult to link to particular service types – as users of the service under study may make up only a fraction of the reported statistics.

(b) Data can be at quite high levels of aggregation and may not lend themselves to detailed subgroups analyses. So, for example, it may be possible to look at the effect of variables such as ethnicity when studied separately – but not together.

(c) Detail may also be limited about care provided and patient characteristics – so, for example, studies which isolate selected causes of death may be difficult.

(d) These data sets often rely on an annual cycle of publication – which means that it can be difficult to track short-term changes. Longer-term analyses are then fraught with the problems of consistent recording of data – where definitions of specific recorded data of interest may change over time.

These factors mean that the use of aggregated data is mainly limited to descriptive analyses. These can be very important in helping to understand local needs and to inform planning of services – but offer less in terms of evaluation of particular services or models of care. For studies of specific service and innovations, a different approach is needed that captures information at the level of an individual patient. These mean enabling access to the source data sets at the level of the individual.

4.4 Using Linked Person-Level Data Sets

Over the past few years, there has been an increasing interest in using data linkage approaches to exploit person level data sets [23, 24], allowing analysts to overcome the drawbacks of the aggregate data. Electronic records that capture individual transactions have become the norm in all walks of life – whether borrowing a library book, sending a parcel, paying for car tax or even for buying seemingly unnecessary goods from popular on-line auction sites.

In the health and care sector, person level electronic records are used to manage the day to day business of care. One's consultation with a family doctor is now usually a three-way interaction between the patient, doctor and computer – recording clinical observations, tests and treatment, helping the professional do their job and allowing the sharing of information across a practice for use in subsequent consultations. When individual records/events contain person-level identifiers, it is possible to string records of different episodes of care together to show patient care over time. This very simple idea is central to many assessments of outcomes which look at changes in health status over time.

Though the pioneering work on data linkage began in Oxford in the early 1960s [25], it is only in the last decade that record linkage has become more accessible. Moreover the NHS has some distinct advantages in this area:

- A system of primary care registration that applies to the vast majority of the population and a unique person-level identifier – the NHS number
- The dominance of NHS provision over private or voluntary care
- A system that has been capturing hospital data that has been operating in a more or less consistent fashion – with unique patient identifiers – that makes it possible to track a person's hospital use over time

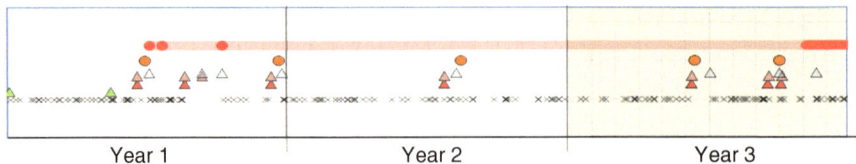

Year 1   Year 2   Year 3

Fig. 4.1 Health and social care event timeline for one person. This chart shows how one person accessed health and social care over a three year period including contacts with a GP (x) A&E attendance (*red triangle*); outpatient visit (*green triangle*); hospital stay admission to discharge (*orange to white triangle*), social care assessment (*red circle*) and social care service (*red line*)

And so in terms of care delivery, there are data sets recording important information about whether a person sees a GP and is admitted to hospital or whether the local authority is funding a home care service. These information systems are essential to perform these basic functions of care. Normally this information is contained in isolated data sets – yet is now increasingly common to be able to link these together for care planning and analysis.

Figure 4.1 gives an example of the sort of view that can be extracted when data sets are linked across sectors. In these cases the events shown are only summaries of what happened in terms of visits to the GP, hospital and social care inputs. These were first published in a study to look at predicting social care admissions [26]. In this case it shows individual's health and social care history over a period of 3 years summarising activity in terms of contact with GP hospital visits and admissions and social care supports

One way to use these data sets is in descriptive studies of service use. For example, one study looked at social care use at the end of life by linking data sets from health service commissioners and local authority social care providers [27]. By using anonymised[1] person-level records from whole populations of eight different local authorities, this study was able to analyse records from over 72,000 people who died. Figure 4.2a, b show how these studies were used to track the pattern of both hospital use and social care use in the last 12 months of life. Figure 4.2a illustrates the dramatic rise in hospital use, especially emergency inpatient admissions that occur in 3 months before a person died. In contrast Fig. 4.2b shows how costs of local authority-funded care increased only gradually through the year.

This report was also able to look at levels of hospital use for people in receipt of local authority social care. It noted a broadly inverse relationship between hospital costs and social care costs across all age groups – implying that the people incurring higher social care costs (mostly those in a care home) tended to use less hospital care. This observation has also been made in other studies (e.g. [28]). There are a variety of possible explanations including that a hospital admission can sometimes be avoided by support provided in a residential care setting – a substitution effect. People within care homes may feel (or be perceived to be) better able, or better supported, to cope outside of the hospital.

---

[1] This study used an approach of pseudonymisation at source whereby secure patient-level identifiers were created by the different agencies. Sensitive information such as individual names and addresses were removed before being sent to the research team.

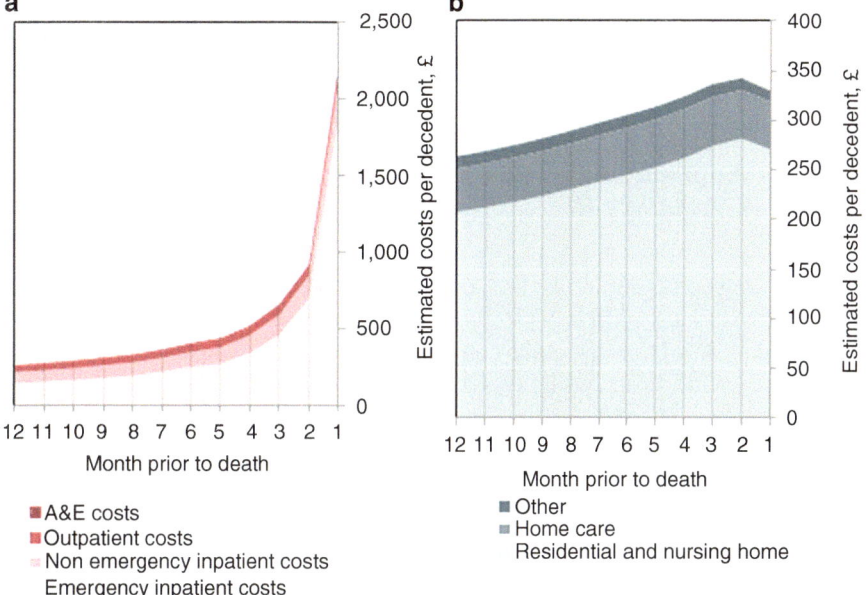

Fig. 4.2 Estimated average costs of care services in each of last 12 months of life split by type of service, hospital care (**a**) and social care (**b**). ($N = 73,243$)

4.5 Retrospective Matching Methods

In addition to descriptive analyses, the use of person-level linked data sets also makes it possible to undertake evaluative studies of particular interventions and services. Linked data can be used to track people over time before and after the intervention. Most importantly such data sets can also be used to creating comparator or control groups through the use of approaches such as propensity or prognostic scoring [29, 30]. These techniques have been applied and widely discussed in evaluations of medical interventions such as pulmonary artery catheterisation [31, 32] and are increasingly being used to study large-scale evaluations of complex community-based interventions.

The idea is to select potential control cases retrospectively, based on identifying cases that are similar across a range of baseline variables. A variety of techniques exist to select matched controls including 'propensity score methods collapse' which summarise a series of baseline variables to a single quantity, which is the estimated probability of an individual receiving the intervention given certain baseline characteristics. A control is then selected on the basis that it has a similar propensity score to the individual receiving the intervention.

More recently, prognostic score methods have been developed [29]. These use different measures based on the estimated probability of an individual receiving the outcome without the intervention. So for a study of hospital admissions, it would be the predicted risk of admission. The prognostic approach weights variables by how predictive they are of future outcomes and so seeks to balance variables that are strongly predictive of future events. The following sections discuss how these methods have been used in one study of end-of-life care.

4.6 An Application: Evaluation of a Home Nursing Service at the End of Life

The following sections describe how this method was used in one study of a home nursing service at the end of life [33, 34]. The Marie Curie Nursing Service (MCNS) was introduced in 1958 to provide nursing care and support to people in their own home. The MCNS is staffed by registered nurses and senior healthcare assistants who provide home-based care to around 28,000 people at the end of life annually in the UK. Although it initially focused on caring for people with cancer, it has increasingly provided care to people with other conditions. The service is commissioned by many local NHS organisations in England. The MCNS offers a number of different models of care:

* Planned – 8 or 9-h shifts of usually overnight nursing care, booked in advance
* Reactive – similar to planned care, but available at short notice
* Multi-visit – shorter episodes of care, usually with multiple visits per nursing shift
* Rapid response – urgent support in response to crises occurring 'out of hours'. May involve either home visits or telephone support

There have been some studies of the MCNS. A 2004 review [35] suggested the care offered by the MCNS was likely to be cost-effective, with potentially £2 saved for every £1 spent on such services. However, this was based on estimated costs rather than being an empirical study of the actual impact of MCNS care. Another study looked at the place of death of over 26,000 people who received MCNS care [36]. It found that 94 % of people were able to die at home, with increasing likelihood of home death associated with a shorter time from referral to death.

In this study the Nuffield Trust was commissioned by Marie Curie Cancer Care (MCCC) to conduct an independent evaluation of the impact of the MCNS on patient outcomes and hospital usage. The key questions were:

* Are people who receive MCNS care more likely to die at home?
* Does the MCNS reduce unplanned hospital use at the end of life?

As a secondary aim, we also wanted to investigate whether the impact (if any) of MCNS care varied as a function of factors such as having a history of cancer, the number of long-term conditions and the type of service received.

The study was therefore pragmatic in that it looked at the reality of everyday care provided by the nursing service. The approach to analysis was therefore to be inclusive and consider all those who received MCNS care between January 2009 and

November 2011. For these patients data would be linked to show their patterns of hospitalisation, and these would be compared to a set of matched controls patients. Ideally, the matched controls would have had the characteristics that were used to identify cases as being eligible for MCNS care. These would include being at the end of life and considered suitable for care at home. However, these criteria do not map naturally onto variables that are recorded in HES, so instead we used proxies. We matched cases and controls individually on a range of demographic, diagnostics and prior hospital use variables.

4.7 Identifying the Person-Level Data Sets

The starting point for this analysis was to identify patients who had been in receipts of MCNS care during a given time period. This data was kept on the routine information systems. Using these systems, we identified a potential study cohort of 38,728 people who received care from the nursing service during that time. The data from the Marie Curie routine information systems were then split into two parts, but each shared a unique study number.

One data file containing person-level identifiers (such as names, postcodes) was sent to through a secure route to the NHS Information Centre (now called Health and Social Care Information Centre). This was then used to identify the key field that linked to electronic hospital records. These keys (HESIDs) were sent to the research team – but without any of the personal identifying information. The vast majority of this group (97 %) could be linked to the hospital records data base, and so only 1,146 individual records were excluded.

The remaining information with details about when a person received a service and the type of service – together with the study number – was sent to the research team and could be linked to the hospital records using the study number. The end result was that we able to identify the summary hospital records for the vast majority of the Marie Curie patients – even though we could not identify who those individual patients were. After cleaning to remove records with missing or inconsistent data, the final cohort consisted of 31,107 people which represented the vast majority of cases of mainstream home nursing care across the country.

4.8 Matching to Find a Control Group

For each Marie Curie patient in the cohort, we looked for individuals to act as control. Ideally, the matched controls would have had the characteristics that were used to identify cases as being eligible for MCNS care. These would include being at the end of life and considered suitable for care at home. We used a two-stage process to identify controls. Stage one created a pool of potential controls based on people who have died within 90 days of the case (to avoid possible confounding effects of

Table 4.1 Characteristics of Marie Curie patients and matched controls

	Mean (sd)	
Measure	Marie Curie	Matched controls
Age	74.8 (12.1)	74.7 (11.4)
Female	47 %	47 %
Deprivation (IMD)	20.1 (14.3)	19.5 (13.3)
Number of chronic conditions	1.50 (1.52)	1.43 (1.42)
Number of conditions associated with ageing	0.70 (0.97)	0.65 (0.96)

service changes over time) and matched on an overall history of cancer recorded on hospital records in the previous 3 years. From this pool of possible controls, we selected the control who was most similar to the case across a number of variables, using the multidimensional distance measure known as the Mahalanobis metric [37]. The variables included in this matching stage were:

- Age
- Area-level socioeconomic deprivation score (IMD (Index of Multiple Deprivation) 2010 score for the LSOA of the postcode)
- Number of emergency admissions in the month/year before the index date
- Number of elective admissions in the month/year before the index date
- Number of outpatient attendances in the month/year before the index date
- Number of A&E attendances in the month/year before the index date
- Number of chronic conditions based on a list of 12 specific conditions, e.g. diabetes and asthma
- History of six cancer types (lung, upper and lower GI (gastrointestinal), sarcoma, CUP (cancer of unknown primary origin), brain and CNS (central nervous system)
- Number of different cancers/conditions associated with ageing

We selected a single control per case using matching without replacement so that the control group would consist of unique individuals (Table 4.1). Sometimes these methods choose multiple matched controls for a single case or consider controls as eligible for more than one case. The choice of single or multiple matches is dependent on the relative numbers of cases in the intervention group and potential pools of controls – which needs to be much bigger for multiple matches which offer a little more power.

4.9 Quality of the Matching

The process of selecting cases as suitable matches relies on complex statistical algorithms, and there are a series of trade-offs to be made during the process. At the heart of these decisions are measures of balance between intervention and controls groups on individual variables. The best matching variables are usually judged on the standardised differences between them (defined as the difference in

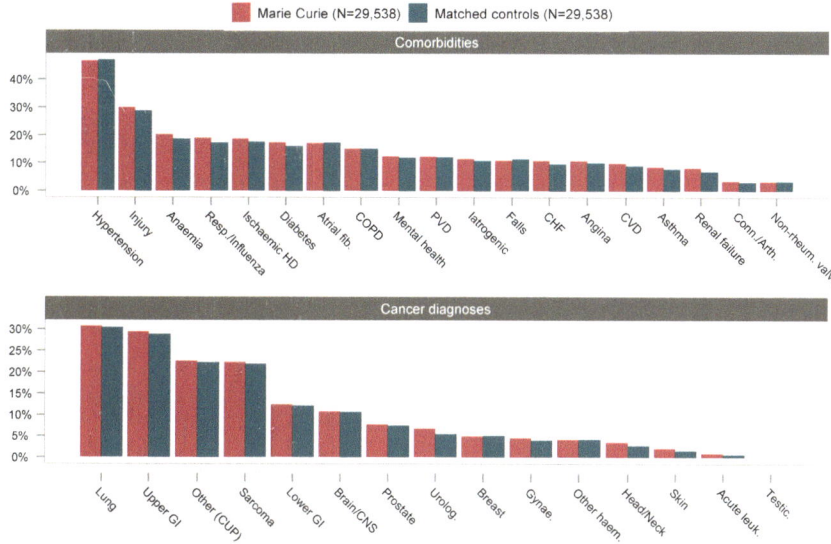

Fig. 4.3 Comparing the frequency of key variables describing chronic health conditions and cancer types in cases and matched

sample means as a percentage of the square root of the average of sample variances). A general rule of thumb is that a standardised difference of >10 % denotes a meaningful imbalance [38].

Before matching, there were a number of significant differences between the groups. For example, compared to the potential controls, those who received MCNS care were younger and less deprived, but much more likely to have been diagnosed with cancer. Potential controls were much more likely to have been diagnosed with dementia or congestive heart failure and to have had a recent history of falls and fractures. However after matching, the subset of cases identified as controls were much more like the MCNS patients in terms of demographic characteristics, morbidity and prior hospital use variables, with no standardised differences of >10 %. As an example Fig. 4.3 compares the frequency of variables identifying chronic health problems and cancer diagnoses between the MCNS groups and the selected control group – across all these variables the differences are very small between the two groups.

4.10 Findings

Having identified matched cases and controls is then possible to compare the groups on some key outcomes. Place of death was a key outcome measure with the hope that the MCNS service would lead to a greater proportion of patients dying at home rather than hospital.

Table 4.2 Place of death for Marie Curie patients and controls

	Place of death			
Group	Home	Hospital	Hospice	Others
Marie Curie	76.7 %	7.7 %	13.0 %	2.5 %
Matched controls	34.9 %	41.6 %	21.5 %	2.0 %

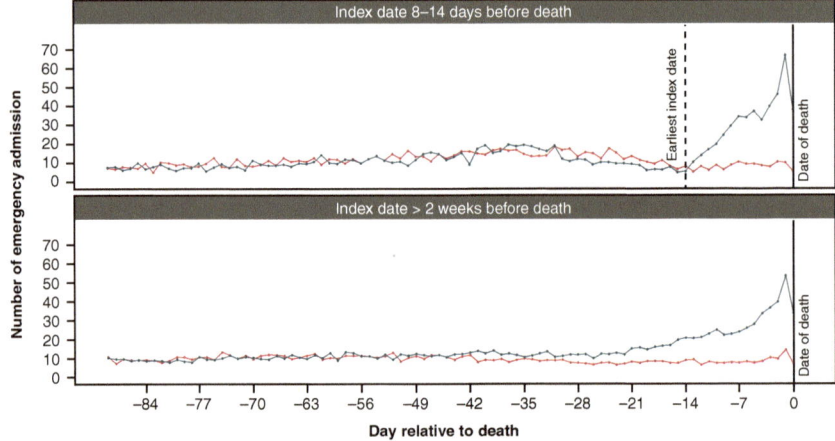

Fig. 4.4 Comparing emergency hospital admissions in the last 90 days according to the starting time of nursing service

The results were positive. 76.7 % of those who received MCNS care died at home, with 7.7 % dying in hospital. In contrast, 34.9 % of the matched controls died at home, with 41.6 % dying in hospital (Table 4.2). The difference in the proportion dying at home was highly statistically significant (unadjusted odds ratio = 6.16, $p<0.001$). The effects remained statistically significant in a more complex model that adjusted for demographic, diagnostic and prior hospital use variables ($p<0.001$).

In this case there is particular interest on how these types of intervention impact on hospital use. Figure 4.4 displays the number of emergency hospital admissions per 1,000 people by day for those who received MCNS care starting 8–14 days before death and their matched controls. The two lines show how in the period from 12 to 2 weeks before death the cases and controls were well matched in terms of the frequency of emergency admissions. However in the final few weeks, the differences between the two groups emerge. Whilst emergency admissions for those using the nursing service stay at a low level, the control group showed a sharp increase in admissions.

The differences between these two lines indicate a lower level of emergency hospital use that was observed across the whole group of people using the nursing service. In fact these differences were observed across range of different measures of hospital activity.

Table 4.3 Hospital activity for Marie Curie patients and matched controls

Activity type	Mean (sd) activity per person		Crude difference	Rate ratio	P value
	Marie Curie	Matched controls			
Emergency admissions	0.15 (0.48)	0.44 (0.73)	−0.29	0.34	<0.0001
Elective admissions	0.06 (0.78)	0.14 (1.16)	−0.08	0.47	<0.0001
Outpatient attendances	0.25 (1.65)	0.52 (2.01)	−0.27	0.46	<0.0001
A&E attendances	0.10 (0.38)	0.34 (0.63)	−0.24	0.28	<0.0001
Emergency bed days	1.32 (5.59)	3.60 (8.97)	−2.28	0.37	<0.0001
Elective bed days	0.25 (2.38)	0.45 (3.35)	−0.20	0.58	<0.0001

Table 4.4 Comparing average hospital costs for Marie Curie patients and matched controls (after index start date for nursing service)

Activity type	Mean (sd) hospital costs per person		Crude difference	F value	P value
	Marie Curie	Matched controls			
Emergency admissions	£463 (£1,758)	£1,293 (£2,531)	−£830	2464.2	<0.0001
Elective admissions	£106 (£961)	£350 (£1,736)	−£244	369.8	<0.0001
Outpatient attendances	£33 (£212)	£76 (£340)	−£43	329.1	<0.0001
A&E attendances	£9 (£34)	£31 (£60)	−£22	3586.3	<0.0001
All hospital activity	£610 (£2,172)	£1,750 (£3,377)	−£1,140	2682.3	<0.0001

Table 4.3 summarises the estimated effects. The use of all types of hospital care was significantly lower in those who received MCNS care compared to matched controls. Across most forms of activity, MCNS patients had between a third and half of the level of hospital use seen in controls. All these differences were significant.

The use of linked person level data also means that the costs of hospital activity to the commissioners of care can be estimated relatively simply using a combination of casemix based tariffs, with some additional use of standard costs (following the methods used in [39]). These measures weight the different forms of activity to give an estimate of what the commissioners of hospital services may pay for patients receiving the nursing service and contrast with usual care as represented by the costs in the control group.

Table 4.4 summarises the average costs per person of hospital care in the period after the index date until death. These figures suggest that overall a person who received MCNS care incurred over £1,100 less in hospital costs in the time between the index date and death, compared to a control over the same period. The vast bulk of the difference was accounted for by reductions in emergency admission costs, although significant reductions were seen across all types of hospital care.

4.11 Discussion

This study demonstrates the way that existing routinely collected data can be used to show an impact on the use of hospital care at the end of life for patients receiving the MCNS. Together these results point to a positive benefit of the MCNS in terms of the impacts of the service on place of death and avoidable hospital admissions. These findings of a higher rate of home deaths, and lower hospital use and costs amongst those who received home-based end-of-life care, are broadly consistent with the existing literature [2, 3, 40–48].

But in addition it is important to note that this study was based on analysing the intervention as applied in practice and on a large scale – rather than in the controlled environment of specific trial or study. In fact the results were derived from studying almost all users of this service so goes a long way to calm any concerns about issues of transferability or sustainability of a model of care. Moreover by using large cohorts for analysis enables researchers to undertake viable studies of subsets of the population which are large enough to show significant differences – for example, the comparison of cancer and non-cancer patients.

Our results showed that the type of home-based end-of-life care was a significant factor on hospital utilisation and costs [33]. People who received the 'standard' planned service of 9-h/day or overnight care (either alone or in conjunction with other types of MCNS care) were much more likely to die at home than those who only received multi-visit or rapid response services. Similarly, for people who received the planned package of care, the average cost reduction compared to controls was around £1,100, whilst it was significantly smaller for those who received only multi-visit or rapid response care at around £900 and £500, respectively. Those who received multi-visit or rapid response care in addition to planned care had the biggest reduction in costs compared to controls. However, the number of MCNS patients who received a service other than planned care alone was small, and so significant caution is needed in interpreting these results.

Of course these approaches do have limitations. The most important are the potential problems arising in non-randomised studies where there is a danger that there are hidden systematic differences between intervention and non-intervention patients. The groups in this evaluation were selected to be as similar as possible on a wide range of variables – but these are limited to information available in the records. There are likely to be characteristics that influence individuals' suitability for home-based end-of-life care that are not recorded in routine administrative data. For example, groups could have differed in terms of the availability of family or other carer support, as well as their preferred place of death. This could potentially have a large impact on the findings if, for example, MCNS patients were more amenable to home care or had greater informal support than controls. Future research should aim to explore the potential impact of these factors, for example, through an RCT.

Secondly, we also have to recognise that this study was not a full economic evaluation, and so it is likely that at least some of these cost differences might be accounted for by other services [15]. Obviously there is the cost of providing the MCNS itself. However, it is also possible that keeping people at home at the end of life would increase the demand for other community services, including district nursing, primary care and social care. Future work should explore the impact of home-based nursing services on the broader set of health and care services [49]. The Palliative Care Funding Pilot sites set up as a result of the recent palliative care funding review may provide relevant information on the costs of these services [1].

The size of the end-of-life population who might benefit from the type of home-based care offered by the MCNS is unclear. It is possible that such services are already provided to most of those for whom they would be suitable, that is, the saturation point has been reached. However, a recent review of palliative care funding in England [1] suggested that around 75 % of the nearly 500,000 people who die each year would be suitable for some form of palliative care. They also estimated that around 90,000 people who would benefit from palliative care die each year without receiving any. This suggests that there is significant potential to increase the number of people who have access to such services.

A recent initiative to improve NHS productivity, QIPP (Quality, Innovation, Productivity and Prevention) programme [49], included work streams in end-of-life care that sought to increase the number of people dying in their usual place of residence and to reduce the number of emergency admissions in the last year of life. Overall these findings are clearly relevant to the policy goals of this programme, in that they provide evidence of the potential benefits of home-based end-of-life nursing schemes, such as that operated by Marie Curie.

4.12   Conclusion

In an increasingly tight financial climate for public services, there is a drive to identify models of service delivery that can reduce demand for expensive hospital care whilst maintaining or improving the quality and experience of patient care. Whilst there is not a shortage of ideas about how new services may be provided, the evidence around this is often lacking – and out of step with policy. So, for example, the NHS is grappling with an increase in emergency hospital care – yet despite the wide range of solutions proposed to solve this problem, very few have been found to be effective (Purdy et al. 2014). As ever more initiatives emerge, there is an urgent need to understand 'what works', yet there is often little time, money or inclination to establish prospective trials. There is therefore a critical role for observational studies that exploit the mass of data we collect already. By using more advanced methods, such as the matching discussed here, we can generate much more robust evaluations. These should be more timely and stand more chance of influencing the managerial decisions that have to be made over investment, or disinvestment, in any particular services.

References

1. Hughes-Hallett T, Craft A and Davies C (2011) Funding the Right Care and Support for Everyone - An independent review for the Secretary of State for Health. Accessed janury 2016. https://www.gov.uk/government/uploads/system/uploads/attachment_data/file/215107/dh_133105.pdf
2. Lorenz KA, Lynn J, Dy SM, Shugarman LR, Wilkinson A, Mularski RA, Morton SC, Hughes RG, Hilton LK, Maglione M, Rhodes SL, Rolon C, Sun VC, Shekelle PG (2008) Evidence for improving palliative care at the end of life: a systematic review. Ann Intern Med 148(2):147–159
3. National Audit Office (2008) End of Life Care. HC 1043, Report by the Comptroller and Auditor General, Session 2007–2008. TSO (The Stationery Office) London. https://www.nao.org.uk/report/end-of-life-care/
4. Gomes B, Higginson IJ (2008) Where people die (1974–2030): past trends, future projections and implications for care. Palliat Med 22(1):33–41
5. Gomes B, McCrone P, Hall S, Koffman J, Higginson IJ (2010) Variations in the quality and costs of end-of-life care, preferences and palliative outcomes for cancer patients by place of death: the QUALYCARE study. BMC Cancer 10:400
6. Gomes B, Calanzani N, Higginson IJ (2012) Reversal of the British trends in place of death: time series analysis 2004–2010. Palliat Med 26(2):102–107
7. Higginson IJ (2003) Priorities and preferences for end of life care in England, Wales and Scotland. The Cicely Saunders Foundation, London
8. Office for National Statistics (2011b) National bereavement survey (VOICES) Published by ONS Statistical Bulleting July 2012. http://www.ons.gov.uk/ons/rel/subnational-health1/national-bereavement-survey--voices-/2012/stb---national-bereavement-survey-2012.html
9. Office for National Statistics (2011a) Mortality statistics: deaths registered in England and Wales (Series DR). 2010. Published by ONS, London. http://www.ons.gov.uk/ons/rel/vsob1/mortality-statistics--deaths-registered-in-england-and-wales--series-dr-/2011/stb-deaths-registered-in-england-and-wales-in-2011-by-cause.html
10. Gomes B, Higginson IJ, Calanzani N, Cohen J, Deliens L, Daveson BA, Bechinger-English D, Bausewein C, Ferreira PL, Toscani F, Meñaca A, Gysels M, Ceulemans L, Simon ST, Pasman HR, Albers G, Hall S, Murtagh FE, Haugen DF, Downing J, Koffman J, Pettenati F, Finetti S, Antunes B, Harding R (2012) Preferences for place of death if faced with advanced cancer: a population survey in England, Flanders, Germany, Italy, the Netherlands, Portugal and Spain. Ann Oncol 23(8):2006–2015
11. Cohen J, Bilsen J, Addington-Hall J, Lofmark R, Miccinesi G, Kaasa S, Onwuteaka-Philipsen B, Deliens L (2008) Population-based study of dying in hospital in six European countries. Palliat Med 22(6):702–710
12. Cohen J, Houttekier D, Onwuteaka-Philipsen B, Miccinesi G, Addington-Hall J, Kaasa S, Bilsen J, Deliens L (2010) Which patients with cancer die at home? A study of six European countries using death certificate data. J Clin Oncol 28(13):2267–2273
13. World Health Organization (2004) In: Davies E, Higginson IJ (eds) Better palliative care for older people. WHO, Copenhagen. See http://www.euro.who.int/__data/assets/pdf_file/0009/98235/E82933.pdf
14. Department of Health (2009) End of life care strategy. First annual report. Department of Health, London
15. Murtagh FEM, Groeneveld EI, Kaloki YE, Natalia C, Claudia B, Higginson IJ (2013) Capturing activity, costs, and outcomes: the challenges to be overcome for successful economic evaluation in palliative care. Progress Palliat Care 21(4):232–235
16. Sculpher MJ, Pang FS, Manca A, Drummond MF, Golder S, Urdahl H et al (2004) Generalisability in economic evaluation studies in healthcare: a review and case studies. Health Technol Assess 8(49):iii–iv, 1–192
17. Roland M, Torgerson DJ (1998) Understanding controlled trials: what are pragmatic trials? BMJ 316(7127):285–285

18. Gheorghe A, Roberts TE, Ives JC, Fletcher BR, Calvert M (2013) Centre selection for clinical trials and the generalisability of results: a mixed methods study. PLoS ONE 8(2):e56560
19. McCarney R, Warner J, Iliffe S, van Haselen R, Griffin M, Fisher P (2007) The Hawthorne effect: a randomised, controlled trial. BMC Med Res Methodol 7(1):30
20. Rothwell PM (2005) External validity of randomised controlled trials: "to whom do the results of this trial apply?". Lancet 365(9453):82–93
21. Black N (1996) Why we need observational studies to evaluate the effectiveness of health care. BMJ 312:1215–1218
22. Osinowo A, Verne J (2011) External Causes of Death. National End of Life Care Intelligence Network. ISBN: 978-0-9569225-7-1. Available from http://www.endoflifecare-intelligence. org.uk/view?rid=117
23. Maddams J, Utley M, Moller H (2011) Levels of acute health service use among cancer survivors in the United Kingdom. Eur J Cancer 47(14):2211–2220
24. Roos LL, Brownell M, Lix L, Roos NP, Walld R, MacWilliam L (2008) From health research to social research: privacy, methods, approaches. Soc Sci Med 66:117–129
25. Acheson DM, Evans JG (1964) The Oxford record linkage study: a review of the method with some preliminary results. Proc R Soc Med 57:269–2
26. Bardsley M, Georghiou T, Chassin L, Lewis G, Steventon A, Dixon J (2012) Overlap of hospital use and social care in older people in England. J Health Serv Res Policy17(3):133–9. doi: 10.1258/jhsrp.2011.010171. Epub 2012 Feb 23
27. Bardsley MJ, Georghiou T, Dixon J (2010) Social Care and Hospital Use at the End of Life. Nuffield Trust. London
28. Hollander MJ (2009) Costs of end-of-life care: findings from the province of Saskatchewan. Healthc Q 12(3):50–58
29. Hansen B (2008) The prognostic analogue of the propensity score. Biometrical 95:481–488
30. Rosenbaum PR, Rubin DB (1983) The central role of the propensity score in observational studies for causal effects. Biometrical 70:41–55. doi:10.1111/j.1475-6773.2008.00834.x, Health Research and Educational Trust
31. Austin PC (2008) A critical appraisal of propensity-score matching in the medical literature between 1996 and 2003. Stat Med 27:2037–2049
32. Sekhon JS, Grieve R (2008) A New non-parametric matching method for bias adjustment with applications to economic evaluations. iHEA 2007 6th world congress: explorations in Health Economics Paper. Available at SSRN: http://ssrn.com/abstract=1138926
33. Chitnis X, Georghiou T, Steventon A, Bardsley M (2012) The impact of the Marie Curie Nursing Service on place of death and hospital use at the end of life. Nuffield Trust, London
34. Chitnis X, Georghiou T, Steventon A, Bardsley MJ (2013) Effect of a home-based end-of-life nursing service on hospital use at the end of life and place of death: a study using administrative data and matched controls. BMJ Support Palliat Care 3:422–430. Published Online First: 5 June 2013. doi:10.1136/bmjspcare-2012-000424
35. Taylor DG, Carter S (2004) Valuing choice – dying at home. A case for core equitable provision of high-quality support for people who wish to die at home. Marie Curie Cancer Care. MCCC London
36. Higginson IJ, Wilkinson S (2002) Marie Curie nurses: enabling patients with cancer to die at home. Br J Community Nurs 7(5):240–244
37. Mahalanobis PC (1936) On the generalised distance in statistics. Proc Natl Inst Sci India 2(1):49–55
38. Normand ST, Landrum MB, Guadagnoli E, Ayanian JZ, Ryan TJ, Cleary PD, McNeil BJ (2001) Validating recommendations for coronary angiography following acute myocardial infarction in the elderly: a matched analysis using propensity scores. J Clin Epidemiol 54(4): 387–398
39. Dixon J, Smith P, Gravelle H, Martin S, Bardsley M, Rice H, Georghiou T, Dusheiko M, Billings J, De Lorenzo MI (2011) A person based formula for allocating commissioning funds to general practices in England: development of a statistical model. BMJ 343:d6608. doi:10.1136/bmj.d6608, Published 22 November 2011

40. Alonso-Babarro A, Astray-Mochales J, Domínguez-Berjón F, Gènova-Maleras R, Bruera E, Díaz-Mayordomo A, Centeno C (2012) The association between in-patient death, utilization of hospital resources and availability of palliative home care for cancer patients. Palliat Med. doi: 10.1177/0269216312442973 [Epub ahead of print: http://pmj.sagepub.com/content/early /2012/04/03/0269216312442973.full.pdf+html]

41. Brumley R, Enguidanos S, Jamison P, Seitz R, Morgenstern N, Saito S, McIlwane J, Hillary K, Gonzalez J (2007) Increased satisfaction with care and lower costs: results of a randomized trial of in-home palliative care. J Am Geriatr Soc 55(7):993–1000

42. Costantini M, Higginson IJ, Boni L, Orengo MA, Garrone E, Henriquet F, Bruzzi P (2003) Effect of a palliative home care team on hospital admissions among patients with advanced cancer. Palliat Med 17(4):315–321

43. Gomes B, Higginson IJ (2006) Factors influencing death at home in terminally ill patients with cancer: systematic review. Br Med J 332(7540):515–521

44. Gómez-Batiste X, Caja C, Espinosa J, Bullich I, Martínez-Muñoz M, Porta-Sales J, Trelis J, Esperalba J, Stjernsward J (2012) The Catalonia World Health Organization demonstration project for palliative care implementation: quantitative and qualitative results at 20 years. J Pain Symptom Manag 43(4):783–794

45. Gomes B, Calanzani N, Curiale V, McCrone P, Higginson IJ (2013) Effectiveness and cost-effectiveness of home palliative care services for adults with advanced illness and their caregivers. Cochrane Database Syst Rev (6):CD007760. doi:10.1002/14651858.CD007760.pub2

46. Purdy S, Lasseter G, Griffin T et al. (2015) Impact of the Marie Curie Cancer Care Delivering Choice Programme in Somerset and North Somerset on place of death and hospital usage: a retrospective cohort study. BMJ Support Palliat Care. 2015;5(1):34–39. doi:10.1136/bmjsp-care-2013-000645. Epub 2014 May 16

47. Serra-Prat M, Gallo P and Picaza JM (2001) Home palliative care as a cost-saving alternative: evidence from Catalonia. Palliative Medicine 15(4):271–8.

48. Tamir O, Singer Y, Shvartzman P (2007) Taking care of terminally-ill patients at home – the economic perspective revisited. Palliat Med 21(6):537–541

49. National End of Life Care Programme (2012) Reviewing end of life care costing information to inform the QIPP end of life care work stream. NHS National End of Life Care Programme. http://socialwelfare.bl.uk/subject-areas/services-activity/health-services/nhsnationalendoflife-careprogramme/reviewing12.aspx

Chapter 5
Preference Elicitation at the End of Life

Terry N. Flynn, Charlie Corke, and Elisabeth Huynh

5.1 Introduction

Given that potential end-of-life (EOL) situations for older people frequently render the patient incapacitated or unconscious, with low chances of recovery, patients and citizens are encouraged to construct advance care plans (ACPs) that set out their wishes for care in such scenarios [1]. An ACP constitutes a set of treatment wishes under each of a potentially large number of "what if?" scenarios. Previous research to understand what elements of these ACP scenarios drive treatment preferences have identified outcomes such as "a good death", "quality of death and dying" and "quality end-of-life care" [1–3]. The particular outcomes elicited, however, typically, depend on the setting and the population studied, demonstrating that people's preferences regarding life-extending care are context specific. For instance, previous work has suggested that in certain circumstances westerners may value maintaining control over decision-making, whilst in some Asian cultures (e.g. Japan), the patient is more inclined to delegate decisions to their physician or the family [4]. Therefore, clinicians and policymakers also need good individual-level data regarding preferences for such care.

However, elicitation of ACPs across the entire population is probably impossible. On the one hand, younger adults typically have better cognitive skills to consider complex treatment scenarios due to lower rates of cognitive impairment. On the other hand, older adults may have better formed (and more informed) views

T.N. Flynn (✉)
TF Choices Ltd, Nottingham, UK
e-mail: drterryflynn@gmail.com

C. Corke
Barwon Health, University Hospital Geelong, Geelong, VIC, Australia

E. Huynh
Institute for Choice, University of South Australia Business School, Sydney, NSW, Australia

© Springer International Publishing Switzerland 2016
J. Round (ed.), *Care at the End of Life: An Economic Perspective*,
DOI 10.1007/978-3-319-28267-1_5

because they are more likely to have thought about the issues and/or witnessed others in EOL scenarios. Thus, if EOL discussions take place, clinicians often find themselves eliciting EOL views amongst vulnerable adults who are on a potentially EOL care pathway already and/or who are experiencing age-related cognitive impairment.

One solution, the "Gold Standard Framework" [5] utilised in practice in the UK, requires the respondent to name specific treatments that are not wanted and elements of care that are wanted. Whilst short and cognitively easy, this assumes preferences are independent of the wider clinical situation and give no indication of the trade-offs the patient is willing to make when their stated "wants" come into conflict and cannot all be achieved simultaneously.

Perhaps as a result, studies in the clinical literature increasingly formulate ACPs as a series of structured "vignettes" [6]. These are constructed using a standardised set of features, such as "life-saving treatment on offer", "assumed pretreatment cognitive state" and "health deterioration leading to an EOL situation", and each of these is varied in repeated questions. Respondents must then decide whether, in each structured vignette, they would wish the life-saving treatment on offer to be administered. However, it has been noted that these structured vignette studies are, in fact, simple types of discrete choice experiment (DCE) [7], a preference elicitation technique with a 30-year history.

5.2 Why Use Discrete Choice Experiments to Capture Preferences for End-of-Life Care?

Discrete choice experiments (DCEs) were initially developed to understand public preferences in transport and marketing [8]. They began to be used to elicit patient preferences in health in the early 1990s [9]. Their principal strength is that they are rooted in a well-tested psychological theory of human decision-making – random utility theory [10] – which, unlike some economic theories, explains key phenomena observed in practice: people making inconsistent choices, being sure or less sure of preferences in different circumstances and being influenced by context effects [11].

The intuition behind random utility theory is simple: when choosing between two options, A and B, how often the respondent chooses A over B in repeated choices gives an indication of how much (s)he values A over B. Broadly speaking, choice frequencies define value, and their predictive power in subsequent real-world decisions won Daniel McFadden the economics Nobel prize in 2000. Random utility theory also assumes people are not perfectly consistent: people reverse their decision sometimes, and this random component allows the analyst to gain insights into issues such as the respondent's certainty of their preferences.

In this context, a DCE would use the observed choice frequencies in a regression model to provide quantitative estimates of how much all the possible features describing EOL scenarios (indeed all possible EOL scenarios themselves) are disliked. If the analyst wishes to remain within the wider medical paradigm based on odds ratios, a well-designed DCE can provide the odds of an individual patient refusing treatment in a particular scenario. Thus, in some respects, DCEs merely extend the between-subject paradigm of clinical trials to provide within-subject inferences.

5.3 Issues with the Use of DCEs (and Clinical Vignette Studies) to Elicit Patient Preferences for End-of-Life Care

There is a wealth of evidence to show that the acceptability of many end-of-life scenarios depends on their specific features [12]. The invasiveness of the treatment, likely post-treatment outcomes in the event of survival and whether the individual is required to assume he/she is already living with severe cognitive impairments like dementia, influences answers to the question "would you wish for this particular treatment, if it were required to keep you alive?" Asking every possible combination of such features – every possible "what if?" scenario – is clearly not feasible, given the complexity and number of modern treatment care paths.

To solve this problem and radically reduce the number of "what if?" scenarios required to elicit the respondent's preferences, DCEs use statistical designs [13, 14]. For example, suppose an individual would wish never to be kept alive if they were to experience severe dementia, there is no need to present (more) scenarios that include dementia. Design theory can also reduce the number of scenarios by making assumptions about which combinations of features "are simply the sum of their parts". In principle, the size of the DCE survey can then be manageable – often of the order of 8–24 questions.

However, since many people complete an ACP quite late in their lives when they are vulnerable and/or suffering from age-related cognitive decline, even small statistical designs may be too large. The best-worst scaling (BWS) technique [15] addresses this by obtaining more information per question: it asks the individual for the "least preferred/acceptable" in addition to the "most preferred/acceptable" item in each question. There are three "cases" (types) of BWS, which differ primarily in terms of the complexity of the items being chosen. Cases 2 and 3 both involve consideration of complete EOL scenarios and, as such, are unlikely to reduce cognitive burden beyond that required in existing clinical vignette studies.

Therefore, researchers may be forgiven for asking if they are back to square one when it comes to the use of discrete choice tasks in eliciting ACPs. If they remain within a traditional DCE framework, then arguably, in some circumstances, yes. Yet health researchers may have an alternative, if they look to the third type of BWS, Case 1, used frequently in other disciplines but largely unknown in health [15]. The remainder of this chapter will discuss how Case 1 BWS can provide an easy way of eliciting patient EOL attitudes. It will also refer to emerging work that may convince any readers sceptical of the value of answers to hypothetical scenarios.

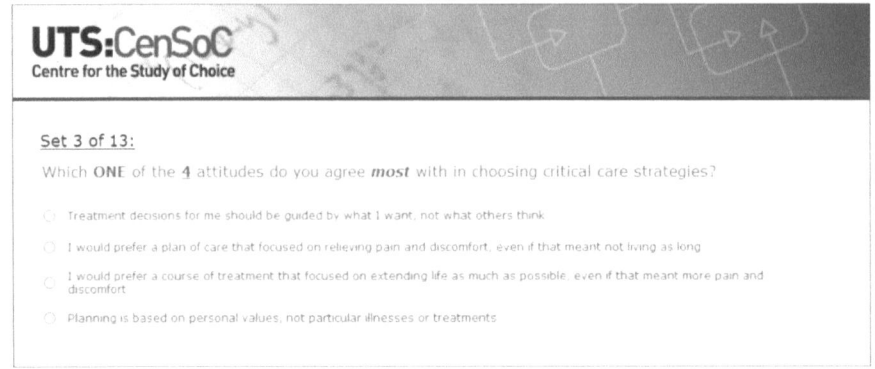

Fig. 5.1 Example of a choice set

5.4   Methods: Australian End-of-Life Care Study

The aims of this pilot study funded by the Australian Victoria State Government were:

1. To understand what older Australians' preferences were for EOL scenarios using a simple DCE of the vignette style used in the clinical literature
2. To establish whether more general EOL attitudes elicited from an easier Case 1 BWS study might provide a suitable proxy for conventional DCE "accept/reject the treatment" responses

The study recruited 1186 Australians aged 55+ from two online panels. It elicited their yes/no treatment choices to eight DCE end-of-life care scenarios, together with their attitudes elicited from the 13-question Case 1 BWS study. Case 1 best-worst scaling (BWS) is most easily described using a real example. A "choice set" (question) from an Australian EOL study is given below in Fig. 5.1:

Respondents had to consider the four attitudinal statements in the choice set and first decide which they agreed with most. Their chosen option was then eliminated, and they had to decide which, from the remaining three, they agreed with least. The respondent saw 13 subsets of four attitudinal statements (items) from a master list of 13. This repetition served a crucial purpose: it allowed each item to "compete" the same number of times with every other and thereby give insights into whether the respondent strongly (dis)agreed with particular items (chose them consistently as most/least agreed with) or felt less strongly/wasn't sure about items and never chose them or chose them only rarely as most or least. For each of the 13 items, the number of times it was chosen as "agreed with least" was subtracted from the number of times it was chosen as "agreed with most"; ordering the 13 items by these "best minus worst scores" provides the average level of agreement of them on a scale with known mathematical properties – it being a function of probabilities. Full details of the full study are available in Flynn et al. [16], but summary results and some follow-up analyses follow.

5.5 Results: Australian End-of-Life Care Study

A latent class analysis of the DCE data found three broad "types" – "do not treat" (61 %), "treat" (7 %) and "it depends" (32 %). Amongst the younger group (those aged under 75), there was a fourth group that had no real preferences at all, suggesting that younger groups contain larger numbers of people who don't seem to have any actionable views at all. Figure 5.2 reproduces the results of the sample level analysis of degree of agreement with the 13 attitudes.

The predominance of "quality of life is more important" type attitudes is clear, in line with the size of the "no treatment" segment in the DCE analysis. However, a key issue in this study was whether these "attitudinal agreement scores" elicited in the BWS study might predict the DCE choices. If so, it offers clinicians and policy-makers confidence that such easier tasks might serve as an adequate proxy for more complex DCE tasks for cognitively impaired patients. This would obviously increase the likely penetration of ACP amongst the older population.

Unfortunately latent class analyses of the BWS data had difficulty identifying the same, relatively clearly defined clusters found in the DCE data. This was because the algorithm failed to recognise the structure in the data: whilst two rounds of piloting had reduced the list of attitudes to 13, there remained many attitudes that seemed to load onto the same construct. Thus two attitudes "all human life is sacred" and "I would prefer a course of treatment that focused on extending life as much as pos-

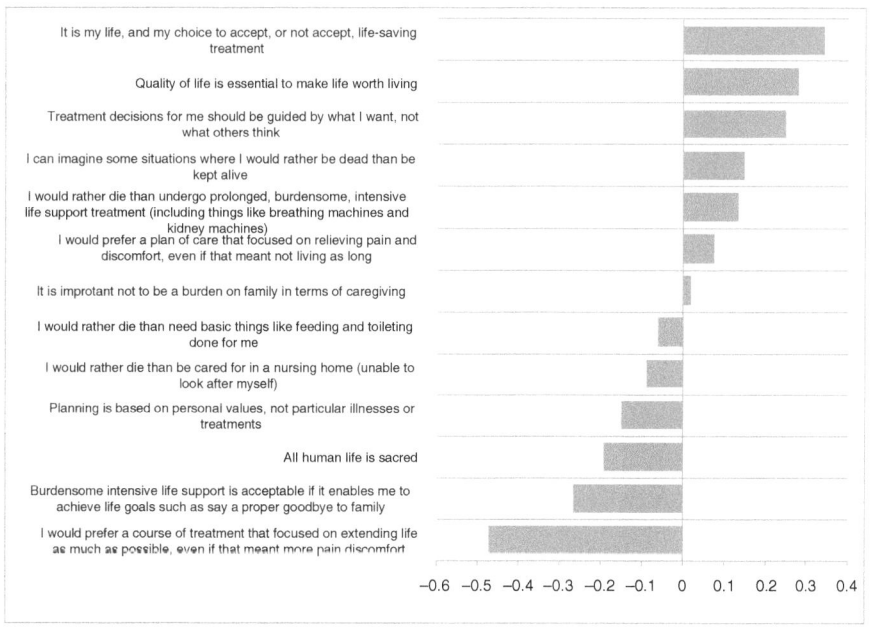

Standard errors all lie between 0.0115 and 0.0142.

Fig. 5.2 Results of the sample level analysis of degree of agreement with the 13 attitudes

sible even if that meant more pain and discomfort" were hypothesised to load onto a latent construct reflecting a belief that quantity of life is more important than quality of life. A priori it was unknown whether the former "gut instinct" or the latter "homo economicus" type attitude would be better in predicting DCE preferences.

5.6 Follow-Up Results: Validation Using Response Times

DCEs, like all ACP techniques, are vulnerable to the criticism that they may lack external validity. Their reliance on "stated preferences" – "what *would* you want *if...*" – means limited ability to validate them: economists would assume these techniques would induce Kahneman's "slow" method of thinking, involving considered responses to scenarios that typically present a wealth of information to show both sides of the argument. However, it is well known that preferences can be altered by context effects that might induce "fast", emotional thinking – the influence of distraught family members may encourage "every option to be tried" even though preferences for palliative, not life-saving, care are on file. For this reason, and given the lack of well-designed studies that alter such context effects, validating most ACP techniques is difficult.

Validation of DCE data is being attempted using a variety of methods that collect physiological data: EEG, eye tracking and response times being the main three. This study, being a pilot, was considered a suitable vehicle for a new programming platform which logged (in milliseconds) when every single choice was made by the respondent across the BWS study. Given the difficulties the latent class analysis had with statements that might differ in terms of their "emotional impact", the distributions of the response times for the 13 attitudes were plotted. Figure 5.3 presents these for the two "pro-length of life" attitudes.

These times are averaged over the entire design, and since all attitudes competed with all others the same number of times, the longer reading time of the second attitude has been netted out. It appears that a decision to agree most with "all life is sacred" was made far more quickly than a decision to agree most with "I would prefer a course of treatment that focused on extending life as much as possible, even if that meant more pain and discomfort". This seemed to be an example of Daniel Kahneman's "fast" and "slow" decision-making styles [17]. Perhaps the former statement reflected spiritual or religious beliefs, whilst the latter statement forced the respondent to consider exactly what negative consequences life prolongation might have. More formal analysis which combines the response time and choice data is ongoing, using the well-established Linear Ballistic Accumulator model [18, 19], to validate random utility theory-based conclusions from DCEs.

Whether society considers "fast" decisions more or less valid is a normative issue that this chapter does not seek to address. However, it does finally allow discrepancies between fast and slow decisions to be identified, which provide opportunities for further qualitative work to explore to what extent patients might want their "fast" decision to rule, when it is inconsistent with a previous "slow" decision made before the crisis situation.

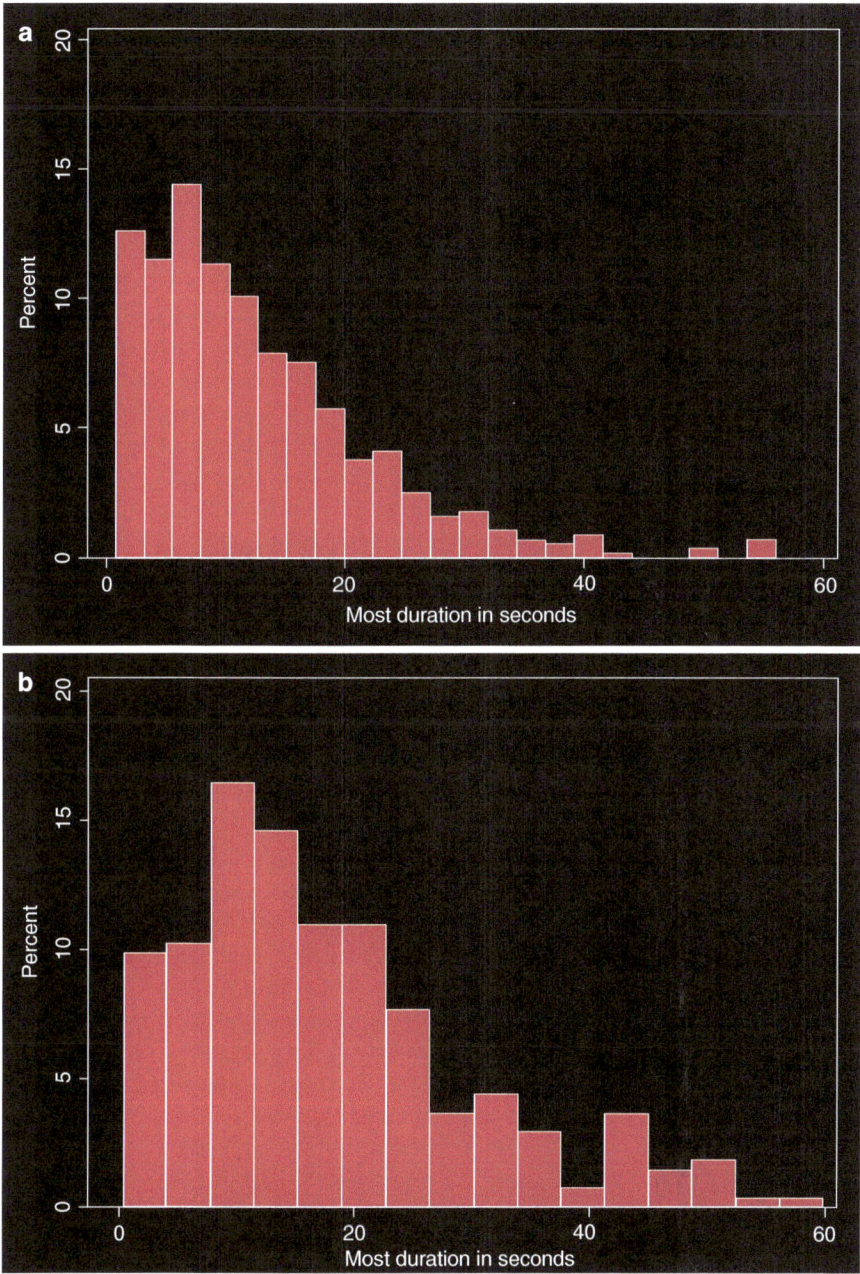

Fig. 5.3 Emotional versus considered responses – how quickly respondents selected "most" agreement. (**a**) "All human life is sacred". (**b**) "I would prefer a course of treatment that focused on extending life as much as possible even if that meant more pain and discomfort"

5.7 Conclusions and Implications of Such Work

Recent clinical work to construct advance care plans has effectively reinvented discrete choice experiments, a technique that has been used in health for many years [9]. It is important that methodological developments in the DCE field are adequately recognised and understood if patients and citizens are to have their wishes properly understood and documented.

Although there have been developments in BWS that provide more information (and potentially fewer scenarios to consider), it may be that the simplest type of DCE with a yes/no response might be the best since it most closely replicates the choice on offer in real life. However, its continued reliance on cognitively demanding complete care scenarios means that Case 1 BWS, hitherto underutilised in health, offers promise. It can be used to elicit general attitudes towards end-of-life care, as opposed to their traditional use in eliciting preferences for specific end-of-life care scenarios, defined by specific treatments and outcomes. Such work is exploratory at this stage, but results are promising. Unfortunately the study reported here could not demonstrate whether such attitudes can unequivocally be shown to predict preferences in specific ACP scenarios. However, the study was a pilot and had an unintended, significant, benefit. The collection of response times provided valuable insights into which attitudes induce "fast", probably emotional reactions and which induce "slow", probably considered reactions. Future work should separate out the "fast" from the "slow" attitudes and conduct separate Case 1 BWS studies on each set. It will then be interesting to observe which set of attitudes best explains treatment preferences in complete care scenarios.

Exploiting the power of response times requires DCEs to be administered electronically, whether via the web, or as stand-alone apps on tablets, PCs and phones. This has another crucial benefit: a picture of the respondent's views can be fed back to them in real time [16]. This overall "picture" of their views can, at the very least, provide a starting point for discussions with family, friends and clinicians. For these reasons DCE-based methods offer an attractive, user-friendly method of eliciting ACPs.

In terms of weaknesses of the method, the need for repeated choice sets is often questioned. It is certainly the case that vulnerable individuals may have difficulty even with a small DCE. However, this repetition is very important. Since humans are frequently inconsistent, unless completely certain about something, it quantifies exactly how often the respondent would agree with a given attitudinal statement in competition with any other. The resulting odds ratio framework is consistent with that used in the wider medical one, albeit at the level of the individual, not the population. Nevertheless, it does not provide a decision rule for the clinician at the bedside as to what constitutes "an acceptable level of patient certainty". As with much health economics decision-making, it provides the data which will allow societal discussion and debate on the normative issue of what level of patient uncertainty necessitates a conservative (life-prolonging) approach to care.

Another development that may prove problematic is in the DCE field itself. The "conjoint analysis" moniker is used for this technique in North America and has largely been influenced by the work of Green and others [20] which sought to decompose value of total scenarios into those attributable to each of the attributes describing it [21]. A problem is that "adaptive conjoint" has become popular as a way of shortening the survey. This seeks to use computing power to tailor the scenarios offered to the respondent on the basis of prior answers. Behaviourally this is suspect because it doesn't adequately recognise that people are inconsistent, and a properly designed DCE will allow for this, rather than effectively assuming that a respondent's first answer reflects their "true, fixed" view. Adaptive conjoint sends the respondent down a path that might not be the right one, had (s)he been allowed to show that (s)he actually doesn't have strong views, or, even worse, has views that would only have formed if (s)he had actually seen the various scenarios that span the treatment space, rather than be "forced" down the path defined by her/his first answer.

Finally, it is worth providing a brief exposition of how the work here links with other user-friendly approaches. The Q-method, currently gaining popularity in health economics [22], is a related technique to the best-worst methods described here. It asks individuals, in largely qualitative interviews, to put the full selection of competing attitudes into an empirical distribution (often one that looks Gaussian, with successively smaller columns of attitudes as one moves away from the centre), with "most agreed with" and "least agreed with" at opposite ends. In terms of aims, this has much to commend it and superficially seems to do exactly what best-worst does. However, there are a number of limitations that may make its use in routine practice impossible. First, the use of largely qualitative format makes it expensive compared to the online surveys used to elicit best-worst data. Second, it is a "one-shot" task. The analyst gains no insights into the true uncertainty in the respondents' answers: would the respondent put the same attitudes in the tails on another occasion? It is a repeated decision-making that gives insights into a person's certainty of their views. Thirdly, the respondent is encouraged to put statements into some sort of unimodal (ideally roughly normal) distribution. In practice this might not be consistent with what they believe at all – best-worst empirically estimates such distributions naturally, and they are frequently not unimodal at all.

This chapter has sought to show that preference elicitation amongst older people to help advance care planning is difficult, but thanks to modern technology, it is not impossible. Discrete choice experiments, and their best-worst variants, offer a way to make the ACP process relatively short and scalable up to the population level. DCE answers are now finally being validated with physiological data in terms of response times. We can finally distinguish between a "fast" answer, drawing on intrinsic values, and a "slow" one, based on a cost-benefit analysis of what is presented. As to whether "fast" or "slow" is most valid, like so many issues in health economics, it is a normative question that must be answered by patients, and by society as a whole, before the data now available can be used to aid decision-making in routine practice.

References

1. Singer PA, Martin DK, Kelner M (1999) Quality end-of-life care: patients' perspectives. JAMA: J Am Med Assoc 281(2):163–168
2. Hales S, Zimmerman C, Rodin G (2008) The quality of dying and death. Arch Intern Med 168(9):912–918

3. Steinhauser KE, Clipp E, McNeilly M, Christakis NA, McIntyre LM, Tulsky JA (2000) In search of a good death: observations of patients, families, and providers. Ann Intern Med 132(10):825–832
4. Hirai K, Miyashita M, Morita T, Sanjo M, Uchitomi Y (2006) Good death in Japanese cancer care: a qualitative study. J Pain Symptom Manage 31(2):140–147
5. CIC GSFC (2013) Thinking ahead – GSF advance care planning discussion. Retrieved from thinking ahead – the gold standards framework advance care planning discussion. Website: http://www.goldstandardsframework.org.uk/cd-content/uploads/files/Library%2C%20 Tools%20%26%20resources/ACP%20General%20July%202013.v21.pdf
6. Dodson JA, Fried TR, Van Ness PH, Goldstein NE, Lampert R (2013) Patient preferences for deactivation of implantable cardioverter-defibrillators. JAMA Intern Med 173(5):377–379. doi:10.1001/jamainternmed.2013.1883
7. Beattie JM, Flynn TN, Clark AM (2013) Patient preferences for deactivation of implantable cardioverter-defibrillators: a response. JAMA Intern Med 173(16):1556–1557
8. Louviere JJ, Hensher DA (1982) On the design and analysis of simulated choice or allocation experiments in travel choice modelling. Transp Res Rec 890:11–17
9. Propper C (1990) Contingent valuation of time spent on NHS waiting lists. Econ J 100:193–199
10. Thurstone LL (1927) A law of comparative judgment. Psychol Rev 34:273–286
11. Louviere JJ (2001) What if consumer experiments impact variances as well as means: response variability as a behavioural phenomenon. J Consum Res 28(3):506–511
12. Kass-Bartelmes BL, Hughes R, Rutherford MK (2003). Advance care planning: preferences for care at the end of life. Rockville (MD): Agency for Healthcare Research and Quality 12: AHRQ Pub No. 03-0018, pp.1–20
13. Rose JM, Bliemer MCJ (2009) Constructing efficient stated choice experimental designs. Transp Rev 29(5):587–617
14. Street DJ, Burgess L (2007) The construction of optimal stated choice experiments: theory and methods. Wiley, Hoboken
15. Flynn TN (2010) Valuing citizen and patient preferences in health: recent developments in three types of best-worst scaling. Expert Rev Pharmacoecon Outcomes Res 10(3):259–267
16. Flynn TN, Huynh E, Corke C (2015) Attitudes towards end-of-life care. In: Louviere JJ, Flynn TN, Marley AAJ (eds) Best-worst scaling: theory, methods and applications. Cambridge University Press, Cambridge
17. Kahneman D (2011) Thinking, fast and slow. Farrar, Straus and Giroux, New York
18. Hawkins GE, Marley AAJ, Heathcote A, Flynn TN, Louviere JJ, Brown SD (2014) The best of times and the worst of times are interchangeable. Decision 1(3):192–214
19. Hawkins GE, Marley AAJ, Heathcote A, Flynn TN, Louviere JJ, Brown SD (2014) Integrating cognitive process and descriptive models of attitudes and preferences. Cognit Sci 38(4):701–735
20. Green PE, Rao VR (1971) Conjoint measurement for quantifying judgmental data. J Mark Res 8:355–363
21. Louviere JJ, Flynn TN, Carson RT (2010) Discrete choice experiments are not conjoint analysis. J Choice Model 3(3):57–72
22. Baker R, Thompson C, Mannion R (2006) Q methodology in health economics. J Health Serv Res Policy 11(1):38–45

Chapter 6
An Introduction to Handling Missing Data in Health Economic Evaluations

Gianluca Baio and Baptiste Leurent

6.1 Introduction

Missing data is a problem commonly encountered in health intervention studies. It is particularly prevalent in palliative care research where collection of complete data is often hampered by the deteriorating health and sometimes death of the study participants. Missing data is a limitation for the validity of an economic evaluation. If missing data is not dealt with appropriately during analysis, there is a risk of bias occurring in the estimates of the outcomes, both benefits and costs, associated with the interventions being compared. Such biased results would in turn effectively invalidate any inferences made to guide the decision-making process.

Given the importance of dealing properly with missing data to making correct inferences from study results, we present here a guide paying specific attention to problems that might arise when studying end-of-life populations in a health economic setting. We begin by describing what it means for data to be missing and how this affects inference. We then outline methods for dealing with different types of missing data, progressing from simple (and often unsatisfactory) methods such as complete-case analysis to more sophisticated and computationally expensive approaches such as multiple imputation, which generally produce more meaningful results. We finish by considering specific issues around end-of-life populations.

G. Baio (✉)
Department of Statistical Science, University College London,
Gower Street, London, UK
e-mail: g.baio@ucl.ac.uk

B. Leurent
London School of Hygiene and Tropical Medicine,
Keppel Street, London, UK

© Springer International Publishing Switzerland 2016
J. Round (ed.), *Care at the End of Life: An Economic Perspective*,
DOI 10.1007/978-3-319-28267-1_6

6.2   Understanding Missing Data

Generally speaking, missing data can arise in two different ways. Some study participants may not be able or willing to complete the planned assessment; we generically
term these as *nonresponders* or *dropouts* and this form of missingness is sometimes
referred to as "unit" nonresponse. In addition, some people may provide only limited
information, e.g. by responding to only some of the questions from a questionnaire
or by refusing to provide some information (e.g. data on salary, wealth or other personal characteristics). This case is sometimes labelled as "item" nonresponse.

One important concept to understand the discussion around missing data and its
resulting potential bias is the classification of the missingness mechanisms proposed by Little and Rubin [1], who distinguish between the case in which data are
missing *completely at random* (MCAR), missing *at random* (MAR) or missing *not
at random* (MNAR). Data can be assumed to be MCAR when missingness occurs
for reasons independent of the variables of interest. For example, if some individuals who were scheduled for an interview could not be reached because the surveyor
was ill on a specific day, we could assume the mechanisms to be MCAR, since the
absence of information about a subset of the intended recipient seems to be a purely
random circumstance. Thus, while on the one hand the assumption of MCAR intuitively produces little impact on the resulting analysis, it is on the other hand often
untenable. We discuss this in more detail later in the chapter.

A less restrictive condition is when data are said to be MAR: this happens when the
reasons for missingness could be related to observed data but are independent on the
missing value itself. For example, if younger people are more likely to drop out of a
study, the missing data mechanism can be considered MAR conditionally on age:
among the same age group, the chance of missingness is constant and does not depend
on any other factor. MAR is a more realistic assumption than MCAR and several
methods have been developed to model data characterised by this feature. Nevertheless,
one can never exclude the possibility that data are in fact generated from an MNAR (or
"informative missingness") mechanism: this happens when, after taking into account
the observed data, the chance of being missing is also associated with the unobserved
value itself. For example, if (after controlling for individual characteristics, such as age
and sex) participants in a smoking cessation trial who did quit smoking are less likely
to report it, the missing data mechanism should be considered MNAR.

The distinction between MAR and MNAR mechanisms has an important implication. When data are MAR, the observed evidence can be used to "recover" (to
some extent!) the missing information. By contrast, when data are MNAR, part of
the information of interest is contained in the very fact that it is missing itself.
Consequently, MNAR information simply cannot be recovered using the observed
data. In addition, it is important to realise that the differences between MAR and
MNAR are effectively "untestable assumptions" on the data-generating process
mechanism: it is often possible to distinguish MCAR from MAR, using the observed
data, but not between MAR and MNAR. Thus, one can never totally exclude the
possibility that missingness is informative, unless other (generally untestable)
assumptions are made.

6.2.1   Effects of Missing Data on Interpretation of Results

As mentioned earlier, missing data are extremely relevant, as they can affect the results of a study in two ways, firstly, by reducing the amount of information available and resulting in a loss of statistical power. High drop out in a trial can result in a sample size lower than planned and the power may not allow statistical test of hypotheses with sufficient confidence. This can partially be controlled by anticipating realistic response rates and inflating the sample size accordingly when designing a study. While a loss of power affects the uncertainty of parameter estimates or statistical tests, it does not make them invalid. The second, and probably more important, problem is the risk of bias caused by missing data. For example, if participants with poorer health and higher resource use are less likely to complete a survey, the mean healthcare cost observed in completers will be an underestimate of the true mean cost in the population. This can lead to serious consequences, if the analysis is taken at face value and used for policymaking. Such a situation is likely to arise in end-of-life care research, where research populations often include many frail or elderly patients at risk of death during the study period. The risk of bias being introduced into results will depend on the amount of missing data, the question being investigated and the missing data mechanism. Because the missingness mechanism can never be fully known, the risk of bias can also be difficult to assess. When the amount of missing data is large (indicatively, in excess of 5–10 % of the data), it is therefore important to: (i) describe the amount and reasons for missingness, (ii) perform extensive sensitivity analyses assuming different mechanisms and (iii) consider the risk of bias possibly caused by the missing data as part of the discussion of the results and the implications in terms of decision-making.

Although we will be discussing below some possible approaches to "limiting the damage" in the face of missing data, we cannot emphasise enough that the ideal solution is to avoid their presence completely. The potential for incomplete data really needs to be considered carefully at the study design stage and limited as much as practically possible. A substantial amount of missing data can render any meaningful inference impossible and jeopardise the whole point of a study. In end-of-life studies in particular, completed outcome measures (such as questionnaires on quality of life or resource use) can be expected to have a large amount of missing values. Thus, alternative methods for data collection, such as the use of routine care data for resources use, or relative or care staff completed questionnaire for health measures, should be considered.

6.3   Dealing with Missing Data

There are several methods that can be used to model data subject to missingness. In the next sections, we give some examples highlighting the main characteristics of each. Specifically, we make a basic distinction between simpler (but often extremely unsatisfactory) procedures and methods based on modelling, which require higher statistical sophistication but are able to produce more robust and reliable results. The technical issues related with the statistical models used to handle the presence of missing data are generally quite complex and are beyond the scope of this book. Therefore, we will only sketch some of the main ideas underlying them here. For the interested reader, we recommend more comprehensive textbooks such as Molenberghs and Kenward [2], Carpenter and Kenward [3], Enders [4] and Molenberghs [5].

6.3.1 Simpler Methods

6.3.1.1 Complete Case Analysis (CCA)

The simplest way of dealing with data sets characterised by missingness is to just restrict the analysis to the "valid" (or "complete") cases. This is the approach taken by many statistical packages by default when, for example, running regression analyses. In CCA, if some of the variables included in the model are affected by missing values for a given respondent, then *all* the variables associated with that unit are discarded from the analysis. Analysis is then conducted on only the cases that have valid observations across all the variables under consideration.

If, on the one hand, this clearly renders the analysis much simpler (because effectively it overcomes the problem of missing data entirely), it has on the other hand several disadvantages. First, because it artificially reduces the sample size (by discarding the missing points), the analysis will certainly produce estimations associated with larger standard errors (i.e. less precision). Second, and more importantly, the assumption underlying CCA is that missingness is noninformative, or in other words completely at random, which, as mentioned earlier, is hardly ever a tenable assumption.

Despite these shortcomings, CCA is probably the most frequently used option in health economic evaluation [6]. The implications of using CCA, for resource allocation decision-making in spite of its unsuitability in most analyses, are unclear and warrant investigation.

6.3.1.2 Last Observation Carried Forward

This is another simplistic way to deal with missing data, often used in clinical trial settings when there are repeated measurements for the individuals in the sample. For example, suppose that we wish to record data on quality of life at baseline and then at successive visits. Ideally, all the patients in the sample will provide a preference score at all the time points. However, it is highly likely that there will be some missing data (e.g. because some individuals withdraw from the study, e.g. because of death). This has implications on our ability to compute an overall utility score, as well as perform cost-effectiveness analysis.

The assumption underlying last observation carried forward (LOCF) is that all unobserved measurements are identical with the last available measurement – the value of the measurement in t_2 for a given participant is assumed to be the same as measured in t_1. As with CCA this method is extremely simple. And, as with CCA it is extremely unsatisfactory, from both the statistical and substantive point of view. There is no reason to assume that somebody who has stopped giving information is "similar" to the individuals who are still alive and willing to participate. There is also no reason to assume that for those who stop giving information, there has been no change in the value of a variable over time. In fact, it is quite likely the opposite that external factors and individual variability would lead to a series of different values for any given individual [7].

6.3.1.3 Mean Imputation

The basic idea behind "imputation" procedures is to replace the values that have not been observed with some suitable obtained summary computed using the available data. For example, consider the case where a response (such as a measure of quality of life) is observed for a set of $n = 10$ individuals. Of these, $m = 4$ does not have complete data. Table 6.1 shows a fictional data set with these characteristics.

If we can assume that the missing units are not substantially different from those that have been observed, the easiest strategy for analysis without discarding the missing observations is to replace them with the observed mean for the available units. In the above case, the mean of the six valid cases can be computed as 0.551, and then, assuming that this is the value for the unobserved cases too, it would be possible to thus artificially "complete" (or "impute") the data set.

While extremely easy, this approach is however not ideal. Firstly, it assumes that the unobserved values of a variable are well represented by the observed ones; arguably, this is unlikely to be the case if we think participants with missing values substantially differ from those with observed values (i.e. any missingness mechanism other than MCAR). Secondly, mean imputation considers all the participants with missing values as having *exactly* the same one, ignoring the possible effect of

Patient	Response
1	?
2	0.597
3	0.585
4	0.788
5	?
6	0.149
7	?
8	0.691
9	?
10	0.494

Table 6.1 A fictional data set including missing data

other factors which differ between individuals. This clearly affects the standard error of the resulting analysis by artificially reducing the natural variation between any measurements, which in turn leads to serious bias in the results and their implications.

6.3.2   Modelling-Based Methods

A more sophisticated statistical approach (which is becoming increasingly popular in biostatistics but worryingly not as much in health economics [6]) involves more comprehensive analyses aimed at modelling (at least some aspects of) the missing mechanism. These can be broadly categorised into *weighting* and *imputation* methods.

6.3.2.1   Weighting

The intuition behind weighting is that in the actual data set, not all observations carry an *information weight* of 1, due to the presence of the missing values. Intuitively, the idea is that units associated with missing data should be weighted up, to adjust for the fact that those individuals are under-represented in the whole sample, because of missingness. For example, consider a randomised study in which it had been originally planned, following careful sample size calculations, to observe n participants from each treatment arm and to conduct an economic evaluation. However, among the patients treated with the active drug, not all patients are completely observed – that is, some number of patients m have some missing data. As mentioned earlier, this may mean that either costs or benefits are not available but also that the record is only partial, i.e. only costs or, more likely, only benefits have been recorded for that patient.

The basic argument is that the value observed for the available units has an information weight that is inversely proportional to the probability that they are observed: if a unit is not observed, then their profile is under-represented in the sample, and to correct for this, they are weighted up. Thus, the idea is to first estimate the probability that each unit (or group of units, for instance, with respect to a combination of prognostic factors) is actually observed. This can be indicated by the quantity $\hat{p}_i$ (the "hat" notation indicates that this quantity is estimated by the available sample data and the subscript i indicates that this refers to the i-th subject in the data set). Then, each unit is given a revised information weight by the inverse of this estimated probability $\hat{w}_i = \dfrac{1}{\hat{p}_i}$ to adjust for the fact that the available sample size is not as big as originally planned by effect of the missing data. Units, for whom the probability of being observed is estimated at high values (or equivalently, the probability of being missing is low), are then given a low information weight. Conversely, units with a low probability of being observed are given a larger weight as they are

Table 6.2 Examples of imputation

			Quality of life values after imputation					
Observed data			Single-imputation methods			Multiple imputation		
Patient	Age	Quality of life	Mean	Regression	Stochastic	1st data set	2nd data set	3rd data set
1	47	?	*0.551*	*0.604*	*0.653*	*−0.137*	*0.412*	*0.798*
2	33	0.597	0.597	0.597	0.597	0.597	0.597	0.597
3	49	0.585	0.585	0.585	0.585	0.585	0.585	0.585
4	39	0.788	0.788	0.788	0.788	0.788	0.788	0.788
5	61	?	*0.551*	*0.439*	*0.693*	*−0.353*	*0.246*	*1.052*
6	71	0.149	0.149	0.149	0.149	0.149	0.149	0.149
7	65	?	*0.551*	*0.392*	*0.471*	*0.739*	*0.316*	*−0.373*
8	55	0.691	0.691	0.691	0.691	0.691	0.691	0.691
9	59	?	*0.551*	*0.462*	*0.686*	*0.508*	*0.624*	*0.699*
10	62	0.494	0.494	0.494	0.494	0.494	0.494	0.494

Examples of imputation. For each method, the imputed values are typeset in italics, while the observed values are typeset as normal text

considered to be "representative" of those that have not been observed, too. Thus, this procedure inflates the weight for subjects who are under-represented due to a large degree of missing data.

In a sense, weighting can be seen as a compromise between the CCA (which simply discards missing data) and more complex methods (which explicitly account for them); the analysis is still performed only on the units that are completely available, but these are given different weights. Inverse probability weighting (IPW) is a valid methodology under the assumption of MAR, conditionally on the model used to compute the weight.

In our example in Table 6.2, we have now reported information about the subjects' age, which we assume is available for all cases. Looking at the data, it seems that older patients are more likely to have their quality of life missing. In this case, we would want to give higher weight to observations from the older participants, to compensate for the other older participants whose data could not be collected.

6.3.2.2 Regression Imputation

A limitation of mean imputation is to ignore the observed characteristics of a given observation and that all imputed values will be exactly the same. One way to overcome this it to make use of observed variables to try and predict the missing data. For example, if we expect age and quality of life to be linearly related, we can perform a linear regression of quality of life on age on the participants with complete data and then use the regression curve to predict a "likely" value of quality of life at a given age (see Fig. 6.1).

This approach can easily be generalised to using more than one predictor and to more complex models, including non-linear structures. This seems already a more attractive approach, as it is trying to get the "best prediction" for each missing value, based on the observed data. However, it will still underestimate the natural variations of the data by assuming the imputed values are perfectly predicted by the regression model.

6.3.2.3 Stochastic Imputation

One method that overcomes the limitation of using the "best" estimate as the imputed value is that of *stochastic* imputation. In this case, the missing value is imputed from a random draw made from a suitable probability distribution (which is usually based on an underlying regression model). In other words, the imputed value is estimated by a predicted value, just as in a regression imputation, to which random noise is added to represent the part of unpredictability (or variation) beyond the one that is captured by the model. An example of stochastic imputation is shown in Fig. 6.1 and Table 6.2.

As is possible to see, the values imputed for the regression and stochastic method are generally different – the latter are *based* on the former but have an extra layer of uncertainty which depends on "how well" the regression model captures the underlying relationships among the variables considered in the analysis. In any case, the analysis of the imputed data set will treat in a same way the observed and imputed values and in a sense ignore the fact that estimations are only uncertain guesses.

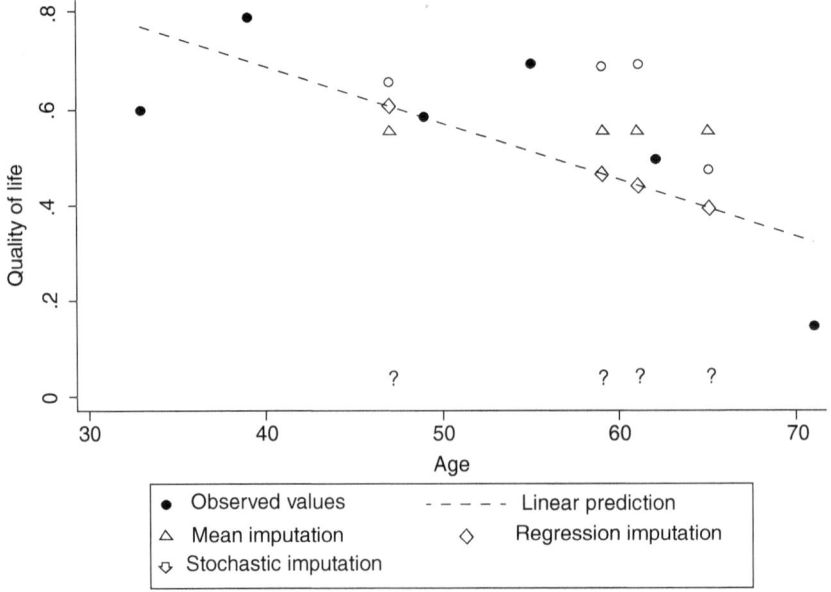

Fig. 6.1 Example of mean, regression and stochastic imputations for quality of life values, by observed age

6.3.2.4   Multiple Imputation

As mentioned above, stochastic imputation ignores the uncertainty in the estimated value that arises from an imperfect prediction model. When used in the analysis, values from the stochastic imputation are treated as known with absolute certainty when in actual fact they are only single estimates of possible values. The method of multiple imputation was developed to address this problem. As a method it has gained wider recognition by analysts conducting cost-effectiveness analyses in recent years [6, 8–10].

The principle of multiple imputation [11, 12], which can be thought of as an extension of the models described above, is to generate multiple estimates of possible values for the missing data, creating multiple versions of the data set in the process. All imputed data sets are then used in the analysis. This method accounts for both the uncertainty in the imputation model and the natural variation of the variables. The more uncertain the imputation is (in terms of prediction of the unobserved value), the larger differences will be generated from one imputed data set to another. This uncertainty is then taken into account in the overall analysis.

In a nutshell, the steps necessary to perform multiple imputation can be seen as follows:

 (i) Perform a suitable regression analysis on the observed data in order to identify the parameters of the imputation model (the regression coefficients).
 (ii) Select a random draw from the estimated distribution to fill the missing values.
(iii) Repeat steps (i) and (ii) a number of times, giving multiple, different and complete data sets (with these differences accounting for the underlying sources of uncertainty).

The analysis is then performed in two further steps:

(iv) Analyse each data set separately using standard methods.
 (v) Pool the results from each multiple data set analysis into one final result using appropriate formulae (e.g. "Rubin's rule").

An example of multiple imputation on our data set can be seen in Table 6.2, with three imputed data sets. As we can see, each of these data sets contains different estimates for the missing values.

The number of imputations necessary to obtain reliable results will depend on the amount of missing data. Ideally, the Monte Carlo error (the uncertainty due to performing only a limited number of imputations) should be verified to ensure it cannot significantly affect the results. Some rule of thumbs have been suggested, such as performing three or five imputations [13] or using the percentage of incomplete observations, i.e. performing 20 imputations if 20 % of data are missing [14]. In general, there is a trade-off to be considered between the computational effort required to perform the analysis and its robustness in terms of inference. Thorough sensitivity analysis (see below) is, as usual, recommended.

6.4   Further Issues

6.4.1   Sensitivity Analyses

We have seen that some approaches can perform well to provide valid estimates even when some data are unobserved, under a number of often questionable assumptions. In reality, some uncertainty will always remain in the presence of missing data and it is difficult to be fully confident in a result which depends on information which is not observed. More importantly, it is fundamental to realise that no statistical model in itself will be able to perform some type of "magic" on the data and that any result derived from an analysis based on data subject to missingness will be in some sense partial. For this reason, it is important to complement the partially observed available data with as much subject-matter-specific information as possible. Bayesian methods (e.g. see [15]) can be brought to bear to this effect.

Most of the approaches discussed above assume MAR. However if data really are generated by an MNAR mechanism, there are some extra information contained in the fact that a unit is missing, which cannot be recovered only by looking at what is observed. This is particularly relevant for end-of-life studies, where patients with worsening health may well be less likely to complete the measures of interest. We note, however, that MNAR sensitivity analyses remain uncommon in economic evaluation [9].

One relatively simple approach to problems of MNAR is to perform sensitivity analyses, comparing the result of interest when the data is analysed under a range of different assumptions. In cost-effectiveness analysis, this is often done based on the individual parameters or the distributional assumptions. If the results do not vary substantially across the different scenarios, this can be assumed as indication that the missing data are unlikely to importantly affect the conclusion. However, it is important to assess the robustness under a wide range of plausible assumptions (rather than for several methods based on the same set of assumptions). For example, it would not be very relevant to show that an inverse probability weighting and multiple imputation analysis give similar results when they both rely on identical MAR assumptions. Ideally, one may want to consider the estimate of interest under the best and worst possible cases for the missing values, but this is often difficult in practice (e.g. with continuous outcomes).

It is often the case that the results will be sensitive to the missing data assumptions, which can make it difficult to draw a simple conclusion. We argue however that this uncertainty should be embraced; instead: it is more honest and scientific to recognise that some results are not fully robust to model specifications and then present the full range of possible results, perhaps trying to investigate the potential for the collection of further information (e.g. new studies or combination of different data sets).

6.4.2   Missing Data Due to Death

As opposed to data which happen to be unobserved but are in principle observable, dealing with missing data due to death raises different issues. One could argue that the term "missing" is not appropriate in this case, since the data (e.g. observations after a patient has died) are actually not existing or "not applicable". Nonetheless, for some research questions, death can be considered as a form of censoring, i.e. some data aimed to be measured are not available, due to the concurrent event of death. There is still a lack of consensus about how to best approach the issue, but some points can be considered:

(i) It is important to formulate the exact question being investigated. A question such as "Is treatment A more effective that treatment B to reduce symptoms of depression after two months?" implicitly assumes "for a patient alive at two months" (patients who die before could therefore be excluded from the analysis). However this needs to be done cautiously: for example, if survival in a randomised trial is dependent on the treatment arms, then the comparison excluding those who died will give a biased treatment effect.

(ii) Imputation of "non-existing" data is not necessarily wrong. Even if it feels unnatural to impute non-existing values, this procedure could allow us, in some situations, to answer better a question of interest than the alternative approaches, such as a complete-case analysis. Imputation should be seen more as a statistical way to estimate a parameter of interest than a way to "predict" values which do not exist. However, if imputing values after death, one will have to be clear about what question one is trying to answer and what assumptions are being made.

(iii) Using QALYs (or DALYs) is an interesting approach, as it combines mortality and quality of life into a single measure. When the treatment affects both health outcomes and survival, the question of comparing QALYs appears much more meaningful than a single outcome at a specific point in time.

(iv) Palliative care interventions often aim at improving the quality of life of patients and not at affecting their survival. If this can be reasonably assumed, then a comparison of the observed outcomes in a randomised trial will give unbiased estimates. However the absence of effect on survival is usually difficult to demonstrate, even if it is not a direct aim of the intervention; for example, better quality of life could well have an indirect effect on the survival time of patients.

6.4.3   Imputation of Skewed Data

Economic analysis often involves working with skewed data, such as counts of resource use (and as a result, costs), which can be problematic for modelling approaches which may rely on assumptions of normality [16]. Often, data are transformed (e.g. using logs): in these cases, care is needed to back-transform the results to the scale which is meaningful for cost-effectiveness analysis.

Alternatively, some methods of imputation will better handle non-normally distributed data; for example, in multiple imputation (and any regression imputation), predictive mean matching can be used, which will associate the closest observed values for the outcomes and therefore preserve the distributional shape from the observed data. Multiple imputation has also been combined with non-parametric bootstrapping [8, 9], although this is a topic under current research and thus recommendations and guidelines are less established.

6.5 Conclusion

We have seen that missing data is a common problem in end-of-life care research, which has the potential to affect conclusions in a substantial way. We have introduced a set of methods, which can be considered when dealing with a data set affected by the presence of missing data. Although some simple methods have the appeal of being more straightforward, they are often unsatisfactory, and more sophisticated approaches, such as inverse probability weighting or multiple imputation, are usually to be preferred. These methods allow to fully capturing the uncertainty caused by the missing data under specific assumptions. This is important as the very fact that some information is missing needs to be accounted for – with the obvious implication of rendering the analysis less precise. However, it is also important to assess how robust conclusions are to different missingness assumptions. It is particularly critical in end-of-life research, where missing data are likely to be related to patient's health. Finally, we would like to highlight that the question of missing data should not only be considered at the analysis stage but, probably, more importantly, when designing a study. This is likely to require the involvement of different expertise, such as patient representative, investigators and analysts to seek possible solutions as early as possible when designing a new study. If this issue is not considered appropriately, the whole point of a study may be at stake, resulting in a waste of resources and precious participant time.

References

1. Little RJ, Rubin DB (2014) Statistical analysis with missing data. Wiley, Hoboken, NJ (US)
2. Molenberghs G, Kenward M (2007) Missing data in clinical studies, vol 61. Wiley, Chichester
3. Carpenter JR, Kenward MG (2008) Missing data in randomised controlled trials – a practical guide. National Institute for Health Research, Birmingham, Publication RM03/JH17/MK. Available at http://www.missingdata.org.uk
4. Enders CK (2010) Applied missing data analysis. Guilford Publications, New York, NY
5. Molenberghs G, Fitzmaurice G, Kenward MG, Tsiatis A, Verbeke G (eds) (2014) Handbook of missing data methodology. CRC Press, London New York, NY (US)
6. Noble SM, Hollingworth W, Tilling K (2012) Missing data in trial-based cost-effectiveness analysis: the current state of play. Health Econ 21(2):187–200
7. Hunter RM, Baio G, Butt T, Morris S, Round J, Freemantle N (2015) An educational review of the statistical issues in analysing utility data for cost-utility analysis. Pharmacoeconomics, 33(4):355–366
8. Burton A, Billingham LJ, Bryan S (2007) Cost-effectiveness in clinical trials: using multiple imputation to deal with incomplete cost data. Clin Trials 4(2):154–161
9. Faria R et al (2014) A guide to handling missing data in cost-effectiveness analysis conducted within randomised controlled trials. Chichester (UK). Pharmacoeconomics 32(12):1157–1170
10. Manca A, Palmer S (2005) Handling missing data in patient-level cost-effectiveness analysis alongside randomised clinical trials. Appl Health Econ Health Policy 4(2):65–75
11. Rubin DB (2004) Multiple imputation for nonresponse in surveys. Wiley, New York, NY (US)
12. Sterne JAC et al (2009) Multiple imputation for missing data in epidemiological and clinical research: potential and pitfalls. BMJ 338:b2393

13. Schafer JL, Olsen MK (1998) Multiple imputation for multivariate missing data problems: a data analyst's perspective. Multivar Behav Res 33:545–571
14. White IR, Royston P, Wood AM (2011) Multiple imputation using chained equations: issues and guidance for practice. Stat Med 30(4):377–399
15. Baio G (2012) Bayesian methods in health economics. CRC Press, Boca Raton, FL (US)
16. Baio, G (2014) Bayesian models for cost-effectiveness analysis in the presence of structural zero costs. Statistics in Medicine 33:1900–1913

Part III
Measuring and Valuing Outcomes

Chapter 7
Measuring and Valuing Outcomes for Care at the End of Life: The Capability Approach

Joanna Coast, Cara Bailey, Alastair Canaway, and Philip Kinghorn

7.1 Introduction Why a Capability Approach?

Although the QALY approach considered has been well defended as a basis for evaluating end-of-life care [1], and it has clear benefits in terms of maintaining consistency with the approach that is used across the evaluation of health interventions [1], there are also arguments for thinking more broadly about how best to evaluate end-of-life care [2]. Decision-making in health care can be underpinned by many different normative bases [3, 4]. Economists are usually concerned about efficiency – the maximisation of outputs given the inputs available – but even where the focus is efficiency, there are a number of different paradigms or approaches that can form the basis for this assessment of efficiency. The most usual are characterised as welfarist (the maximisation of utility on the basis of achieving a Pareto optimum where no one person's utility can be increased without another person's utility being decreased [5]) or extra-welfarist health maximisation (as discussed already in relation to QALYs [4]). A third approach, however, has recently generated interest. This is the capability approach initially developed by Amartya Sen [6–8]

J. Coast (✉)
School of Social and Community Medicine, University of Bristol, Bristol, UK
e-mail: Jo.coast@bristol.ac.uk

C. Bailey
Health Economics Unit, Institute of Applied Health Research, University of Birmingham, Birmingham, UK

Nursing, Institute of Clinical Sciences, University of Birmingham, Birmingham, UK

A. Canaway
Warwick Clinical Trials Unit, Warwick Medical School, University of Warwick, Coventry, UK

P. Kinghorn
Health Economics Unit, Institute of Applied Health Research, University of Birmingham, Birmingham, UK

© Springer International Publishing Switzerland 2016
J. Round (ed.), *Care at the End of Life: An Economic Perspective*,
DOI 10.1007/978-3-319-28267-1_7

but since associated with the work of authors such as Martha Nussbaum [9], Sabina Alkire [10, 11] and Ingrid Robeyns [12–14].

Core concepts of the capability approach are capabilities and functionings. Sen defines functionings as the achievements of a person (observed outcomes). The concept of functionings represents some overlap or common ground between QALYs and the capability approach, with instruments such as the EQ-5D assessing health functioning in terms of mobility, self-care, usual activities, pain and discomfort and anxiety/depression. Outcome-based assessments of well-being incorporate non-utility information (hence the term 'extra-welfarist' being associated with QALYs). However, only in its most basic form does the capability approach measure well-being in terms of functionings [15]. Functionings are usually used as a proxy for capability, defined as the set of potentially achievable functionings. The full (or extended) form of the capability approach therefore conceptualises well-being as freedom. Focus on ability and freedom makes this extended form of the capability approach respectful of individual autonomy and human heterogeneity. Through consideration of how an outcome was reached, the extended form of the capability approach also allows for a finer distinction to be drawn between states.

The capability approach has been extended into health by those focusing on health justice [16–19] and patient experience [20, 21] and more specifically into health economics by a number of authors [22–34]. The application of the capability approach within health economics involves, for most authors, at least a shift in the focus of outcomes towards a broad assessment of capability rather than health or utility.[1] It may also be associated with different decision rules, for example, a greater focus on achieving capability thresholds rather than maximising total gain [16, 35].

The capability approach has largely been focused on what is needed to achieve a good life; in relation to end-of-life care, its application has been minimal. One detailed exploration of specialist palliative care services in relation to age used Ruger's account of health capability [36], to suggest that 'equity should be assessed by considering how far experiences of Specialist Palliative Care fall short of the agreed standard of care all patients are expected to receive' [37, p. 367]. Burt's research was more focused on the decision criterion aspect of Ruger's work, finding that there were different levels of access to specialist palliative care services amongst different groups where the level of need was similar, suggesting a violation of the principles of Ruger's framework [37]. A second application utilises Nussbaum's list of central human capabilities to explore issues around euthanasia, concluding that there are arguments within the list that can be used to assess the relevance of a right to die [23]. Neither of these applications focuses on issues around measuring outcome in relation to a good death.

---

[1] Although a small number of economists see the possibility of re-shaping the QALY as a measure of capability [25, 29], a key concern is that reducing the scope of the capability approach to just health is to essentially undermine one of its key strengths and principles, which is the multi-dimensional assessment of wellbeing.

Work within health economics has, however, started to consider the application of the capability approach as a broad conceptual framework for evaluating end-of-life care, as well as some of the issues that are involved in applying the approach to this complex area [2]. This chapter extends the work in this earlier review, by making the case for using a broadly conceptualised capability approach that includes aspects of outcome related to 'a good life' and 'a good death' and, in relation to 'a good death', consideration of both the individual at the end of life and those close to them. It then focuses on issues around identifying domains for inclusion in outcomes and valuing such domains.

7.2 A Broad Conceptual Approach Within the Capability Framework

End-of-life care is complex. It has been defined as helping 'all those with advanced, progressive, incurable illness to live as well as possible until they die. It enables the supportive and palliative care needs of both patient and family to be identified and met throughout the last phase of life and into bereavement. It includes management of pain and other symptoms and provision of psychological, social, spiritual and practical support' [38, p. 47]. End-of-life care can include aspects of health care (such as pain relief), aspects of social care (such as availability of support, dignity) and the provision of care that aims to enhance aspects of well-being that go beyond both of these (such as autonomy, completion and spirituality). Because there are aspects of end-of-life care where the objectives clearly differ from an exclusive focus on generating health gain, the relevant framework for evaluation might need to have more in common with the broad methods advocated for evaluating social service interventions [39], where health outcomes are not routinely seen as the focus of evaluation. It has recently been argued that the focus of the evaluation of end-of-life care within a capability approach should be the opportunity for a good death [2].

There is the additional complication that people do not shift in an instant from a state of focusing on a good life to one of focusing on a good death. Reflecting work from a number of sources [40–44], a starting framework for thinking about capabilities is shown in Fig. 7.1. This outlines two capability objectives that should be included within an integrated framework for evaluating end-of-life care. The first is to live a good life and the second is the opportunity to have a good death [2]. Whilst the capability to live a good life focuses, as with most current economic evaluation, on individual well-being (or utility or health in other frameworks), the opportunity for a good death is more broadly conceived as being related, but in different ways, to both the dying individual and those close to them [45, 46]. This reflects the importance of the impact of the death on loved ones [47]. This integrated framework for evaluation reflects the blurring of boundaries in which curative and palliative interventions are often delivered concurrently [48–50] as well as that the failure to recognise the need for transition to palliative care has significant implications for patient care [51–53] and satisfaction with care amongst bereaved relatives [54–56].

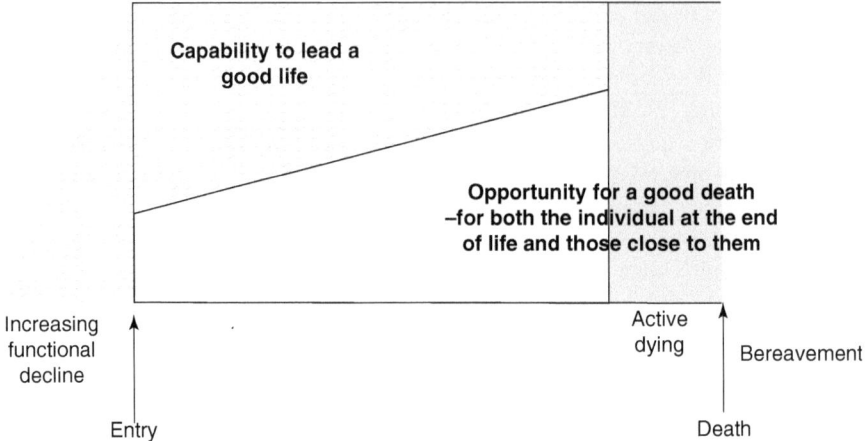

Fig. 7.1 A conceptual framework for evaluating capability at the end of life

7.3 Populating the Integrated Framework

7.3.1 Capability to Lead a Good Life

There are an increasing number of measures available that focus on measuring capability for use in economic evaluation. These include both generic measures aimed at the whole (adult) population [20, 30, 57, 58] and specific measures focused on particular groups of people, such as older people [26, 27, 31], or on particular conditions/interventions, including mental health conditions [33], pain [59], social care [39, 60, 61] and public health interventions [62]. For the purposes of this framework, generic measures of a good life are most helpful, suggesting that either generic measures for the whole population or for particular sectors of it should be included in the framework. To make the framework applicable to all population groups, a generic measure such as ICECAP-A would be most appropriate.

The ICECAP-A is a brief measure of capability containing five attributes: autonomy, attachment, achievement, enjoyment and stability [22]. The conceptual attributes were generated through in-depth interviews with adult members of the general population and refined through follow-up interviews intended to confirm the conceptual attributes and generate meaningful expressions for their use in a questionnaire [22]. Each attribute has four levels that range from having no capability to having full capability [22]. Index values have been generated from the general population through a best-worst scaling exercise, with values anchored at zero for no capability on any attribute and one for full capability on every attribute [30]. With these values, it is possible to consider capability over time. The measure is intended for self-completion. Recent work has assessed the validity of the measure in the general population [57, 58], and it is currently being assessed alongside other measures for feasibility of use amongst hospice patients, both for self-completion and completion by family members and health professionals [63].

7.3.2 Opportunity for a Good Death

7.3.2.1 For the Individual at the End of Life

Research has suggested that a number of factors are important to people at the end of life. These may be important to capture in assessing the capability for a good death and may include such things as spirituality [64], dignity [65], autonomy and choice [64–67], completion [64, 67], preparation for death [64, 67, 68], support and love [69, 70] as well as freedom from pain, adverse symptoms and emotional distress [64–67]. These sorts of capabilities are also upheld by practical policy with, for example, a recent document on palliative care in Australia suggesting that key issues for health professionals would go beyond medical issues, logistical issues and health gain, and include a focus on wishes at the end of life including: views on euthanasia and advance directives; family support, including taking account of the needs of carers; 'emotional, physical, spiritual, social and cultural well-being' (p. 9); autonomy, including seeking out and respecting people's wishes about their preferences for care and support; and human dignity [71].

Although many service documents also focus on service issues such as the location of care [38, 72–75], conceptually, it is important to separate the attributes associated with a good death from those factors, such as service provision, that influence whether a good death is achieved. This, in part, differentiates economic measures from broader survey or quality of life instruments where the aims differ from those of economic evaluation and suggests the need for instruments specific for use in the economic evaluation context.

One measure has been generated specifically with the aim of measuring capability at end of life for use in economic evaluation. This is the ICECAP Supportive Care Measure (ICECAP-SCM) [76]. Like the ICECAP-A, this measure was generated using in-depth interviews, although in this case the measure focused on those who could be conceived as having started to think about end of life to varying degrees. Interviews were conducted with older people in the general population, older people in residential homes and patients receiving palliative care. The resultant measure is, again like the ICECAP-A, a brief measure, with seven attributes each with four levels. For the ICECAP-SCM, the seven attributes are choice (expressed as having a say), love and affection, freedom from physical suffering, freedom from emotional suffering, dignity, support and preparation [76]. The use of the measure with hospice patients and potential proxies (those close to the patient and health professionals) is currently being evaluated [63], and values are currently being generated. An important issue in relation to both measure completion and valuation is who should provide these assessments. In relation to measure completion, there are practical issues of whether a person at the end of life is able to complete the measure, issues around whether adaptation in different groups is differential and (for completion by proxies) informational issues [2]. With respect to valuation, there is the question of whether the values used should be those of the general population (who may be seen as important in terms of their role as citizens and taxpayers) or of people at the end of life (who may have particular knowledge about end-of-life states, but where there may be logistical and ethical problems in accessing values and where values may be subject to adaptation).

As measures such as the ICECAP-SCM are generated and developed, it will be possible to consider the impact on an individual of a good death, although there are clearly challenges that will be important in terms of future research. One of these is the issue of how to account for time in relation to a good death. Whilst some research has found that people refuse to trade quality of life for quantity [77], other research has found that individuals with very poor health and limited life expectancy may prefer to live only a very limited amount of time – referred to as a maximum endurable time [78]. Given the latter finding particularly, length of survival might not be an appropriate element of outcome in terms of a good death.

7.3.2.2 For Those Close to the Individual at the End of Life

Individuals close to the person at the end of life (close persons) may assume greater importance than in most health-care interventions [79, 80]. There is evidence that loved ones and caregivers of dying patients experience significant social and economic burden [81, 82], and bereavement has been found to be particularly strong in terms of its impact on a person's well-being [83–85]. There is also evidence of impact of bereavement on mortality, physical health and mental health of close persons [47, 86–88].

Interventions for those close to a person at the end of life may take place both prior to death and during bereavement. There is also evidence that provision of supportive care to the patient can benefit their family members in terms of reductions in psychological symptoms and grief [47, 89, 90] and that these benefits of end-of-life care can continue into the future for the loved ones of the deceased [47]. The holistic approach to end-of-life care also means that caring interventions may be targeted jointly at the dying person and those close to them – for example, the provision of day hospice services for the patient may also provide much needed respite for family members to relax or attend to other issues [91]. For those who die suddenly, there may be different implications for family in terms of lack of preparedness for the death. From the family's perspective, it may be a poor death if they are unable to say goodbye, are left without a will and so on. Essentially, the benefits of end-of-life care may extend beyond the benefits to the individual at end of life [80, 92]; as Dame Cecily Saunders, a pioneer of the hospice movement, said, 'how people die remains in the memory of those who live on' [93].

There are important challenges in capturing these benefits to those who live on. One important question is around what these benefits are and whether they vary between the pre-death and post-death period. Early qualitative work within the EconEndLife project suggests that there are a number of aspects that it may be important to capture in a measure of benefit to close persons. These include the ability to achieve good communication, the ability to access physical and emotional support, the ability to have privacy and space, the ability to prepare and cope and the ability to be free from emotional distress related to the condition of the dying person.

A second important challenge focuses on whose benefits should be captured. Here there is a need to clarify both who should be included as a close person and whether there are degrees of 'closeness' which affect the level of benefit from end-of-life care. The valuation of a close person measure also requires attention; such valuation could use similar methods to those of other capability indices [94], but could also draw on more deliberative methods [95] perhaps more associated with Sen's view that values should rest on democracy and debate [96].

7.4 Achieving an Integrated Framework

Clearly, these individual components are all important in developing a more integrated framework for evaluating end-of-life care, with this framework based on the notion that a person at the end of life and those close to them may concurrently have quality of life and quality of dying issues, with shifting perceptions and expectations leading to different goals becoming more or less prominent along the dying trajectory. Important, therefore, is how this integration might take place so that the framework is valuable to decision-makers choosing between alternative interventions at the end of life.

Capturing the shifting relevance of different goals along different dying trajectories is clearly a complex challenge; nevertheless, there are a number of options here. One would be to explicitly leave the deliberation to decision-makers (who could be seen as the agents of citizens [97, 98]), to trade off the different aspects of benefit within the decision-making process. This would be akin to a cost-consequence approach [99, 100] or to the use of cost/QALY gained alongside other considerations as within the process conducted by the National Institute for Health and Care Excellence (NICE) [101]. There are, however, also alternatives for more formal integration that could be used to obtain specific weights, either from aggregations of the weights chosen by individuals or through consensus means. These might include methods such as multi-criteria decision analysis [102], discrete choice modelling [103], Delphi techniques [104] or deliberative methods [95]. These methods could be used to explicitly give weights to the different aspects within the end-of-life capability framework, such that they could be formally integrated within the decision-making process. Exploratory work is required here and, if successful, could be utilised more generally in economic evaluation where benefits beyond health or beyond the individual are important to capture in the decision-making framework.

A further part of the integrated framework is its use in decision-making, in particular whether the focus should be on maximising the (integrated/summary measure of) capability well-being or on some other decision rule, aligned more closely with the ideas of shortfall and the reaching of a particular minimum threshold, as recently explored in relation to the ICECAP-A [35]. Again, further research is required, both in terms of the desired or appropriate normative basis for decision-making and the practicalities of operationalising the approach.

7.5 Discussion

This chapter has focused on the possibilities for applying the capability approach within the economic evaluation of end-of-life care. It essentially outlines both a framework for the assessment of capability at the end of life and a challenging research agenda. The framework comprises components relating to both the capability for a good life and the opportunity for a good death and thus potentially brings a rich set of relevant information to the decision-making process. Although methods for accessing this rich set of information are still in their infancy, the normative approach of focusing on capability well-being has much support, and it may be more important to imperfectly measure what is important to people; as Sen argues 'if an underlying idea has an essential ambiguity, a precise formulation of that idea must try to capture that ambiguity rather than lose it' [6, p. 48–49].

Amongst the many challenges already outlined is the further challenge of how to relate this framework for evaluating capability at the end of life to the more general frameworks for economic evaluation. One way is to envisage a shift from one framework to another, perhaps at a point defined by the health-care process (diagnosis, prognosis) or through particular decisions by the patient regarding treatment. There are clear challenges in identifying such points, particularly where people do not receive such a clear terminal diagnosis – for example, those entering long-term care and suffering a gradual decline, eventually dying in a care home. Nevertheless, there is increasing research interest in identifying such individuals so that appropriate services can be put in place, and such research will also be important for this type of evaluative work. More generally, this shift between frameworks could be conceptualised within a life-course approach, in which measures developed using the same basic principles but focused on particular aspects of the life course are used in succession as people's lives move into different phases. The ICECAP measures perhaps offer a means of thinking in this way, as people move from an adult phase (ICECAP-A), generally (although of course not always) via an older person phase (ICECAP-O), to a phase at the end of life where the more complex framework outlined here would be utilised in decision-making.

The integrated framework proposed here provides a challenging and ambitious agenda for the future; nevertheless, it also provides existing tools for measuring the opportunity for a good death for a person at the end of life, and research is also well on the way to developing a tool for measuring the impact on capability of end of life care for those close to the person at the end of life. Utilising these tools will provide more information about their relative strengths and weaknesses; their feasibility, validity and sensitivity to change; and their value in decision-making. In turn, this will provide an increasingly firm basis for taking forward the capability approach in evaluating end-of-life care.

Funding Acknowledgements This work was supported by the European Research Council [261098 ECONENDLIFE].

References

1. Round J (2012) Is a QALY still a QALY at the end of life? J Health Econ 31:521–527
2. Coast J (2014) Strategies for the economic evaluation of end-of-life care: making a case for the capability approach. Expert Rev Pharmacoecon Outcomes Res. doi:10.1586/14737167.2014.914436
3. Brouwer WBF, Culyer AJ, van Exel NJA, Rutten FFH (2008) Welfarism vs. extra-welfarism. J Health Econ 27:325–338
4. Coast J, Smith RD, Lorgelly P (2008) Welfarism, extra-welfarism and capability: the spread of ideas in health economics. Soc Sci Med 67:1190–1198
5. Boadway RW, Bruce N (1993) Welfare economics. Blackwell, Oxford
6. Sen A (1992) Inequality reexamined. Russell Sage Foundation, New York
7. Sen A (1993) Capability and well-being. In: Nussbaum MC (ed) The quality of life. Clarendon Press, Oxford
8. Sen A (2009) The idea of justice. Allen Lane, London
9. Nussbaum MC (2003) Capabilities as fundamental entitlements: Sen and social justice. Fem Econ 9(2–3):33–59
10. Alkire S (2005) Why the capability approach? J Hum Dev 6:115–133
11. Alkire S, Deneulin S (2009) The human development and capability approach. In: Deneulin S, Shahani L (eds) An introduction to the human development and capability approach. Freedom and agency. Earthscan, London, pp 22–48
12. Agarwal B, Humphries J, Robeyns I (2003) Exploring the challenges of Amartya Sen's work and ideas: an introduction. Fem Econ 9(2–3):3–12
13. Robeyns I (2005) The capability approach: a theoretical survey. J Hum Dev 6:93–114
14. Robeyns I (2006) The capability approach in practice. J Polit Philos 14:351–376
15. Kuklys W (2005) Amartya Sen's capability approach. Theoretical insights and empirical applications. Springer, Berlin
16. Prah Ruger J (2010) Health capability: conceptualization and operationalization. Am J Public Health 100:41–49
17. Ruger JP (2004) Health and social justice. Lancet 364:1075–1080
18. Ruger JP (2004) Millenium development goals for health: building human capabilities. Bull World Health Organ 82:951–952
19. Venkatapurum S (2011) Health justice: an argument from the capabilities approach. Polity Press, Cambridge
20. Entwistle VA, Watt IS (2013) Treating patients as persons: a capabilities approach to support delivery of person-centred care. Am J Bioeth 13(8):29–39
21. Ryan M, Kinghorn P, Entwistle VA, Francis JJ (2014) Valuing patients' experiences of healthcare processes: towards broader application of existing methods. Soc Sci Med 106:194–203
22. Al-Janabi H, Flynn TN, Coast J (2012) Development of a self-report measure of capability wellbeing for adults: the ICECAP-A. Qual Life Res 21:167–176
23. Anand P (2005) Capabilities and health. J Med Ethics 31:299–303
24. Anand P, Dolan P (2005) Equity, capabilities and health. Soc Sci Med 60:219–222
25. Bleichrodt H, Quiggin J (2013) Capabilities as menus: a non-welfarist basis for QALY evaluation. J Health Econ 32:128–137
26. Coast J, Flynn TN, Natarajan L, Sproston K, Lewis J, Louviere JJ, Peters TJ (2008) Valuing the ICECAP capability index for older people. Soc Sci Med 67:874–882
27. Coast J, Peters TJ, Natarajan L, Sproston K, Flynn TN (2008) An assessment of the construct validity of the descriptive system for the ICECAP capability measure for older people. Qual Life Res 17:967–976
28. Coast J, Smith RD, Lorgelly P (2008) Should the capability approach be applied in health economics? Health Econ 17:667–670
29. Cookson R (2005) QALYs and the capability approach. Health Econ 14:817–829

30. Flynn TN, Huynh E, Peters TJ, Al-Janabi H, Clemens S, Moody A, Coast J (2015) Scoring the ICECAP-A capability instrument. Estimation of a UK general population tariff. Health Econ 24(3):258–269

31. Grewal I, Lewis J, Flynn TN, Brown J, Bond J, Coast J (2006) Developing attributes for a generic quality of life measure for older people: preferences or capabilities? Soc Sci Med 62:1891–1901

32. Lorgelly PK, Lawson KD, Fenwick EAL, Briggs AH (2010) Outcome measurement in economic evaluation of public health interventions: a role for the capability approach? Int J Environ Res Publ Health 7:2274–2289

33. Simon J, Anand P, Gray A, Rugkasa J, Yeeles K, Burns T (2013) Operationalising the capability approach for outcome measurement in mental health research. Soc Sci Med 98:187–196

34. Smith RD, Lorgelly P, Al-Janabi H, Venkatapurum S, Coast J (2012) The capability approach: an alternative paradigm for health economics? In: Jones A (ed) Elgar companion to health economics. Edward Elgar Publishing, Cheltenham

35. Mitchell PM, Roberts TE, Barton PM, Coast J (2015) Applying the sufficient capability approach in economic evaluations to aid decision-making. *Social Science and Medicine* 139:71–79

36. Ruger JP (2006) Health, capability and justice: toward a new paradigm of health ethics, policy and law. Cornell J Law Publ Policy 403:403–482

37. Burt JA (2010) Equity, need and access in health care: a mixed methods investigation of specialist palliative care use in relation to age. UCL, London

38. Department of Health (2008) End of life care strategy. Promoting high quality care for all adults at the end of life. Department of Health, London

39. Forder JE, Caiels J (2011) Measuring the outcomes of long term care. Soc Sci Med 73(12):1766–1774

40. Gott M, Ingleton C, Bennett MI, Gardiner C (2011) Transitions to palliative care in acute hospitals in England: qualitative study. BMJ 342:1773

41. Lunney J, Lynn J, Foley D, Lipson S, Guralnik J (2003) Patterns of functional decline at the end of life. JAMA 289:2387–2392

42. Lunney J, Lynn J, Hogan C (2002) Profiles of older medicare decedents. J Am Geriatr Soc 50:1108–1112

43. Murray SA, Kendall M, Boyd K, Sheikh A (2005) Illness trajectories and palliative care. BMJ 330:1007–1011

44. Porock D, Parker-Oliver D, Zweig SC, Rantz M, Petroski GF (2003) A profile of residents admitted to long-term care facilities for end-of-life care. JAMDA 4(1):16–22

45. Field M, Cassel C (1997) Approaching death: improving care at the end of life. National Academy Press, Washington, DC

46. Kehl KA (2006) Moving toward peace: an analysis of the concept of a good death. Am J Hosp Palliat Med 23(4):277–286

47. Stroebe M, Schut H, Stroebe W (2007) Health outcomes of bereavement. Lancet 370(1960):1973

48. Coventry P, Grande G, Richards D, Todd C (2005) Prediction of appropriate timing of palliative care for older adults with non-malignant life-threatening disease: a systematic review. Age Ageing 34:218–227

49. Lloyd L (2004) Mortality and morality: ageing and the ethics of care. Ageing Soc 24:235–256

50. Shah S, Blanchard M, Tookman A, Jones L, Blizard R, King M (2006) Estimating needs in life threatening illness: a feasibility study to assess the views of patients and doctors. Palliat Med 20:205–210

51. Boyd K, Murray SA (2010) Recognising and managing key transitions in end of life care. BMJ 341:4863

52. Ellershaw J, Ward C (2003) Care of the dying patient: the last hours or days of life. BMJ 326:30–34

53. Hewison A, Lord L, Bailey C (2014) "It's been quite a challenge." Redesigning end-of-life care in acute hospitals. Palliat Support Care 28:1–10
54. Bussmann S, Muders P, Zahrt-Omar C, Escobar P, Claus M, Schildmann J, Weber M (2013) Improving end-of-life care in hospitals: a qualitative analysis of bereaved families' experiences and suggestions. Am J Hosp Palliat Med. doi:10.1177/1049909113512718
55. Edmonds P, Rogers A (2003) 'If only someone had told me…' a review of the care of patients dying in hospital. Clin Med 3:149–152
56. Ellershaw J, Dewar S, Murphy D (2010) Achieving a good death for all. BMJ 341:4861
57. Al-Janabi H, Keeley T, Mitchell P, Coast J (2013) Can capabilities be self-reported? A think aloud study. Soc Sci Med 87:116–122
58. Al-Janabi H, Peters TJ, Brazier J, Bryan S, Flynn TN, Clemens S, Moody A, Coast J (2013) An investigation of the construct validity of the ICECAP-A capability measure. Qual Life Res 22:1831–1840
59. Kinghorn P, Robinson A, Smith RD (2014) Developing a capability-based questionnaire for assessing well-being in patients with chronic pain. Soc Indic Res. doi:10.1007/s11205-014-0625-7
60. Malley JN, Towers A-M, Netten AP, Brazier JE, Forder JE, Flynn T (2012) An assessment of the construct validity of the ASCOT measure of social care-related quality of life with older people. Health Qual Life Outcomes 10(21):1–14
61. Netten A, Burge P, Malley J, Potoglou D, Towers A-M, Brazier J, Flynn T, Forder J, Wall B (2012) Outcomes of social care for adults: developing a preference-weighted measure. Heath Technol Assess 16(16):1–166
62. Lorgelly PK, Lorimer K, Fenwick EA, Briggs AH, Anand P (2015) Operationalising the capability approach as an outcome measure in public health: the development of the OCAP-18. Social Science and Medicine 142:68–81
63. Bailey CJ, Orlando R, Kinghorn P, Armour K, Perry R, Coast J (2014) Measuring quality of end of life using ICECAP-SCM: feasibility and acceptability. BMJ Support Palliat Care 4:112
64. Steinhauser KE, Christakis NA, Clipp EC, McNeilly M, McIntyre L, Tulsky JA (2000) Factors considered important at the end of life by patients, family, physicians, and other care providers. J Am Med Assoc 284:2476–2482
65. Byock IR, Corbeil YJ, Goodrich ME (2009) Beyond polarization, public preferences suggest policy opportunities to address aging, dying and family caregiving. Am J Hosp Palliat Med 26(3):200–208
66. Singer P, Martin D, Kelner M (1999) Quality of end-of-life care – patients' perspectives. JAMA 281:163–168
67. Steinhauser KE, Clipp EC, McNeilly M, Christakis NA, McIntyre L, Tulsky JA (2000) In search of a good death: observations of patients, families and providers. Ann Intern Med 132:825–832
68. Steinhauser KE, Christakis NA, Clipp EC, McNeilly M, Grambow S, Parker J, Tulsky JA (2001) Preparing for the end of life: preferences of patients, families, physicians, and other care providers. J Pain Symptom Manag 22:727–737
69. Daveson BA, Alonso JP, Calanzani N, Ramsenthaler C, Gysels M, Antunes B, Moens K, Groeneveld EI, Albers G, Finetti S, Pettanati F, Bausewein C, Higginson IJ, Harding R, Deliens L, Toscani F, Ferreira PL, Ceulemans L, Gomes B, PRISMA (2013) Learning from the public: citizens describe the need to improve end-of-life care access, provision and recognition across Europe. Eur J Publ Health 24(3):521–527
70. Singer MA (1995) Community participation in health care decision making? Is it feasible? Can Med Assoc J 153(4):421–424
71. National Health, Medical Research Council (2011) An ethical framework for integrating palliative care principles into the management of advanced chronic or terminal conditions. National Health and Medical Research Council, Canberra
72. Department of Health and Ageing (2010) Supporting Australians to live well at the end of life. National palliative care strategy 2010. Department of Health and Ageing, Canberra

73. Health Canada (2007) Canadian strategy on palliative and end-of-life care. Final report of the coordinating committee. December 2002 to March 2007. Health Canada, Ottawa
74. Ministry of Health (2012) Resource and capability framework for integrated adult palliative care services in New Zealand. Ministry of Health, Wellington
75. The Scottish Government (2008) Living and dying well: a national action plan for palliative and end of life care in Scotland. The Scottish Government, Edinburgh
76. Sutton E, Coast J (2014) Development of a supportive care measure for economic evaluation of end-of-life care, using qualitative methods. Palliat Med 28:151–157
77. Arnesen T, Norheim O (2003) Quantifying quality of life for economic analysis: time out for time trade off. Med Humanit 29:81–86
78. Dolan P, Stalmeier P (2003) The validity of time trade-off values in calculating QALYs: constant proportional time trade-off versus the proportional heuristic. J Health Econ 22(3):445–458
79. Gomes B, Harding R, Foley KM, Higginson I (2009) Optimal approaches to the health economics of palliative care: report of an international think tank. J Pain Symptom Manag 38:4–10
80. Haycox A (2009) Optimizing decision making and resource allocation in palliative care. J Pain Symptom Manag 38(1):45–53
81. Emanuel E, Emanuel L (1998) The promise of a good death. Lancet 351:S21–S29
82. Emanuel E, Fairclough D, Slutsman J, Emanuel L (2000) Understanding economic and other burdens of terminal illness: the experience of patients and their caregivers. Ann Intern Med 132:451–459
83. Broman CL, Riba ML, Trahan MR (1996) Traumatic events and marital well-being. J Marriage Fam 58:908–916
84. Li J, Laursen TM, Precht DH, Olsen J, Mortensen PB (2005) Hospitalization for mental illness among parents after the death of a child. N Engl J Med 352(12):1190–1196
85. Oswald AJ, Powdthavee N (2008) Death, happiness and the calculation of compensatory damages. J Leg Stud 37(Suppl 2):S217–S251
86. Buckley T, Sunari D, Marshall A, Bartrop R, McKinley S, Tofler G (2012) Physiological correlates of bereavement and the impact of bereavement interventions. Dialogues Clin Neurosci 14(2):129–139
87. Jones MP, Bartrop RW, Forcier L, Penny R (2010) The long-term impact of bereavement upon spouse health: a 10-year follow-up. Acta Neuropsychiatr 22(5):212–217
88. Song J, Floyd FJ, Seltzer MM, Greenberg JS, Hong J (2010) Long-term effects of child death on parents' health related quality of life. Fam Relat 59(3):269–282
89. Cameron J, Parkes CM (1983) Terminal care: evaluation of effects on surviving family of care before and after bereavement. Postgrad Med Educ 59:73–78
90. Ransford HE, Smith ML (1991) Grief resolution among the bereaved in hospice and hospital wards. Soc Sci Med 32:295–304
91. Douglas H, Higginson I, Myers K, Normand C (2000) Assessing structure, process and outcome in palliative day care: a pilot study for a multicentre trial. Health Soc Care Community 8:336–344
92. Becker G, Murphy K, Philipson T (2007) The value of life near its end and terminal care. NBE Working Paper 13333. National Bureau of Economic Research, Cambridge, MA
93. Saunders C (1989) Pain and impending death. In: Wall P, Melzak R (eds) Textbook of pain. Churchill Livingstone, Edinburgh, pp 624–631
94. Flynn TN, Louviere J, Peters T, Coast J (2007) Best-worst scaling. What it can do for health care research and how to do it. J Health Econ 26:171–189
95. Fishkin JS, Luskin RC (2005) Experimenting with a democratic ideal: deliberative polling and public opinion. Acta Polit 40:284–298
96. Sen A (2005) Human rights and capabilities. J Hum Dev 6:151–166
97. Coast J (2001) Citizens, their agents and health care rationing: an exploratory study using qualitative methods. Health Econ 10:159–174

98. Mooney G (1994) Key issues in health economics. Harvester Wheatsheaf, New York
99. Coast J (2004) Is economic evaluation in touch with society's health values? Br Med J 329:1233–1236
100. Mauskopf JA, Paul JE, Grant DM, Stergachis A (1998) The role of cost-consequence analysis in healthcare decision making. Pharamacoeconomics 13(3):277–288
101. Rawlins M, Barnett D, Stevens A (2010) Pharmacoeconomics: NICE's approach to decision-making. Br J Clin Pharmacol 70(3):346–349
102. Thokola P, Duenas A (2012) Multiple criteria decision analysis for health technology assessment. Value Health 15:1172–1181
103. Lancsar E, Louviere J (2008) Conducting discrete choice experiments to inform healthcare decision making: a user's guide. Pharmacoeconomics 26(8):661–677
104. Powell C (2003) The Dephi technique: myths and realities. J Adv Nurs 41(4):376–382

Chapter 8
Identifying Objects of Value at the End of Life

Christopher J. Sampson

8.1 Introduction

As end-of-life care rises up the political and research agenda, methods of economic evaluation are coming under increased scrutiny from researchers both inside and outside of the health economics field. Such scrutiny is warranted – end-of-life care has a number of characteristics that make economic evaluation particularly challenging. These include proximity to death, the improbability of survival gain, individuals' changing priorities, declining cognition and effects on close persons (for a fuller discussion of these issues, see Chap. 2). In view of these particularities of end-of-life care, some researchers have determined that current 'extra-welfarist' approaches to defining outcomes – in terms of quality-adjusted life years (QALYs) – do not adequately reflect well-being. As a result, suggestions are being made that would see the QALY approach either replaced or subject to significant redefinition.

In relation to end-of-life care, the debate is still in its infancy, with few substantive discussions about appropriate outcome measurement for the purpose of resource allocation. A number of alternatives have been proposed, most notably the capability approach and the palliative care yardstick (PalY) framework [1–3]. The purported goal of adopting these alternative evaluation approaches is to extend the evaluative space 'beyond health' – that is, to include non-health outcomes when considering the benefits of interventions in economic evaluations. In addition to these proposed alternative frameworks, more specific aspects of life that are not currently considered within the evaluative space, such as the 'provision of a good death' or 'being treated with dignity', have also been suggested for explicit consideration in the evaluation process (though it is not immediately clear how – or why – these items should be counted in economic evaluation).

C.J. Sampson
Division of Rehabilitation and Ageing, School of Medicine, Queen's Medical Centre, University of Nottingham, Nottingham NG7 2UH, UK
e-mail: Chris.Sampson@nottingham.ac.uk

© Springer International Publishing Switzerland 2016
J. Round (ed.), *Care at the End of Life: An Economic Perspective*,
DOI 10.1007/978-3-319-28267-1_8

The purpose of this chapter is to guide the definition of what should be included in the evaluative space in end-of-life care, but also more broadly. I consider which outcomes – what Sen has called 'objects of value' – might be included within an economic evaluation, in relation to *what* we value (the domains) and *why* we value it (its consequents). My focus is upon judgements about the effectiveness of interventions in end-of-life care, rather than issues surrounding equity or decision criteria in the allocation of resources. Such issues are discussed elsewhere in this volume (see, e.g. Chaps. 9 and 10). I argue that alternative evaluative frameworks are currently ill-defined. I identify some gaps in the apparent normative foundations of these alternative approaches and some flaws in the operational proposals that arise in efforts to implement the alternative frameworks. Finally, I consider some criticisms of the use of QALYs but suggest that current approaches should be maintained, with some changes.

8.1.1   Objects of Value

Central to this discussion is the identification of 'objects of value'. Objects of value are those items that we might wish to consider in an evaluation and which might be influenced by interventions in end-of-life care or other health-care settings. They might include such objects as being free from pain, being worried, owning a TV, having independence, being fertile or being in employment. Some objects of value might be easily observable, while others may be intangible. There is no limit to the number of possible objects of value, but we might have reason to believe that not all objects are worthy of consideration. There may be some potential effects of interventions (whether positive or negative) that we might not want to include in an analysis. For example, we might wish to exclude income from employment as an object of value (even if people seek to maximise their incomes) either because we do not consider it an end in itself or because it is not relevant to the context of health and social care. This therefore raises the inevitable question of which objects of value should be included.

Taken together, the objects of value that are considered in an analysis define the evaluative space of the economic evaluation. Because any aspect of a person's life experience could potentially be included as an object of value, the sum of all potential objects of value defines a person's state of being. Those objects that we determine to be of value to the individual define their well-being. In this chapter I provide some guidance on the process of identifying objects of value. Failure to appropriately identify which objects of value should be included in the evaluative space could result in inefficient and inequitable allocations of resources.

8.1.2   The Meaning of Extra-Welfarism

The cost-per-QALY approach currently used in the UK and elsewhere has become known as extra-welfarism. Much debate has taken place (and continues) around the definition of extra-welfarism. In this chapter I take at face value the definition provided by Brouwer et al. [4]. This is a broad conception of extra-welfarism, and, generally speaking, proponents of alternative approaches to economic evaluation in end-of-life care do not completely reject it. Therefore, I interpret these alternatives as (potentially) representing adjustments to the evaluative space within the scope of extra-welfarism.

Tony Culyer – one of the key architects of extra-welfarism in health economics – has discussed the notion of 'characteristics of people' and identifies these as the objects of value within the extra-welfarist evaluative space [5]. Characteristics of people include such notions as 'being able to feed oneself' and 'being reassured'. In this vein, Brouwer et al. suggest 'characterizing the evaluative space of extra-welfarism... as an assembly of other characteristics of individuals' [4]. However, while this limits the evaluative space to characteristics of people (rather than resources or their characteristics), it does not determine whether all characteristics of people should be included within the evaluative space or how one might identify specific characteristics of people to consider. Hurley states that part of the extra-welfarist evaluation process is to, 'from the set of all characteristics of people, define the set of characteristics that are normatively relevant for evaluation in the health sector' [6]. In this chapter I present a means of more clearly defining the evaluative space within such an extra-welfarist framework.

8.2   Domains and Consequents: The What and Why of the Evaluative Space

Sen identifies two questions in regard to evaluation: (i) what are the objects of value and (ii) how valuable are these respective objects. He describes the former as defining the 'evaluative space' [7], and it is this question that is explored throughout this chapter.

Here I present reason and basis for demarcation in the definition of the evaluative space, adding the question of *why* particular objects are valuable to Sen's questions of *what* is valuable and *how valuable* it is. These are normative questions, and researchers should define objects of value in terms of what I will call 'domains' – the *what* of the evaluative space – and their 'consequents' – the *why*.

8.2.1   Definitions

8.2.1.1   Domains

Domains are those realms of human life in which we would deem improvements to be valuable. There is no limit to the number, scope or specificity of domains that might be included within the evaluative space, but each needs clear justification. Domains are not mutually exclusive and might have any number of subdomains across physical, psychological and spiritual constructs. A domain of particular relevance in the economic evaluation of health care is health. Other examples might include mobility, employment, nourishment, autonomy, relationships or any other aspect of life that we think might be relevant and worthy of consideration.

8.2.1.2   Consequents

Consequents have not previously been specified in the literature. They represent *in what respect* we value particular objects. That is, they are the reason *why* we value states within domains and are the means by which well-being (in its broadest sense) might be improved.[1] Consequents represent the consequential effect on well-being (however understood) of a given state, not the consequential result of a particular intervention. Relevant consequents to economic evaluation in health care might include (though are not limited to):

- Capabilities [8]
- Functionings [8]
- Preference satisfaction [9]
- General satisfaction [10]
- Need satisfaction [11]

Consequents are not necessarily mutually exclusive. Individual preferences might be valued in their own right as a consequent, or might be used as a proxy for utility (another consequent), while both might also reflect changes in capability sets. However, this does not mean that these are equivalent or that the choice of consequents is – for lack of a better word – inconsequential. What is important is the extent to which each approach adequately reflects the value provided by a state. For example, a wide choice set may be valuable to a person but not adequately reflected in their preferences. This is one of the primary arguments in favour of adopting capabilities as the consequent of value, because adaptation might lead to people's preferences not adequately reflecting the value associated with particular capability sets.

Later I will discuss means of identifying which domains and consequents should be included in the evaluative space and the extent to which different approaches are explicit in their attempts to do so. For now it will suffice to acknowledge that we *might* not want to include all possible domains or consequents within the evaluative space.

8.2.2   Defining the Evaluative Space

A substantial philosophical literature has developed around the notion that 'health' holds special moral significance [47] and similar ideas have developed in the context of economic evaluation in health care. Consider the often-repeated claim made

---

[1] The use of the term 'consequent' should not be understood to imply consequentialism, the notion that the outcomes of actions are the basis by which to judge the moral correctness of those actions.

in the extra-welfarist literature that 'health' is something that is valuable *as an end in itself* [11]. Such a claim requires some working definition of health, and any useful definition (i.e. useful as an objective) necessarily relates to particular consequents. One cannot attach value in the absence of definition. Even the most rudimentary definitions of health (consider 'not dead') necessitate a level of functioning as a consequent, even if not explicitly acknowledged. Some definitions of health imply capabilities as the consequent – for example, that of Huber et al. who propose the inclusion of adaptation and self-management as key components of health [12].

Consider mobility as a possible object of value within the domain of health. If our concern lies in the extent to which people are mobile, then the consequent is functioning. If we primarily care about whether or not an individual prefers a given state of mobility, then individual preferences are the consequent. Valuations of these different objects of value might not be equal, and therefore it is important to define in what respect mobility should be included within the evaluative space. The fundamental notion of mobility cannot itself be an object of value (rather, 'mobility' should be considered a domain). Likewise, the notion of health cannot be an object of value. Objects of value might include being in good health, having the opportunity to be in good health or being satisfied with one's health.

Superficially, it might seem reasonable to equate the domains of the evaluative space with specific descriptive systems, while equating the consequents of the evaluative space with specific valuation methods. However, this would be an error. Descriptive systems (e.g. questionnaires) should be developed such that they provide maximum informational content (as is feasible) regarding objects of value within the domains of interest. Attention should also be given to the number of states that the descriptive system is able to define and practical concerns associated with this [13]. Valuation methods should seek to quantify the value of the objects in respect to the consequents. Backward reasoning could lead to misspecification of the evaluative space. Both consequents and domains require ex ante definition in order to avoid this. The conflation of consequents and domains is also common. For example, the 'outcome' of welfarist approaches is usually seen to be utility, while the 'outcome' of extra-welfarism is seen to be health. In this sense each has been interpreted as 'unidimensional' [6]. But utility (as a consequent) and health (as a domain) are not comparable in this way.[2]

Sen states that 'the selection of the evaluative space has a good deal of cutting power' [7], highlighting the importance of clarity in this regard. Failure to clearly define the evaluative space risks including and excluding the wrong objects of value, even in terms of one's own normative position. Extra-welfarism adopts 'characteristics of people' as the objects of value. We can now acknowledge that characteristics of people require definition in terms of both consequents and domains. Consider one example characteristic highlighted earlier in this chapter – being able to feed oneself [5]. The wording 'being able to' implies that this characteristic is valued as a capability, invoking this as the primary (if not exclusive) consequent of interest.

---

[2] Furthermore, determining a single metric for outcome measurement is a feature of the decision rules employed and does not necessitate a unidimensional evaluative space.

'To feed oneself' could be a specific domain of interest, though it seems to imply a domain of autonomy. Thus we could determine that the evaluative space consists the domain of autonomy, valued in respect to the capabilities provided by objects within this domain. However, we could alternatively conclude that this characteristic is of value in terms of health functionings. This retrofitting approach is problematic in at least two ways. First, it can be used to justify any number of domains and conse- quents being included in the evaluative space. The reason for including this charac- teristic remains unknown, and it becomes impossible to establish boundaries to the evaluative space. Second, we cannot know the informational value of these objects as indicators of well-being, and thus their use in evaluation presupposes usefulness. Objects with more informational value within the domain may remain unidentified. As such, the objects may be given undue weight.

8.2.3 Normative Positions

Which domains and consequents should be included in the evaluative space is an unavoidable normative question that cannot be answered exclusively by empirical investigation. There is much discussion both within and beyond health economics about definitions of well-being and recommended normative positions. In general, researchers have tended to focus either on the consequents of value or on the domains of value, while being unclear regarding the other. For example, Sen clearly argues in favour of capabilities, while being reluctant to specify domains [14]. Conversely, Rawls's 'primary goods' clearly outline a set of domains while being unclear about in what respect resources are valued [15] – though one interpretation of Rawls's later writing could be that he accepted capabilities as the consequent of value, stating that Sen's idea is 'needed to explain the propriety of the use of pri- mary goods' [16]. A strict welfarist could be an exception in clearly defining the consequent (individual utility) and valuing all domains (as might be represented in a simple willingness to pay exercise). Martha Nussbaum is another exception in clearly defining capabilities as the consequent and a narrow set of 'central capabili- ties' (including bodily health, emotions and practical reason) as domains [17].

Some authors have discussed the idea of 'context' in the capabilities literature [8]. The context of evaluation being discussed here is health care or, more specifi- cally, end-of-life care. Depending on an individual's normative position, the context of the evaluation might or might not be allowed to inform the selection of domains. Later I argue that it should.

8.3 New Vistas for Extra-Welfarism in End-of-Life Care?

Having specified the basis on which the evaluative space should be defined (i.e. in terms of domains and consequents), we can now explore the extent and manner in which alternative frameworks for economic evaluation in end-of-life care expand the evaluative space as they claim. In this section I consider the health-related QALY approach and its alternatives. For each I consider the supposed normative basis of the approach and the consistency and validity in its application – both generally and with specific reference to end-of-life care – and assess to what extent each determines a different evaluative space. Because it has undergone the most development in the health economics literature, my focus will be upon the capabilities approach. Definitions of extra-welfarism have been widely discussed [4, 6, 18, 19]. Here I simply wish to assert that extra-welfarism is an ambiguous concept. The alternatives presented herein are considered broadly within the realm of extra-welfarism. While some have described cost-per-QALY analysis as non-welfarist [20], whether a given evaluative space should or should not be considered extra-welfarist is not the subject of this chapter.

8.3.1 Health-Related QALYs

Extra-welfarism (as currently operationalised) is commonly described as involving 'health maximisation' [21]. Indeed, a focus on the domain of health might be considered extra-welfarism's defining feature, at least as the term is currently used [21]. Extra-welfarism has been criticised as restrictive on this basis, though clear definition of the domains of the evaluative space should be seen as a positive feature of an evaluative framework.

In terms of consequents, the health-related QALY framework is less well defined. There is little agreement in the literature over the principal consequent, even in the narrow understanding of extra-welfarism as health maximisation. There are at least three interpretations of the consequent. First, current QALY approaches might capture health preferences, with preferences over health states as the consequent. This is perhaps the most common understanding of the QALY approach, with the use of valuation tools that explicitly seek to elicit preferences and economic evaluations using QALYs described as 'cost-utility' analyses. Preference elicitation techniques are variously considered to elicit von Neumann-Morgenstern utility or some other form of choice value. As such, the 'preference satisfaction' understanding of the health-related QALY approach could further be interpreted in multiple ways. Second, QALYs might be interpreted as measuring health functionings, using tools such as the EQ-5D. This view is presented by some critics of the health-related QALY, in particular proponents of the capabilities approach [22]. Third, it is possible to interpret QALYs as capturing capabilities [23].

In using the health-related QALY, the evaluative space consists of the domain of health. As such, end-of-life care is only deemed effective to the extent that improvements are observed within the domain of health. However, in practice, some measurement tools have been designed such that they allow for a very broad understanding of health. For example, the EQ-5D includes the dimension 'usual activities', which might be considered beyond the domain of health in some respects (though when completing the questionnaire respondents are asked to consider their answers in respect of their health). Such ambiguities arise because the evaluative space was not clearly defined and used to guide the development of such descriptive systems.

Though there are problems associated with the health-related QALY approach – some solutions for which I outline below – it can be used to evaluate end-of-life care with respect to objects of value that lie within the domain of health [1]. Due to ambiguity in the consequent associated with the health-related QALY approach, there is scope for reinterpretation and minor adjustment to satisfy researchers' preferred normative positions in this regard. However, if objects of value outside the domain of health are to be included, then an alternative approach is necessary. Later I argue that such a change is unwarranted and undesirable.

8.3.2 Capabilities

One major claim, currently gaining traction in end-of-life care, is in favour of the capability approach. Introduced by Sen [8], the capability approach proposes a movement away from an understanding of well-being as 'utility' towards the acknowledgement of functionings (what people are and what they do) and capabilities (the alternative sets of functionings available to a person), with capabilities forming the basis of the evaluative space. The apparent focus of the capability approach is therefore on defining the evaluative space by an alternative consequent. In health economics it has been characterised as a shift in focus 'away from achieved functionings towards the freedom that a person has in their lives to achieve different aspects of well-being' [24]. Such a capability approach has also been described as offering a means of finding balance between autonomy and paternalism [25]. However, as suggested above, health-related QALYs might already be interpreted as reflecting capability sets [23]. Therefore, we must consider what proponents seek to add beyond a simple reinterpretation.

In practice, the focus of the capability approach in health economics has been upon extending the evaluative space to include additional domains of value, rather than its namesake consequent. It has been framed as an 'extension of the informational or evaluative space' [24] that offers a broader understanding of well-being [26]. What people prioritise as being important to their quality of life changes as they approach the end-of-life [27], and this is perhaps the primary reason for the suggestion of alternative outcome measures in end-of-life care. Proponents have suggested that capabilities better reflect what is important to people at the end of life and there is some evidence that people in end-of-life care do value capabilities [28] (though it is not clear to what extent they are valued in relation to alternative consequents such as functionings). An effort to more accurately capture the capabilities associated with particular states – if we determine these to lie within the evaluative space – is a valuable exercise.

Specific objects of value have been identified in relation to end-of-life care (e.g. 'preparing for death', 'receiving spiritual comfort', 'being treated with dignity and respect', 'influencing the care received', 'receiving love and support', 'not feeling like a burden' and 'achieving a sense of completion in life' [2]), and these have been presented as relating to capabilities. However, such objects might also be defined in terms of functioning (e.g. 'did people say goodbye and make preparations?'). The relevance of capabilities is presupposed in the wording of these characteristics. The key distinction being made is not in the objects of value but in the way the question is presented. By extension, objects of value in the EQ-5D could be rephrased to represent capabilities – e.g. 'I have some problems washing or dressing myself' becomes 'If I want to, I am able to wash or dress myself as I need'. Such retrofitted arguments in favour of a capabilities approach should be avoided.

There has also been some suggestion that the capability approach in end-of-life care might be used to justify existing interventions based on their objectives. For example, Coast highlights that 'the objective of care at the end of life is not focused purely on health improvement' [2] and presents this as an argument against current approaches. Here, again, the tail is wagging the dog. What care currently tries to achieve may be entirely misguided and is irrelevant to the definition of the evaluative space.

One specific argument in favour of a capability approach in end-of-life care has focused on the opportunity for a good death [2, 3]. It remains unclear why 'a good death' should necessarily indicate capabilities as the consequent of interest, and its explicit inclusion risks skewing evaluations away from what patients and the public value. There is no clear definition of to which aspects of life (domains) the provision of a good death brings value and no explanation of how it relates to the consequent of capabilities. Regardless, as discussed previously, this retrofitting approach to particular proposed objects of value precludes the definition of the evaluative space. This is not to say that the provision of a good death should not be considered, but rather that it is not the place of economists to specify items at their will. Suppose that 'opportunity for a good death' is identified as being a relevant aspect of the health domain and that we value the capabilities associated with it as a consequent. It does not follow that this should be *the* or even *a primary* object of value identified through outcome measurement. There may be many more important objects of value that might better reflect well-being and provide more information about the evaluative space. Unless this object of value is identified as a relevant indicator within a predefined evaluative space, its inclusion risks misrepresenting patients' priorities and resulting in inefficient allocations of resources.

Aside from the examples cited above, proponents of the capabilities approach are developing improved methods for the development of descriptive systems to reflect a prespecified evaluative space [29–31]. These qualitative approaches are designed such that they elicit information about the most important and informative objects of value within an evaluative space for a given sample. This is in contrast to the methods used to develop health-related preference-based measures such as the EQ-5D, which was based on an assessment of pre-existing instruments [32] (though improved approaches are being developed for health-related preference-based measures [33]). However, it is not clear how one might determine whether particular objects of value are identified because of their importance as a capability or because of their importance as an achieved functioning [34].

Coast has argued that health maximisation is not always important, including in end-of-life care, arguing that individual choice is more important [2].[3] This claim

---

[3] Here I have understood 'choice' in terms of the act of making a choice, which clearly relates to the notion of preferences and is a consequent. However, it might also be interpreted (and it may be Coast's intention to present it) as freedom or autonomy, which should be considered a domain. Thanks to Alastair Canaway for highlighting this.

seems to confuse domains (health) with consequents (individual choice) in the context of a decision rule (maximisation) and inexplicably introduces choice alongside the previously discussed consequent of capabilities. Sen has rejected the choice approach to well-being [8], and it is difficult to see how the capability approach could be used to justify prioritisation of individual choice in end-of-life care. The reason Sen opposes the choice approach is that individual choice probably does not adequately reflect capabilities. In this regard, a focus on individual choice would seem to contradict the purpose of the capabilities approach and instead support the use of individual preferences as the consequent.

8.3.2.1 Measuring Capabilities

The ICECAP family of measures – which purport to capture capabilities – have adopted best-worst scaling and discrete choice experiments for the purpose of valuation. Those involved in the design of ICECAP instruments argue that best-worst scaling might reflect 'values' rather than preferences and therefore be appropriate in capturing capabilities, meanwhile claiming that best-worst scaling is an effective method for capturing utility [35, 36]. This raises the question of whether proponents of such measures make any distinction between the two consequents of capabilities and preference satisfaction and – if they do not – why they seek to adjust the consequent of the evaluative space. This obscures the basis for a rejection of the normative foundations of QALYs, which – as already noted – could be interpreted as reflecting capabilities. These approaches are only likely to capture capabilities to the extent that they are reflected by preferences, undermining their purpose.

Recently, the ICECAP Supportive Care Measure (ICECAP-SCM) has been developed for the purpose of evaluating end-of-life care, based on the factors that older people (at the end of life) consider important [31]. In eliciting objects for inclusion, no evaluative space was clearly predefined. Respondents were not asked about attributes relating to a specific domain, such as health. As such, all of those objects of value that were identified (namely, 'having a say', 'being with people who care about you', 'physical suffering', 'emotional suffering', 'dignity', 'being supported' and 'being prepared') come from an unbounded evaluative space. The first thing to conclude from this is that the measure cannot be directly comparable on equivalent scales – however valued – to a measure based on a restricted evaluative space. This is because the measures are likely to provide information about different constructs; one could not equate information about a person's satisfaction with health with information about their subjective well-being. Indeed, the ICECAP-SCM is not presented as – or intended to be – comparable with measures such as the EQ-5D. Rather, it might be used to achieve technical efficiency – not allocative efficiency – within the restricted context of end-of-life care. This is in contrast to the approach adopted in the recent development of the CHU9D – a paediatric preference-based outcome measure – which asked specifically about health, thus restricting the domain and ensuring comparability in terms of the evaluative space [33].

In relation to end-of-life care, Coast argues that 'death itself may not imply a loss of capability' [2]. However, this creates a conundrum when we observe the approach to valuation that has been applied to the capabilities approach in health economics. Measures like the ICECAP-O assume that the lower boundary of value is 'no capabilities' and also that being dead equates to having no capabilities. Thus, 'dead' cannot be assigned a higher value than any other state, and the only state compared to which death might not represent a loss of capability is that in which an individual already has no capability.

By accepting conveniences in the operation of the capability approach, the family of ICECAP measures may be reduced to little more than a semantic nuance, their focus being on the use of terms such as 'I am able to', 'I can' and 'If I want to'. There may be merit in this, but there is currently no evidence to suggest that the use of these terms results in any substantive difference in response. A simple test could involve comparing two questionnaires – one using functioning terms (e.g. 'I am', 'I do') and the other using capability terms (e.g. 'I am able to', 'I can') – that are identical except in their wording, and to see if individuals either (a) give divergent responses or (b) attach different values to states defined in these terms. Advocates of the capability approach are keen to allow time for further development of measures [24], which could prove fruitful.

As currently presented in relation to end-of-life care, the capabilities approach seems unclear and insufficiently justified. Its primary goal in health economics appears to be to extend the evaluative space 'beyond health'. Therefore, (somewhat confusingly) the capabilities approach indicates changes in the domains of interest rather than necessarily changes in the consequents. The ways in which researchers have operationalised the approach to date support this view. This movement 'beyond health' rather than towards capabilities has received less discussion, and there have been fewer arguments provided in favour of such an extension to the evaluative space.[4] The primary nature of the capabilities argument against health-related QALYs is to extend the domains of the evaluative space from health alone to well-being more broadly, and this view has – for reasons that are not clear – become conflated with a movement towards valuing capabilities rather than functionings.

8.3.3 Other Alternatives

Normand presents an argument against the use of 'standard' outcome measures in end-of-life care, suggesting that 'contextual factors' may be important [3]. This, to some extent, echoes the claims for inclusion of specific objects of value within the evaluative space and is subject to the same errors in reasoning. The more fundamental suggestion by Normand is that the value of time may not be constant and thus the additive assumption of the QALY may not hold. Normand argues that this is

---

[4]Arguments of this kind are more common in relation to the use of subjective well-being as a consequent [37].

particularly relevant at the end of life, when time is limited. The resulting framework proposed is the palliative care yardstick (PalY) [3, 38], which involves two changes to the standard QALY approach. First, additional items would be added in that might not otherwise be adequately measured. Second, nonadditivity of time should be accepted. Normand suggests that nonadditivity of time might be achieved by allowing value to be attached to the components of a 'good death'. In regard to the first suggestion, this approach is flawed insofar as it requires the retrofitting approach previously described. If followed, investigators might adopt similar methods to those used for establishing 'bolt-on' items for preference-based measures [39]. The second suggestion seems to conflate two separate issues – the nonadditivity of time (e.g. greater weight to years immediately preceding death) and the value of a good death (i.e. differential objects of value).

Time exists separately to the evaluative space because it does not define an individual's state of being, and its role should therefore be defined in the valuation process. Current approaches assume that value is additive in time, e.g. that 2 years in a given state is of twice as much value as 1 year in that state. It seems intuitively true that time is more valuable at the end of life because it is more scarce – when a person dies, their time has run out. In this respect, the PalY is not based on any adjustment of the evaluative space, but on how we handle time in the analysis [38]. Valuation processes are beyond the remit of this chapter, and it will suffice here to say that the evaluative space needs definition before we consider how to appropriately handle time.

There are a number of other limitations to the current conception of the health-related QALY that make alternatives worthy of consideration. Some authors have suggested that the concern at end of life may be to provide care rather than health improvement, implying that the receipt of care should be a domain of interest (though providing no justification for this) [31]. It may be more accurate to characterise this as a procedural concern, which is arguably more pertinent to end-of-life care than to other settings. Similarly, end-of-life care also raises additional challenges in terms of caring externalities, adaptation and cognition. The extent to which formal frameworks have been developed to address these challenges is limited, and each could be confronted in a variety of ways. Below I discuss some means of addressing these concerns within a health-related QALY approach.

8.4 Reasons to Use the Health-Related QALY in End of Life

Having highlighted some shortcomings in the ways in which alternative conceptions of the evaluative space in end of life have been promoted by others, I here defend extra-welfarism as currently defined. I argue that it is important to specify which domains constitute the evaluative space and that current approaches provide sufficient flexibility and practical tools to allow for the adequate identification of outcomes in end-of-life care.

8.4.1   Context Relevance

In the past, some researchers have shied away from specifying the domains of value to be included in the evaluative space. In doing so they imply that the evaluative space should consist of everything that might determine well-being. This is not untenable in theory, though it is worth noting that the evaluative space would therefore include those aspects of life that some people value but that we might consider to be in some sense 'bad'. However, it is untenable in practice. Proponents of such an approach for the economic evaluation of publicly funded health care have failed to recognise the decision-making context. There is good reason for the current focus on health, as I will explain.

If domains are not specified – even within the consequents of capabilities or functionings – we arrive at a problem also faced within the welfarist approach to cost-effectiveness analysis (i.e. cost-benefit analysis). Objects of value that we might have reason to believe are important – say, provision of a good death – can be traded against all other things that people might value. For example, cosmetic surgery may be deemed more valuable than reconstructive surgery if patients receiving the former have a capability set that is more greatly influenced by their appearance. It also seems probable that providing a patient with the cash value of their health care would increase capabilities and functionings outside the health domain (without restricting capabilities within it) and that publicly funded health care within a National Health Service should necessarily reduce well-being in these terms.

As outlined above, the researcher should not presuppose which objects of value within the evaluative space provide the most information about the value of a given state. Thus, in allowing objects from an unrestricted domain space, it is possible that health-care providers could become responsible for objects of value that in no way relate to either health or health care. It is possible that the identification of the most informationally rich objects within this unrestricted domain space might relate to wealth, freedom, relationship status, employment, intelligence, or any other aspect of life for which health care has no apparent duty or capacity to provide.

Sen suggests that the grounds for offering assistance – for example, in the form of health care – depend on the decision-making context [7]. As Brouwer et al. state, 'the emphasis in the health care sector is clearly on improving *health*' [4]. It is important to consider this context and that broadly speaking the health service is neither responsible nor equipped to offer assistance to people in achieving whatever is most valuable to them. Health care is suitably equipped to improve people's health; the health service might be particularly bad – compared to other sectors or services – at supporting individuals' non-health goals. This simply represents a recognition of the contexts in which decisions will be made, rather than an explicit 'decision-making' approach to economic evaluation [40]. Even if decision-makers seek to maximise health in some simplistic fashion, there may still be grounds to argue that economic evaluation in health care should incorporate domains beyond health, notably domains that might be more commonly considered social care.

Introducing a different approach specific to end-of-life care is not informative to the problem of resource allocation of health-care budgets. Sen stated that the norms involved in the specification of the evaluative space must depend on the purpose of the evaluation [7]. Accepting an alternative means of outcome measurement in end-of-life care forgets this important point. The purpose of economic evaluation in health care is to allocate resources – usually defined by a fixed health-care budget – as efficiently and equitably as possible. Those resources allocated to end-of-life care are the same resources that might alternatively be allocated to other health care, and allocation decisions therefore require evaluation on an equivalent basis.

The context of end-of-life care, for those whose responsibility is to allocate health resources, *is* health care. Much of what is considered to be end-of-life care takes place in hospitals, surgeries and community care settings. It is administered by doctors and nurses. To distinguish end-of-life care from health care generally would be impossible. The extent to which end-of-life care is distinguishable from other health-care contexts is the same as that for other specific areas (consider the apparent contextual differences between midwifery, psychiatry and emergency care). Existing arguments in favour of separate evaluation of end-of-life care do not stand to reason where care is funded from a fixed health-care budget.

8.4.2   Measurability

Functionings can be measured both objectively and subjectively as necessary and are easy to conceive. Resource-based approaches such as Rawls's primary goods are easily observable. Utility is not observable, but much time and effort has gone into developing methods that are indicative of it. Capabilities are not easily quantified in themselves, and nor is it easy to isolate their value from the value of functionings. As yet, no clear methodology for the successful definition and valuation of capability sets has been developed. As outlined above, the consequent associated with the health-related QALY approach is unclear. My own interpretation is that under certain circumstances preference-based elicitation tools (such as ranking exercises and choice experiments) elicit values associated with both functionings and capabilities. I accept this as the appropriate basis for allocating resources for publicly funded health care.

Central to this is the principle that states should be valued by the general public, rather than by individuals. This means that (most) individuals value hypothetical states in which they have not had cause to select a preferred function set, and thus we might expect respondents to see value in choice.[5] To this extent, appropriate and widely tested methods are available for the purpose of valuing states. There should also be some concern in end-of-life care about the extent to which individuals have the capacity to either describe or value health states. Most approaches require agency assumptions that might not hold in end-of-life care, and the role of these assumptions requires further research.

---

[5] The influence of wider choice sets in the hypothetical should be seen as related to but distinct from the influence of uncertainty.

8.4.3 Flexibility

A descriptive system can never be complete, even within narrowly defined domains. Consider an evaluative space defined by the domain of health and the consequent of individual preference satisfaction. Not only will different groups – say, those in end-of-life care and healthy children – have different preferences, but their health will be differently defined. Any single questionnaire will not provide sufficient information to enable valuation of all objects within the evaluative space for both groups. Within the domain of health, a descriptive system might include any number of items. The goal of the descriptive system is to describe the evaluative space as fully as possible, while maintaining practical value. There is no reason why different descriptive systems – say, for different patient groups – cannot be comparable so long as they both attempt to capture information relating to the same evaluative space.[6] As such, a health-related QALY approach allows for the inclusion – and adequate measurement – of objects of value within the health domain that might only be relevant to specific groups. Interventions for end-of-life care could be evaluated using a descriptive system that more adequately reflects health concerns at the end of life, and this would be entirely consistent with current approaches.

Neoclassical welfare economics employs strict rules of engagement, namely, in demanding utility maximisation, individual sovereignty, consequentialism and welfarism [41]. Extra-welfarism developed by relaxing these rules to enable such mechanisms as interpersonal comparison, weighting of objects and the sourcing of values from parties other than the individual.

The extra-welfarist framework additionally does not prescribe the inclusion or exclusion of externalities or procedural value and does not insist on specific methods of valuation. It is important that these characteristics are maintained. Caring externalities can (and should) be accounted for insofar as they affect outcomes within the evaluative space; there is no requirement for individual sovereignty. The health-related QALY approach can fully consider caring externalities if these relate to the domain of health. The recent development of the ICECAP Close Person Measure (ICECAP-CPM) demonstrates a process by which such a measure could be developed [42], though the ICECAP-CPM itself extends beyond the domain of health. The inclusion of domains beyond health requires justification, bearing in mind that effects on caring externalities will necessarily be traded against health improvements to the individual. Similarly, the health-related QALY approach could be adapted to account for value in the process and delivery of care [43, 44].

In health care we often observe 'irrational' preferences, and it is important that we adopt a framework that does not enforce strict rules regarding appropriate responses and is inclusive of all views. Furthermore, it is necessary to allow for different forms of data collection from different sources, which can accommodate those with reduced capacity.

---

[6] There is practical value in generic instruments that are valid for the majority of patients, but these should not be seen as a panacea.

While the capability approach has fewer strictures than welfarism, it may be seen to limit the extent to which utility, choice and preference information might be taken into account. A simple dualism of domains and consequents, which I have argued to be based on a self-evident distinction, does not insist on any relationship between consequents or between domains. Such a framework does not require strict causal flows, for example, from capabilities to functionings to utility. Therefore, more freedom and clarity is afforded in the definition of a normative position that need not conform to traditional views and which could employ a variety of valuation techniques and decision rules.

8.5   An Agenda for Change

In order to adequately capture value in end-of-life care, and to improve the definition of the evaluative space more generally, I propose the following changes to the health-related QALY approach.

1. Clearer definition by researchers of their own normative position in terms of both consequents and domains

   Much of the debate between different parties in regard to the appropriate evaluation of outcomes in end-of-life care has been hindered by a lack of clarity. Researchers should clearly lay out their normative position in respect to the domains they deem to be worthy of inclusion in the evaluative space and the consequents that they understand to provide value. Clear definition of the evaluative space needs to be provided prior to the development of descriptive systems that identify specific objects of value and should guide the selection of valuation techniques. There is no value in defining differential evaluative spaces for different groups of people when resources are allocated from a single budget, as this precludes efficient and equitable outcomes.

2. Appreciation of value beyond consequences to the individual

   Having defined the evaluative space in terms of domains and consequents, it is necessary when defining a normative position to also assert to whom improvements are deemed valuable. Particularly within a publicly funded health-care system, there seems no reason to limit this to the impact on an individual. Characteristics of people other than the individual recipient of care are valuable. Both positive and negative externalities in terms of the domains and consequents of value should be included within the evaluative space. Likewise, impacts relating to the process rather than the outcome of care should be explicitly acknowledged as being of value.

3. Clearer definition of process in the formulation of descriptive systems

   In order to maintain comparability in outcomes across different measures, it is important that descriptive systems provide information on the same evaluative space. In order to achieve this, clear rules need to be established and adhered to for the qualitative and quantitative methods used to identify specific objects of value for inclusion in a descriptive system. The best descriptive system is that which provides the most information about the evaluative space while maintaining practicality in statistical and operational terms.

4. Acceptance of a multiplicity of descriptive systems

   Much has been made of the comparability or otherwise of different descriptive systems. This is largely due to ambiguity in the definition of the evaluative space. It must be recognised that the role of descriptive systems is not to define the evaluative space but to provide information about it. For any given evaluative space, there should be a great contest to identify descriptive systems and valuation methods that best reflect it. These should be tested in the usual ways in regard to validity and reliability. There should be both generic measures and population-specific measures in order to adequately reflect people's differing priorities. Measures that are condition specific should not be used if this involves the presupposition that particular disease symptoms are relevant to well-being.

5. Recognition of the true nature of valuation processes

   Just as descriptive systems do not define the domains of value, nor do valuation processes define the consequents. Valuation processes in extra-welfarism do not *need* to elicit individual preferences that reflect utility, as utility is expressly not the (only) outcome of value. As such, it is permissible – and here I argue preferable – to use valuation tools that provide information about the extent to which individuals prefer different states for reasons other than their impact on utility. Tools such as visual analogue scales and choice experiments may usefully reflect non-utility information about functionings and capabilities.

6. More research into the fundamental dimensions of value

   There are some universal dimensions relevant to well-being that transcend any definition of the evaluative space. The most pertinent in end-of-life care is time. Another is uncertainty. There are arguments that people value time differently at the end of life [38, 45], though this might also apply to other patient groups [46] and as such should not relate exclusively to end-of-life care. There is a need for more investigation of how people value time and if any differential valuations ought to be considered in economic evaluation. For example, there may be grounds for developing a three-dimensional QALY in which life years are valued in terms of both quality of life and the value of time.

   Each of these suggestions is entirely compatible with extra-welfarism and with the principles of welfare economics more broadly [4].

8.6   Conclusions

Though it seems clear that aspects of life matter 'beyond health' [22, 43], and that people appear to value these items within the context of health care, it does not follow that such items should be included in their own right. Restricting the evaluative space to the domain of health does not mean that only health improvements are achieved, rather it means that we value the extent to which improvements in health can improve well-being more broadly.

The importance of defining the evaluative space has not been adequately recognised by the various approaches to economic evaluation in end-of-life care, which have focused on the development of descriptive systems and valuation techniques. While current approaches fail on a number of counts, the alternatives appear to fail on the same and perhaps more.

Much has been made of differing normative bases for the arguments, but on inspection it is clear that these arguments lack focus, confusing the domains and consequents of the preferred evaluative space. I hope this chapter might assist in the debate between those who support and those who oppose current approaches and enable each to detail with clarity any points of departure.

The end of life is unique; people only experience it once. But there are many things in life that people only experience once, and this is no grounds for special treatment. As currently described and operationalised, alternative outcome measures such as the ICECAP-SCM should not inform the allocation of resources in health care because they are based on an alternative evaluative space and lack context relevance. However, in practice we might expect such measures to converge with existing 'preference-based' approaches due to ambiguity and imprecision in both. The development of a clear and consistent approach to the evaluation of end-of-life care within the health-care context is needed. The alternative is to risk inefficient and inequitable allocations of resources.

Acknowledgements Thanks to Alastair Canaway, Matthew Franklin, David Parkin and Jeff Round for valuable and timely discussion of the issues raised in this chapter and for comments provided on an earlier version. All views, errors and omissions are my own.

References

1. Round JA (2012) Is a QALY still a QALY at the end of life? J Health Econ 31:521–527
2. Coast J (2014) Strategies for the economic evaluation of end-of-life care: making a case for the capability approach. Expert Rev Pharmacoecon Outcomes Res 14:473–482
3. Normand C (2009) Measuring outcomes in palliative care: limitations of QALYs and the road to PalYs. J Pain Symptom Manag 38:27–31
4. Brouwer WBF, Culyer AJ, van Exel NJA, Rutten FFH (2008) Welfarism vs. extra-welfarism. J Health Econ 27:325–338
5. Culyer AJ (1990) Commodities, characteristics of commodities, characteristics of people, utilities, and the quality of life. Quality of life: perspectives and policies. Routledge, London, pp 9–27
6. Hurley J (1998) Welfarism, extra-welfarism and evaluative economic analysis in the health sector. In: Morris L Barer, Thomas E Getzen, Greg L Stoddart (eds), health care and health economics: perspectives on distribution. Wiley, Chichester, pp 373–395
7. Sen A (2007) Capability and well-being. In: Hausman DM (ed) The philosophy of economics: an anthology. Cambridge University Press, Cambridge, pp 270–293
8. Sen A (1999) Commodities and capabilities. Oxford University Press, Oxford
9. Fleurbaey M, Luchini S, Muller C, Schokkaert E (2013) Equivalent income and fair evaluation of health care. Health Econ 22:711–729
10. Ferrer-i-Carbonell A, Frijters P (2004) How important is methodology for the estimates of the determinants of happiness? Econ J 114:641–659

11. Culyer AJ (1989) The normative economics of health care finance and provision. Oxf Rev Econ Policy 5:34–58
12. Huber M, Knottnerus JA, Green L et al (2011) How should we define health? BMJ 343:d4163
13. Flynn TN (2015) Where next for discrete choice health valuation – part one. Terry Flynn PhD. http://www.webcitation.org/6bwtEuQvW. Accessed 1 Oct 2015
14. Sen A (2001) Development as freedom. Oxford University Press, Oxford
15. Rawls J (2009) A theory of justice. Harvard University Press, Cambridge, MA
16. Rawls J (2001) The law of peoples: with, the idea of public reason revisited. Harvard University Press, Cambridge, MA
17. Nussbaum MC (2001) Women and human development: the capabilities approach. Cambridge University Press, Cambridge
18. Birch S, Donaldson C (2003) Valuing the benefits and costs of health care programmes: where's the "extra" in extra-welfarism? Soc Sci Med 56:1121–1133
19. Coast J, Smith RD, Lorgelly P (2008) Welfarism, extra-welfarism and capability: the spread of ideas in health economics. Soc Sci Med 67:1190–1198
20. Tsuchiya A, Williams A (2001) Welfare economics and economic evaluation. In: Drummond M, McGuire (eds.) Alistair, Economic evaluation in health care: merging theory with practice. Oxford University Press, Oxford pp 27–28
21. Coast J (2009) Maximisation in extra-welfarism: a critique of the current position in health economics. Soc Sci Med 69:786–792
22. Coast J, Smith RD, Lorgelly P (2008) Should the capability approach be applied in health economics? Health Econ 17:667–670
23. Cookson R (2005) QALYs and the capability approach. Health Econ 14:817–829
24. Coast J, Kinghorn P, Mitchell P (2014) The development of capability measures in health economics: opportunities, challenges and progress. Patient. doi:10.1007/s40271-014-0080-1
25. Ruger JP (2010) Health capability: conceptualization and operationalization. Am J Public Health 100:41–49
26. Flynn TN, Huynh E, Peters TJ, Janabi HA, Clemens S, Moody A, Coast J (2015) Scoring the ICECAP-a capability instrument. Estimation of a UK general population tariff. Health Econ 24:258–269
27. Normand C (2012) Setting priorities in and for end-of-life care: challenges in the application of economic evaluation. Health Econ Policy Law 7:431–439
28. Douglas H-R, Normand CE, Higginson IJ, Goodwin DM (2005) A new approach to eliciting patients' preferences for palliative day care: the choice experiment method. J Pain Symptom Manag 29:435–445
29. Janabi HA, Flynn TN, Coast J (2012) Development of a self-report measure of capability wellbeing for adults: the ICECAP-A. Qual Life Res 21:167–176
30. Grewal I, Lewis J, Flynn T, Brown J, Bond J, Coast J (2006) Developing attributes for a generic quality of life measure for older people: preferences or capabilities? Soc Sci Med 62:1891–1901
31. Sutton EJ, Coast J (2014) Development of a supportive care measure for economic evaluation of end-of-life care using qualitative methods. Palliat Med 28:151–157
32. EuroQol Group (1990) EuroQol – a new facility for the measurement of health-related quality of life. Health Policy 16:199–208
33. Stevens KJ (2010) Working with children to develop dimensions for a preference based generic paediatric, health related quality of life measure. Qual Health Res 20:340–351
34. Al-Janabi, Keeley T, Mitchell P, Coast J (2013) Can capabilities be self-reported? A think aloud study. Soc Sci Med 87:116–122
35. Coast J, Flynn TN, Natarajan L, Sproston K, Lewis J, Louviere JJ, Peters TJ (2008) Valuing the ICECAP capability index for older people. Soc Sci Med 67:874–882
36. Flynn TN, Louviere JJ, Peters TJ, Coast J (2007) Best – worst scaling: what it can do for health care research and how to do it. J Health Econ 26:171–189
37. Gandjour A (2001) Is subjective well-being a useful parameter for allocating resources among public interventions? Health Care Anal 9:437–447

38. Chochinov HM (2011) Death, time and the theory of relativity. J Pain Symptom Manag 42:460–463
39. Longworth L, Yang Y, Young T, Mulhern B, Mukuria C, Rowen D, et al. (2014) Use of generic and condition-specific measures of health-related quality of life in NICE decision-making: a systematic review, statistical modelling and survey. Health Technol Assess 18. doi:10.3310/hta18090
40. Sugden R, Williams AH (1978) The principles of practical cost-benefit analysis. Oxford University Press, New York
41. Hurley J (2000) An overview of the normative economics of the health sector. Handb Health Econ 1:55–118
42. Canaway A (2015) Capturing the impacts of end of life care on those close to the dying for use in economic evaluation. Retrieved from University of Birmingham eTheses Repository. http://etheses.bham.ac.uk/6084
43. Payne K, McAllister M, Davies LM (2013) Valuing the economic benefits of complex interventions: when maximising health is not sufficient. Health Econ 22:258–271
44. Brennan VK, Dixon S (2013) Incorporating process utility into quality adjusted life years: a systematic review of empirical studies. Pharmacoeconomics 31:677–691
45. Round J (2012) Death, time, and the theory of relativity: a brief reply? J Pain Symptom Manag 43:e2–e6
46. Sampson C (2012) Considering time perception. The Academic Health Economists' Blog. http://aheblog.com/2012/07/10/considering-time-perception. Accessed 27 Aug 2015
47. Daniels N (1985) Just health care (studies in philosophy and health policy). Cambridge University Press, Cambridge

Chapter 9
Life at a Premium: Considering an End-of-Life Premium in Value-Based Reimbursement

Christopher McCabe, Mike Paulden, James O'Mahony, Richard Edlin, and Anthony Culyer

9.1 Introduction

The increasingly explicit use of health technology assessment (HTA) continues to generate substantial public and academic policy debates [1–12]. The reasons are twofold. First, the debates are about puzzling issues whose correct resolution is not immediately obvious though they can radically change the implications of HTAs. Second, the very explicitness of HTA's use pinpoints the issues and locates those likely to gain or lose from the solutions, thus making external examination and critique of current approaches both easier and more policy relevant. Stakeholders have different interests (stakes) in the decision-making processes, the methods of analysis, the evidence considered and the values, both social and private, upon which outcomes depend. One specific issue, which raises a host of concerns, is whether it is proper to treat the benefits of treatment for patients close to the ends of their lives relatively favourably. This might be done by, for example, weighting their benefits more heavily or their costs more lightly than those accruing to other patient groups or by using differential discount (interest) rates or by applying an 'easier' threshold

C. McCabe (✉) • M. Paulden
Department of Emergency Medicine, University of Alberta, Edmonton, AB, Canada
e-mail: mccabe1@ualberta.ca

J. O'Mahony
Trinity College Dublin, Dublin, Ireland

R. Edlin
School of Population, University of Auckland, Auckland, New Zealand

A. Culyer
Institute of Health Policy, Management and Evaluation, University of Toronto, Toronto, ON, Canada

Centre for Health Economics, University of York, York, UK

© Springer International Publishing Switzerland 2016
J. Round (ed.), *Care at the End of Life: An Economic Perspective*,
DOI 10.1007/978-3-319-28267-1_9

condition for the technology in question to be approved. Our analysis concludes that the correct treatment of such matters has implications for both the methods of analysis, especially the treatment of opportunity cost, and the design of the decision-making procedures employed, especially regarding the characteristics of those consulted and those who directly participate in it.

It is clear that at the heart of many of these issues lie questions of value and, hence, of value judgments. Values are typically revealed in many ways and with varying degrees of completeness. The most obvious expression of a value attaching to a good or service is monetary: its price. In a well-functioning market (not typical of healthcare markets) a price represents both the minimum that the marginal supplier is willing to receive in order to provide a little more of that good or service and the maximum that the marginal consumer is willing to pay for a little more of it. This is the 'willingness to pay/accept' approach to valuation. It can be distorted in many highly significant ways, as when suppliers have monopolistic powers, consumers are poorly informed about the benefits and risks, their agents (health professionals) have conflicts of interest (e.g. by being paid for low-quality care), or the beneficiaries include people other than the immediate patients (e.g. family, friends, informal carers and the general caring public). The individual willingness to pay approach is unsuited to public decision-making not only on grounds such as these but also because those who may benefit from the care do not typically bear any of the cost. Instead the cost is distributed across the entire system. More resources for those near the end of life means less for others – usually anonymous people, unknown alike to the beneficiaries and to those who minister professionally to them.

In the publicly financed system, 'value' in HTA is typically measured as a 'real' outcome using a metric that corresponds to a (socially defined) notion of 'health' or 'health gain'. Delivering this gain will invariably require monetary expenditures from the budget, but these expenditures represent neither the value (private or social) of the benefit nor the value of what is sacrificed to gain it (i.e. health gain forgone by others). The value of what is both forgone and what is gained is expressed instead directly in terms of the health metric, generally in terms of quality-adjusted life-years (QALYs) or disability-adjusted life-years (DALYs). Value-based reimbursement is the challenge of defining the value of health gain in terms of what the *provider* (the public agency) is willing to pay. This problem has been at the centre of debates in health technology assessments and funding decisions from the outset [2]. In HTA, therefore, a significant part of the value of a health technology is the value of the health that it produces or the value of the health displaced as the use of other technologies has to fall.

'Value' in HTA, as in other regions of public policy, also has wider connotations. For example, a further reason for valuing a technology may be because it makes a contribution to reducing avoidable inequalities in the health of the population. Yet another dimension of value may be the reduced exposure to financial risk of heavy out of pocket expenditures through inclusion of a technology in the insured package (private or public). Other elements may be the contribution made to uniformity in terms of access and a sense of common 'solidarity'. None of these elements of 'value' lends itself easily to financial measurement, but it is not, fortunately, usually necessary for them to be valued in monetary terms. What is necessary is for them to be recognised as expressions of public or social value judgements (with implications for governance and procedure) and for decision-makers to be able to take due account of each in a reasonable way in reaching a conclusion about the inclusion of a technology in the insured package. The only point at which a monetized expression of value is necessary is in the so-called 'threshold' cost per QALY, which is set so far as possible at a level such that no technology inside the insured package has a cost per QALY higher than the threshold and no technology not in the package has one that is lower. That principle assumes that population health maximization is a primary policy objective (though clearly in the light of the foregoing not the only one), and debate about how best to estimate this threshold has been another abiding discussion point since the 1980s.

Arguments for an end-of-life premium, especially in the context of late-stage cancer therapies, have been advanced in a number of jurisdictions [13–15]. However, the grounds for premiums are rarely made clear by the small groups who effectively make the decisions, have not been evidence based (in the sense of being informed by unbiased evidence concerning the views of the general public) [16] and are essentially ad hoc. The role, implicit and explicit, of self-interested technology makers, professional users and organized patient groups (often funded by manufacturers) [17] is doubtless significant (though there is deplorably little firm evidence to corroborate this conjecture). Most importantly of all, the notion that allowing benefits for this group means denying benefits to other groups tends to be ignored: research asking for people's expressed values rarely confronts experimental subjects with the 'price' of forgone care for others; and in the real world those most likely to be denied care as a consequence of resource deployment to this group are never present in consultations or in person within the decision-making process. Methodological guidance issued to advisory committees and research groups rarely mentions the true opportunity cost and never outlines methods for estimating it empirically.

The 'real' as distinct from the monetary costs are incurred at two policy levels. The first is in decisions about the budget. In private insurance systems, the test is essentially a market test of the revenue stream that is judged to be supportable from premiums. Regardless of the risk aversion of the public, higher premiums involve less disposable income available for other purchases, and these forgone purchases, potentially including healthcare, are the opportunity costs and they are implicitly revealed through the public's willingness to pay for different insurance packages. In social insurance and tax-funded systems of healthcare, the test is one made by politicians and relates to the setting of budgets for the various categories of public expenditure: more on healthcare means less on education, transport or defence (at even higher levels, there is the choice between public expenditure as a whole and private consumption as a whole). The second policy level, given a decision about the healthcare budget, concerns the health benefit package to be made available and those who are entitled to receive care. A fully universal system is one in which all have equal entitlements and the range of services is comprehensive – but nonetheless budget constrained. It is this second level of decision-making with which we are concerned here.

Is it possible to develop a theoretically coherent, procedurally transparent and inter-decision-consistent value framework to inform reimbursement decisions [18–21]? In this chapter we describe the landscape in which the debates for such a framework are taking place and critically evaluate the claims made by different groups for different value premiums from a conceptual and empirical perspective. We then review a theoretical framework for value-based reimbursement decisions given a healthcare budget and use this framework to explore how value premiums could be incorporated into the reimbursement/listing process. In the final section we consider the implementation of an end-of-life premium in such a framework and consider the likely impact of doing so on (a) access to healthcare and (b) the health of individuals approaching the end of their lives.

9.2   Policy Challenges in Value-Based Reimbursement

With hindsight, value-based reimbursement appears to be the inevitable destination of a journey that started with the development of health technology assessment in the 1970s [22–24]. Value-based reimbursement is guided by the principle that the monetary price paid for a new technology should be set to ensure that its incremental value in terms of health gain is positive; that is, any additional cost in terms of the resources and consequential health it displaces for the new technology should be less than (and certainly not greater than) the value of the incremental health it produces [16]. The guide price for this is the threshold, indicating the social willingness to pay for an additional QALY or a lost DALY. When decisions are made under the assumption of a fixed budget, this condition ensures that the adoption of a new technology increases the overall health that is produced by the expenditure of that budget. When the budget is not fixed but guided by some private willingness to pay for health, this condition ensures that the technology meets that private willingness to pay criterion.

QALYs combine life expectancy and health-related quality of life in a single measure by weighting the time lived using weights for health-related quality of life experienced in each time period. Whilst weights can be derived in many ways, increasingly they are derived using preference-based health-related quality of life measures such as the EQ-5D, SF-6D or Health Utilities Index [25–27]. These instruments consist of psychometrically validated health state descriptive systems together with a utility algorithm that provides a utility weight for each health state in the descriptive system. The utility algorithm is normally constructed using statistical analyses of population health state preference survey data [28]. However, there have been many critiques of this approach. Some have focused on the inadequacy of the descriptive systems used to capture health [29, 30] and others on the methods for deriving the utility weights [31]; others have argued that the valued effects of healthcare are more than the impact on health and are modified by numerous other factors, such as the availability of alternative treatments, disease prognosis and impact of the condition on economic activity [32]. Even more fundamentally, others have argued that the weights ought to be seen less as expressions of the strength of preferences of the lay population and rather as statements of public policy made on a population's behalf by people judged to be unbiased, competent, sufficiently well informed and accountable. Their judgments might be informed by the opinions of the public but need not follow them slavishly [33–36].

The response of policymakers and HTA institutions to these criticisms has tended towards acknowledgement of the limitations while nonetheless retaining the standard QALY-based evaluation. This seems a reasonable approach pending the resolution of the issues. Members of decision-making panels are charged with taking account of the disputed issues as well as other problems such as the limitations of the quantitative analysis and bridging the gap between the 'health-centric' perspective of most evaluations and political concern for a broader set of social values to be taken into account [10, 18, 19, 37]. In line with this approach, the processes of HTA have developed to create more formal opportunities for the communication of different values to decision-makers. Patients, clinicians, advocacy groups and manufacturers are encouraged and often supported to provide their views on the value of a technology to the decision-makers through written submissions, in-person presentations, consultations on proposed decisions and appeal processes [38].

Academics have produced a steady stream of commentaries, policy documents and empirical studies. In a recent scoping literature review, Paulden and colleagues identified 19 additional value arguments that have been advanced for consideration in HTA in the context of rare diseases. They also proposed that the value arguments could be usefully sorted into four distinct categories: disease-related, technology-related, population-related and socio-economic-related factors [39] (Table 9.1).

Table 9.1 Typology of value arguments proposed for health technology assessment processes

Disease related	Technology related	Population related	Socio-economic related	Opportunity cost
Prevalence	Effectiveness of treatment	Identifiability of beneficiaries	Socio-economic policy objectives	Price of treatment
Severity	Magnitude of benefit	Impact of treatment on the distribution of population health	Industrial and commercial policy objectives	Cost-effectiveness of treatment
Life-threatening/ chronically debilitating	Safety of treatment	Societal impact of treatment	Legal considerations	Budget impact of treatment
Availability of treatment alternatives	Innovative nature of treatment			
Feasibility of diagnosis	Feasibility of delivering treatment			

With so many candidate value arguments – in addition to the complexities already inherent in the form of poor, contested or absent evidence, imperfect models of health and cost consequences for periods outside the trial evidence base, political constraints and the post-decision behaviour of clinicians and patients – the policy challenge becomes clear. It is highly unlikely that decision-makers can consistently, transparently and reproducibly balance so many competing factors given the established limits of human mental processing capacity [40]. Such limitations in human processing capacity are one of the reasons why HTA processes have utilized decision-theoretic models to synthesise large quantities of information from disparate sources [41]. Hence it is unsurprising to observe the emergence of calls to use multi-criteria decision analysis (MCDA) as a tool for use in HTA [30, 42, 43].

As the scope of value arguments proposed has expanded, some authors have sought empirical information on what weight different populations would attach to some of them. Researchers at the University of Sheffield and the Office of Health Economics have examined, amongst other things, whether the general population attach a special value to therapies that extend life at the end of life and report conflicting results [44, 45]. Linley and Hughes undertook a large survey of the UK population and found that respondents did not support an end-of-life premium, a special status for children or socio-economically disadvantaged populations, treatments for rare diseases or cancer therapies. In contrast, they found support for paying a premium for treatments aimed at severe disease, unmet need and innovative technologies [16]. It is noteworthy that this is consistent with the qualitative work undertaken by the NICE Citizens Council [46].

Desser and colleagues undertook two separate surveys, one of the Norwegian general population and the second of Norwegian physicians. Both examined whether a special value should be attached to the rarity of the treated condition. The authors report that neither study found a clear preference for paying a premium for treatments based upon the rarity of the condition, but there was some indication for a generalized preference for equal access to care [47, 48]. A separate study from the same research group, published in the *BMJ*, also found no preference for a premium for orphan diseases [49].

Two recent studies in Canada, one using discrete choice experiments and the other a citizens' jury, examined population preferences for healthcare resource allocation around expensive drugs for rare diseases [50, 51]. Neither study reported substantial support for a value premium based upon the prevalence of the condition, but there was support for a value premium based upon the severity of the condition and the magnitude of benefit. Neither the Canadian nor the Norwegian studies asked the respondents to consider proximity to the end of life.

Whilst there has been extensive discussion concerning the value of health gains, the empirical literature is not large. There is some consistency around value being driven by the effectiveness of a technology and the severity of the condition it treats. The empirical evidence for other proposed value arguments is either absent or conflicting, and overall the evidence base for value premium could hardly be described as mature. The reported studies vary according to the methods, the populations surveyed and the value arguments that were investigated. A number of the value arguments identified in the Paulden scoping review do not appear to have been sub-jected to empirical investigation. As a result, the current literature plays a greater role in complicating the decision problem faced by decision-makers than it does in offering solutions.

We return later to the consideration of the implications of this complexity.

9.3 Somebody Else's Healthcare: Value-Based Choices for Limited Healthcare Budgets

Applying the simple decision rule 'select technologies and their optimal use so as to maximize population health' is, needless to say, made immeasurably more complex given the foregoing issues (both those that are resolved in principle but difficult to assess empirically and those that remain unresolved in principle). It is nonetheless helpful to assume them away in order to see the logical implications of such a deci-sion rule. A useful model of this process was described by Culyer and colleagues, in the context of the United Kingdom National Institute for Health and Care Excellence's use of a cost-effectiveness threshold [9, 52].

In any period of time, we take the budget available for service provision to be given, as determined variously by a parliamentary vote, forecast premium income or forecast hypothecated taxes and 'contributions'. As we saw earlier, the decision rule 'select technologies and their optimal use so as to maximize population health' is equivalent to setting the threshold cost per QALY or incremental cost-effectiveness ratio (ICER) at a level such that no technology inside the insured package has a cost per QALY higher than the threshold and no technology not in the package has one that is lower. It is worth noting that Eckermann and Pekarsky observe that this model assumes that the current allocation of the budget across reimbursed technolo-gies is optimal [53]. For the purposes of our discussion here, if this assumption does not hold, then the consideration of who bears the opportunity cost would expand to include patients whose access to funded therapies was further delayed, as well as patients for whom technologies would cease to be funded. The central tenet of our observations would not be affected.

Let us assume that a healthcare system has solved the selection problem of the correct threshold (we examine later the situation where the threshold has been set too high or too low). All technologies that are provided have an ICER no higher than the threshold and there are no technologies not provided that have an ICER lower than the threshold.

Figure 9.1 illustrates the starting position. On the left-hand side of the figure, we see a portfolio of reimbursed technologies, ranked in the order of their efficiency – where efficiency is measured in terms of health produced per $1,000 of expenditure (the reciprocal of the cost-effectiveness ratio). After the eighth technology has been funded, the available budget is exhausted. On the right-hand side of the figure, we see four technologies that are not reimbursed. All four were previously not available

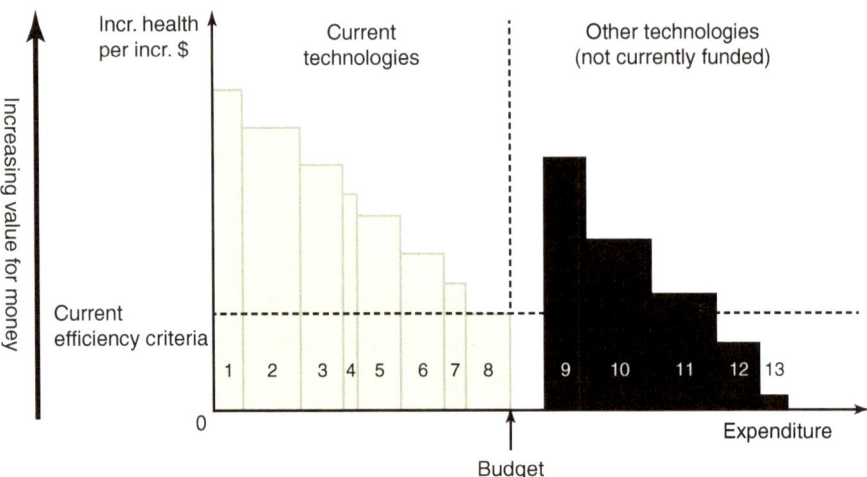

Fig. 9.1 Value-based reimbursement: initial allocation

but two of them have C–E ratios that are lower than the threshold. The question facing the decision-maker is which of any of these technologies should be funded?

Given the fixity of the budget, any new technology must produce at least as much health per extra dollar spent as any technology that it replaces; it is simple to see that technologies 12 and 13 should not be adopted. That is, the appropriate decision by an HTA decision-maker who wishes to maximise population health is to refuse reimbursement to these technologies. However, this still leaves technologies 9, 10 and 11 as likely candidates for funding, since these all produce health more efficiently than (so have an incremental health per incremental dollar higher than) technology 8.

To see which technologies should be funded on efficiency grounds, we can order all 13 technologies in terms of their efficiency. This is shown on Fig. 9.2. Within this diagram, 1–4 and technologies 9 and 10 are provided within the existing budget. Technologies 6, 7 and 8 are no longer funded; *the new investment requires complementary disinvestment*. The unfunded technologies (6–8, 11–13) are not selected because they yield health benefits less efficiently than each of those that were selected; in each case these treatments would yield health benefits but do not do so efficiently – they are relatively cost-ineffective. *To have invested in any of these would have reduced population health*. The opportunity cost (of health foregone) would have exceeded the health benefits that they would have provided.

Note that whilst technology 11 was a likely candidate for funding (as it produces health more efficiently than technology 8), it is not funded when all treatments are taken into account. This is because as technologies 9 and 10 are added, the opportunity cost (of health foregone) increases and so the efficient criteria to obtain funding become more onerous. Whilst technology 11 would have met the old criteria, it does not meet the new.

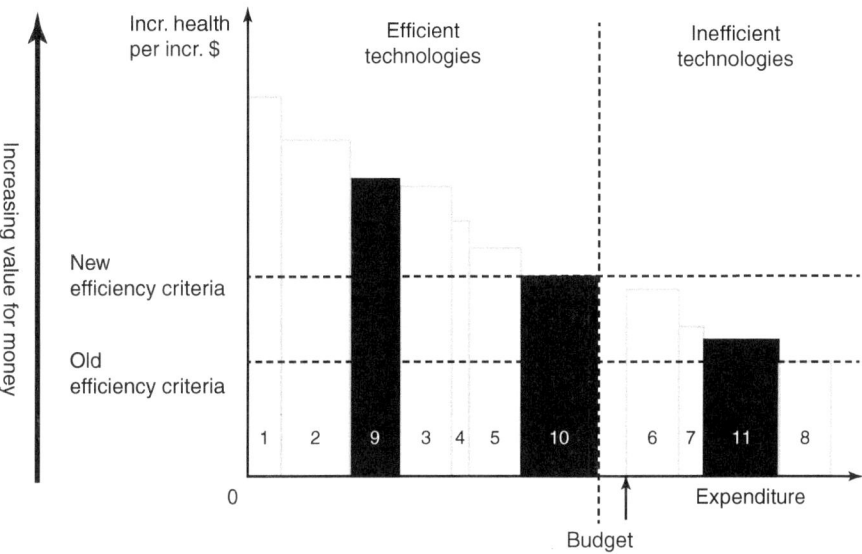

Fig. 9.2 Value-based reimbursement: post-appraisal allocation of resources

The decision to fund new technologies, in the absence of an increase in the budget, certainly means that other people's healthcare has been displaced. It also means that the health generated is greater than the health lost. But the gainers will not normally be the same people as the losers. The question therefore arises: do the displaced individuals, diseases and technologies have characteristics that may be deserving of a 'value premium', as outlined in Table 9.1, that may, after all, keep them in the insured bundle (or warrant an increase in the budget at the next opportunity)?

It is very difficult for HTA decision-makers to know which patients will bear the opportunity cost of the new technology – i.e. which patients will not be able to access previously available treatments or services. Suppose that all patients count equally in the sense that a QALY for each counts as of equal significance so that decision-makers are indifferent as to who gets an additional QALY. This is often expressed as the QALY=QALY=QALY rule. Under these circumstances, knowing the identity of the losers is of little importance – all that is required is that their losses of health are more than compensated by the increases in the health of the gainers. But now suppose that decision-makers regard the beneficiaries as being specially deserving by virtue of their closeness to death. Now not knowing the identity of the losers is problematic for it cannot be assumed that none of them are also 'close to death'. It cannot be safely assumed that the patients who bear the opportunity cost are 'average patients' with no special value characteristics. To assume this would imply that decision-makers use different frameworks to value the health gains of the *identified* beneficiaries of the technology being appraised and the health losses of the unidentified individuals who bear the opportunity cost. The patients may be individually unidentified but something may be known about their prevalence in the population as a whole.

Paulden and colleagues recently described the implications of considering the value characteristics of those bearing the opportunity cost in the same way as the identified beneficiaries [37]. They identified two general principles for taking account of additional value arguments to modify a cost-effectiveness threshold:

> First, the greater the weight that is applied to the value of health for the individuals given special consideration, and the greater the proportion of those individuals amongst the population bearing the opportunity cost, the lower the cost effectiveness threshold should be for technologies that do not affect those individuals.
>
> Second, when there are multiple special value arguments under consideration, if the bearers of the opportunity cost are assigned a greater cumulative weight than the beneficiaries of the technology, then the threshold should be lower compared to when everyone's health is valued equally. Equally if the cumulative weight is greater for the beneficiaries of the technology than for those who bear the opportunity cost, then the threshold should be higher.

9.4 Implementing a Coherent End-of-Life Premium: Mechanisms and Implications

In the UK, NICE has operated an end-of-life premium since 2009. The amendment to the Institute's methods guide identified three criteria that, if fulfilled, justified giving greater weight to QALYs acquired in the later stages of terminal disease. The criteria were [15]:

- The treatment is indicated for patients with a short life expectancy, normally less than 24 months.
- There is sufficient evidence to indicate that the treatment offers an extension to life, normally of at least an additional 3 months, compared to current NHS treatment.
- The treatment is licensed or otherwise indicated, for small patient populations.

When these criteria were met, the Appraisal Committee were to consider 'the magnitude of the additional weight that would need to be assigned to QALY benefits in this patient group for the cost effectiveness of the technology to fall within the current threshold range'.

Despite its superficial attraction, there is a hidden minefield of ethical and political value judgments that warrant explicit identification and discussion. One is whether discriminating in favour of people with a short life expectancy is warranted when one considers that it is tantamount to discriminating *against* those with a longer expectation of life. The merit in valuing extensions in life expectancy over improvements in quality of life at the end of life is not self-evident. The use of arbitrary thresholds – the 3-month life extension and an expected life expectancy less than 24 months – to determine which technologies qualify invites questions about the rightness of these periods compared to others. The apparent unfairness to those who may fall just on the wrong side of these apparently arbitrary timelines seems not to have been openly debated. It is the latter apparent arbitrariness that we discuss in more detail here. Any end-of-life premium plainly requires a definition of 'length of life' – but what ought it to be and by what means ought it to be determined?

Using NICE's specification of the end-of-life premium, consider a treatment for a patient group with a 3-year life expectancy and very poor quality of life. A treatment that both improved their quality of life and extended life expectancy by 6 months would not qualify for the end-of-life premium. By contrast, a treatment that increased the life expectancy of patients with an already good quality of life and an 18-month life expectancy by 3 months would qualify. The first group of patients has fewer remaining QALYs than the second yet are disadvantaged even further by the end-of-life premium. Similarly, a treatment that provides an extra 3 months life expectancy of poor quality of life would qualify though a treatment that offers only 2 months extension but of good quality of life would not. The arbitrary cut-offs introduce apparent injustice in the treatment of people that are consistent with neither common notions of horizontal and vertical justice nor with what we take to be the rationale of the appraisal process. The process by which NICE values health outcomes explicitly adjusts quantity of expected life by its quality. It is not obvious why quality of life is normally an essential component of the value of healthcare save for those with short expectations of life.

Any specification of an end-of-life premium defined in terms of maximum life expectancy and then applied to evaluations that otherwise consider quality, as well as length of life, will necessary lead to this type of incoherence. Any specification of a minimum life expectancy benefit is similarly flawed. Expanding the end-of-life definition to include the quality of life, for example, by specifying a maximum remaining quality-adjusted life expectancy, will introduce the possibility that people with substantial disabilities but long life expectancy may qualify, though the policy could then scarcely be described as an 'end-of-life' policy.

The opportunity cost of this weighting is, let us recall, forgone health for others, including those who have severe health problems and who may themselves have a short expectation of life. It is well established that the majority of healthcare resource consumption takes place in the last years of life. Indeed proximity to death is increasingly accepted as a better predictor of healthcare consumption than age [54]. The end-of-life premium implicit in the current allocation of healthcare resources raises two further questions. The first regards the probability that the opportunity cost of new technology adoption is born by people who would meet the criteria for the end-of-life premium. Unless disinvestment decisions actively target other subgroups in the population, it is credible that some portion of the impact will fall on such people.

Consider a reimbursement decision for an end-of-life therapy, which is expected to produce 1.8 QALYs for each treated patient. However the price of this highly effective therapy means that it will cost 2.1 QALYs through displaced healthcare elsewhere in the system. The application of an end-of-life premium that weighted EOL QALYs 20 % higher than other QALYs values the new therapy as producing

2.16 EOL_QALYs – [1.8*1.2]. Initially, this suggests that the EOL means we should reimburse the new technology, as its outcomes are more highly valued than the healthcare it displaces. However, if 20 % of the people whose healthcare is displaced also meet the EOL criteria, the expected value of the displaced healthcare increases to 2.184 EOL_QALYs [(2.1*0.8)+(0.2 * 2.1 * 1.2)]. When the EOL criteria are applied to both the beneficiaries and those whose care would be displaced, the new therapy is no longer good value.

Internal ethical coherence in the application of the value premium requires that only a minority portion of any premium should be taken into account; and as a result many fewer technologies are likely to clear a premium weighted cost-effectiveness threshold than its advocates expect.

Secondly, the application of an end-of-life premium entails the possible exacerbation of a pre-existing inequity. If there were strong evidence of the public having a preference for a premium price for technologies that extend life but only at the end of life, this favoured discrimination might be justified as 'evidence based'; however, the empirical evidence for such a social value is uncertain at best, and even if it were, it does not follow that public policy ought to follow that preference slavishly. There is at least as strong an evidence base for a social preference for preventive treatments rather than cure [55]. It is hard to make a convincing argument that the application of an end-of-life premium is consistent with our understanding of social preferences.

In the NICE methodological guidance, the reference case recommends that 'the valuation of health-related quality of life … should be based on a valuation of public preferences from a representative sample of the UK population using a choice-based method', this valuation leads to the calculation of 'utility values'. The idea that public values should be 'based on' individuals' preferences or, indeed, on preferences at all opens the question of the extent to which technology appraisers have discretion in setting relative values on outcomes accruing to people with different characteristics. One might normally expect that people appointed to advisory committees like the NICE Appraisal Committees will have suitable characteristics not necessarily found in the general population: their preferences over health states, insofar as preferences are what matters, will arguably be better informed as to probable outcomes, and they will be alert to exaggerated claims made on behalf of technologies and selection bias in the evidence presented to them. With usual clinical and patient representation, these committees will also have a combination of direct and vicarious experience of the conditions being treated before and after treatment. For such reasons, it may be expected that respecting public preferences (however revealed) will be done in a mature and impartial manner. In the matter of applying weights to particular groups, however, like those near the end of life, there is very little to guide decision-makers by way of unbiased evidence as to 'what the public thinks'. It seems highly likely that the evidence about 'what the public thinks' is evidence gathered with no regard to the fact that favouring one group necessarily involves disfavouring another.

Independent of the source of these values, elementary horizontal justice requires that a coherent end-of-life premium should apply to both the identified beneficiaries of the technology being appraised and to the individuals, as best they may be identified, bearing the opportunity cost of its adoption. Further, it would be desirable were it based upon some evidence of social support for the position. The problem of perverse decisions that comes from arbitrary cut-offs along continuous scales (such as life expectancy or quality of life) are unavoidable, but evidence of social support for the specific rationale may at least meet some requirements of procedural justice.

Within the context of value-based resource allocation decisions, coherence would dictate that both quality of life and quantity of life improvements – to patients who meet the end-of-life qualification criteria – are valued and valued at a premium. Hence NICE's three conditions would be replaced by one: the specification of the end-of-life status.

The example above, of NICE's 2009 end-of-life amendment illustrates the difficulties of weighting schemes within CEA. These problems are most apparent when the weighting system to account for an additional value arguments is made explicit. However, most jurisdictions do not have explicit end-of-life schemes. In these cases additional value arguments relating to end-of-life care may be incorporated informally, as decision-makers may use discretion to accept interventions at higher costs than would be justified by strict application of the cost-effectiveness threshold alone. The problems of weighting schemes described above apply equally to such circumstances. Indeed, since they are less apparent, they pose the additional difficulty of typically not being evident to observers. Accordingly, the inconsistencies and potential inefficiencies can be even less obvious and may remain unquestioned.

9.5   Conclusion

An end-of-life premium for health state values is one of many special value arguments that have been advanced to support the reimbursement of technologies that fail standard value for money assessment criteria. Along with rarity, innovation, the lack of alternative treatment and 'discount rate blight', the United Kingdom has been amongst the most enthusiastic champions of its use. However, the evidence for social support for the many of these special value arguments is either negative or contradictory, not just in the UK but in other jurisdictions as well. However, these evidentiary problems do not appear to weaken the advocates' belief in the rightness of their beliefs; and hence the question of how an end-of-life premium should be implemented remains a live policy issue.

The first recommendation we would make is that no single value premium should be implemented in isolation. There are many arguments for special value status and these should be considered in their entirety as most individuals will qualify for one or more of them over the time horizon of most policy analyses [56]. At a minimum, all value arguments that clear a shared evidence threshold should be considered. In the current evidence environment, that is likely to include the majority of the value arguments identified by Paulden and colleagues [37]. An arbitrary adoption of a subset of value premia would open up decisions to challenge on the basis of inconsistent application of rationales to decisions affecting the same healthcare budget and/or failure to take account of relevant evidence. The feasibility of decision bodies being able to do this reproducibly and reliably without recourse to some formal valuation framework, such as a quantitative multi-criteria decision analysis, is dubious given the evidence on human capacity for processing information [38, 57].

Our second recommendation is that whichever value framework is constructed must be applied equally to the identifiable beneficiaries and those who would bear the opportunity cost of adopting new technologies. To do otherwise is to value individuals' health differently solely on the basis of identifiability, leading to inequitable and inefficient reimbursement decisions, creating a systematic bias in favour of new interventions at the expense of existing care.

Third, whichever arbitrary definition of end of life is chosen should be validated against social preferences. The arbitrary and potentially perverse incentives that come from such a definition are unavoidable, but demonstrating social support may make them an acceptable price to pay for a pragmatically tractable decision-making framework.

Fourth, assuming that the components of the conventional QALY are a subset of the value of a technology, the benefit of an end-of-life premium must apply to both improvements in health-related quality of life and life expectancy. To do otherwise creates an unnecessary and unjustified inconsistency in the valuation framework used for end-of-life technologies and all other technologies.

Finally, whilst moving forward with values based upon the best available evidence and expert judgement is a reasonable initial strategy, substantive research to obtain robust evidence on the values of the population affected by the resource allocation decisions will be an urgent priority if decisions that depend on 'special value' arguments are to withstand the challenges that will come from any system that complies with the important principles of procedural justice.

References

1. Jonsen A, Jonsen AR (1986) Bentham in a box: technology assessment and health care allocation. Law Med Health Care 14:172–174
2. Weinstein MC (1988) A QALY is a QALY is a QALY – or is it? JHE 7:289–290
3. Cookson R, Dolan P (2000) Principles of justice in health care rationing. J Med Ethics 26:323–329
4. Daniels N, Sabin JE (2002) Setting limits fairly: can we learn to share medical resources? Oxford University Press, Oxford
5. NICE (2003) NICE Citizens Council report on age. http://www.nice.org.uk/Media/Default/Get-involved/Citizens-Council/Reports/CCReport02Age.pdf. Accessed 23 Sept 2014
6. Harris J (2005) Its not NICE to discriminate. JME 31(7):373–375
7. McCabe C, Claxton K, Tsuchiya A (2005) Orphan drugs and the NHS: should we value rarity. BMJ 331:1016–1019

8. National Institute for Health and Clinical Excellence (2008) Social value judgements: principles for the development of NICE guidance, 2nd edn. http://www.nice.org.uk/media/default/About/what-we-do/Research-and-development/Social-Value-Judgements-principles-for-the-development-of-NICE-guidance.pdf. Accessed 23 Sept 2014
9. McCabe C, Claxton K, Culyer AJ (2008) The NICE cost effectiveness threshold: what it is and what that means. PharmacoEconomics 26(9):733–744
10. Ontario Citizens Council (2011) Towards a value framework. A report to the Ministry of Health and Long Term Care. Toronto. http://www.health.gov.on.ca/en/public/programs/drugs/councils/report/values_framework.pdf. Accessed 23 Sept 2014
11. Porter E (2012) Rationing health care more fairly. New York Times, 21 Aug 2012. Accessed 23 Sept 2014
12. Raftery J. NICE proposes an alternative for value based pricing. BMJ Blogs. http://blogs.bmj.com/bmj/2014/02/25/james-raftery-nice-proposes-alternative-for-value-based-pricing/. Accessed 23 Sept 2014
13. Philipson T, Becker G, Goldman D, Murphy KM (2010) Terminal care and life near its end. NBER Working Paper no 15649. NBER. Cambridge, Massachusetts
14. Pinto-Prades JL, Sanchez-Martinez FI, Corbacho B, Baker R (2014) Valuing QALYs at the end of life. Soc Sci Med 113:5–14
15. NICE (2009) Appraising life extending, end of life treatments. NICE. http://www.nice.org.uk/guidance/gid-tag387/resources/appraising-life-extending-end-of-life-treatments-paper2. Accessed 23 Sept 2014
16. Linley WG, Hughes DA (2013) Societal views on NICE, cancer drugs fund and value based pricing criteria for prioritizing medicines: a cross-sectional survey of 4118 adults in Great Britain. Health Econ 22(8):948–964
17. Moynihan R, Heath R, Henry D (2002) Selling sickness: the pharmaceutical industry and disease mongering. BMJ 324:886–891
18. Claxton K, Briggs A, Buxton MJ et al (2008) Value based pricing for NHS drugs: an opportunity not to be missed? BMJ 336:251
19. NICE (2014) Methods of technology appraisal consultation. NICE. https://www.nice.org.uk/Guidance/InConsultation/GID-INCONSULTATION/html/p/methods-of-technology-appraisal-consultation?id=2cbiqn4bjozoxf4h6trcemndea. Accessed 23 Sept 2014
20. Haute Autorite de Sante (2014) Pricing and reimbursement of drugs and HTA policies in France. HAS. http://www.has-sante.fr/portail/upload/docs/application/pdf/2014-03/pricing_reimbursement_of_drugs_and_hta_policies_in_france.pdf. Accessed 23 Sept 2014
21. IQWIG (2009) General methods for the assessment of the relation of benefits to costs. IQWIG. https://www.iqwig.de/download/General_Methods_for_the_Assessment_of_the_Relation_of_Benefits_to_Costs.pdf. Accessed 23 Sept 2014
22. Wikipedia Congressional Office of Technology Assessment. http://en.wikipedia.org/wiki/Office_of_Technology_Assessment. Accessed 23 Sept 2014
23. Stevens A, Colin-Jones D, Gabbay J (1995) Quick and clean: authoritative health technology assessment for local health care contracting. Health Trends 27(2):37–42
24. Banta D (2003) The development of health technology assessment. Health Policy 63(2):121–132
25. Dolan P (1997) Modeling valuations for EuroQol Health States. Medical Care 35(11):1095–1108
26. Feeny D, Furlong W, Torrance GW et al (2002) Mutliattribute and single attribute utility functions for the Health Utilities Index Mark 3 system. Medical Care 40(2):113–128
27. Brazier JE, Roberts J, Deverill M (2002) The estimation of a preference based measure of health from the SF-36. Journal of Health Economics 21(2):271–292
28. Brazier J, Ratcliffe J, Tsuchiya A, Salomon J (2007) Measuring and valuing health benefits for economic evaluation. Oxford University Press, Oxford
29. Stolk EA, Busschbach JJ (2003) Validity and feasibility of using condition specific outcome measures in economic evaluation. Qual Life Res 12(4):363–371

30. Brazier JE, Dixon S (1995) The use of condition specific outcome measures in economic appraisal. Health Econ 4(4):255–264
31. Whitehurst DGT, Norman RA, Brazier JE, Viney R (2014) Comparison of contemporaneous EQ-5D and SF-6D responses using scoring algorithms derived from similar valuation exercises. Value Health 17:570–577
32. Devlin N, Sussex J (2011) Incorporating multiple criteria in HTA: methods and processes. Office of Health Economics, London, http://www.ohe.org/publications/article/incorporating-multiple-criteria-in-hta-methods-and-processes-8.cfm (accessed 23rd September 2014)
33. Hausman DM (2006) Valuing health. Philos Publ Aff 34:246–274
34. Hausman DM (2010) Valuing health: a new proposal. Health Econ 19:280–296
35. Culyer AJ (2014) Four issues with cost-effectiveness analysis: a view from the side-lines. In: Health technology assessment and health policy today: a multifaceted view of their unstable crossroads, Springer, Madrid, pp 1–18
36. Nord E (1999) Cost-value analysis in health care: making sense out of QALYs. Cambridge University Press, Cambridge, UK
37. NICE (2013) Guide to the Methods of health technology appraisal. NICE, London, http://www.nice.org.uk/article/PMG9/chapter/1-Introduction. Accessed 23 Sept 2014
38. Facey K, Boivin A, Gracia J et al (2010) Patient's perspectives in health technology assessment: a route to robust evidence and fair deliberation. IJTAHC 26(3):334–340
39. Paulden M, Stafinski T, Menon D, McCabe C (2015) Value based reimbursement decisions for orphan drugs: a scoping review and decision framework. PharmacoEconomics 33(3):255–269
40. Miller GA (1956) The magical number seven, plus or minus two: some limits on our capacity for processing information. Psychol Rev 63(2):81–97
41. Claxton K, Sculpher MJ, Ades TE (2005) Cost consequences: implicit, opaque and anti-scientific. (Letter) BMJ. http://www.bmj.com/rapid-response/2011/10/30/cost-consequences-implicit-opaque-and-anti-scientific. Accessed 23 Sept 2014
42. Mitton C, Donaldson C (2004) Health care priority setting: principles, practice and challenges. Cost effectiveness and resource allocation. 2:3. http://www.resource-allocation.com/content/2/1/3. Accessed 23 Sept 2014
43. Airoldi M, Morton A, Smith JAE, Bevan G (2014) STAR – people powered prioritization: a 21st century solution to allocation headaches. Medical decision making 2014 (online ahead of print). http://mdm.sagepub.com/content/early/2014/08/12/0272989X14546376.abstract. Accessed 23 Sept 2014
44. Rowen D, Brazier J, Mukuria C, Keetharuth A, Risa A, Tsuchiya A, Whyte S, Shackley P. Update: eliciting societal preferences for weighting QALYs according to burden of illness, size of gain and end of life
45. Shah K, Devlin N (2012) Understanding social preferences regarding the prioritization of treatments addressing unmet need and severity. Office Health Economics. http://www.ohe.org/publications/article/social-preferences-about-unmet-need-and-disease-severity-126.cfm. Accessed 23 Sept 2014
46. NICE Citizens Council (2004) NICE CC report for ultra orphan drugs. London. http://www.nice.org.uk/proxy/?sourceUrl=http%3A%2F%2Fwww.nice.org.uk%2FniceMedia%2Fpdf%2Fboardmeeting%2Fbrdjan05item4.pdf. Accessed 23 Sept 2014
47. Desser AS, Olsen JA, Grepperud S (2013) Eliciting preferences for prioritizing treatment of rare diseases: the role of opportunity costs and framing effects. PharmacoEconomics 31:s1051–s1061
48. Desser AS (2013) Prioritizing treatment of rare diseases: a survey of preferences of Norwegian doctors. Soc Sci Med 94:56–62
49. Desser AS, Gyrd-Hansen D, Olsen JA, Grepperud SK, Sønbø I (2010) Societal views on orphan drugs: cross sectional survey of Norwegians aged 40 to 67. BMJ 2010:341
50. Stafinski T, McCabe C, Menon D (2014) Determining social values for resource allocation decision making in cancer care: a Canadian experiment. J Cancer Policy 2(3):81–88

51. Mentzakis E, Stefanowska P, Hurley J (2011) A discrete choice experiment investigating preferences for funding drugs used to treat orphan diseases. Health Econ Policy Law 6(3):405–433
52. Culyer AJ, McCabe C, Briggs AH et al (2007) Searching for a threshold not setting one: the role of the national institute for health and clinical excellence. J Health Serv Res Policy 12(1):56–58
53. Eckermann S, Pekarsky B (2014) Can the real opportunity cost please stand up: displaced services, the straw man outside the room. PharmacoEconomics 32(4):319–325
54. Polder JJ, Barendreght JJ, van Oers H (2006) Health care costs in the last year of life – the Dutch experience. Soc Sci Med 63(7):1720–1731
55. Ubel PA, Spranca MD, Dekay ML, Herschey JC, Asch DA (1998) Public preferences for prevention versus cure: what if an ounce of prevention is worth only an ounce of cure? Med Decis Mak 18(2):141–148
56. Wailoo A, Tsuchiya A, McCabe C (2009) Weighting must wait: incorporating equity concerns into cost effectiveness analysis may take longer than expected. PharmacoEconomics 27(12):983–989
57. Cairns J, van der Pol M, Lloyd A (2002) Decision making heuristics and the elicitation of preferences: being fast and frugal about the future. Health Econ 11(7):655–658

Chapter 10
Eliciting Societal Views on the Value of Life-Extending Treatments Using Q Methodology

Rohan Deogaonkar, Rachel Baker, Helen Mason, Neil McHugh, and Marissa Collins

10.1 Introduction

Publicly funded healthcare systems operating with fixed budgets must incorporate rationing mechanisms of some sort in order to set priorities. Efficiency, which might be defined broadly in health terms as maximising health benefits with respect to cost, is a key consideration in setting priorities. However, efficiency is not the only consideration, and members of society may value other issues in relation to the distribution of resources to different groups of beneficiaries. Life-extending treatments for people with terminal illnesses, which are non-curative by definition and often produce relatively small health gains in relation to their costs, are a prime example of technologies that might not satisfy usual cost-effectiveness thresholds [1–4]. It is also an example of a context in which equity arguments (such as those around severity or need) might be brought to bear at the 'expense of' efficiency and a range of ideological, ethical and economic arguments could be invoked to support or oppose the provision of 'end-of-life treatments'.

It is generally accepted that the views and values of members of the public, as taxpayers and potential patients, are relevant in determining priorities in the provision of publicly funded healthcare. One way of including societal preferences (in relation to distributional equity) into measures of cost-effectiveness is by applying differential weights to different types of health gain – the most common measure of which is the quality-adjusted life year or QALY. If the predominant societal view is that relatively short life extensions for people with terminal illnesses are worthwhile based on equity considerations, then the treatment benefits and QALYs gained at the end of life will be valued (weighted) more than QALYs gained by patients with nonterminal illnesses elsewhere in the health system.

R. Deogaonkar • R. Baker (✉) • H. Mason • N. McHugh • M. Collins
Yunus Centre for Social Business and Health, Glasgow Caledonian University, Glasgow, UK
e-mail: rachel.baker@gcu.ac.uk

© Springer International Publishing Switzerland 2016
J. Round (ed.), *Care at the End of Life: An Economic Perspective*,
DOI 10.1007/978-3-319-28267-1_10

To date most studies examining the issue of end-of-life treatments have adopted quantitative approaches to preference elicitation [5–9]. A range of methods have been used but typically, in preference elicitation studies, a selected number of attributes, which are hypothesised to be important, are presented to respondents in scenarios which attempt to isolate the relative impact of different attributes on respondents' choices. The evidence, however, remains limited and equivocal. Linley and Hughes [5], Olsen [10] and Shah et al. [8] find no, or limited, support for an end-of-life premium. In contrast, Pennington et al. [11], Shah et al. [9], Pinto-Prades et al. [6] and Rowen et al. [7] find evidence suggestive of an end-of-life premium. These studies have taken quantitative approaches, including discrete choice survey methods [7, 8], person or benefit trade-off questions [5, 6] and willingness to pay (WTP) [6, 11]. This literature is reviewed in more depth by Shah in Chap. 11 in this volume, and so is only discussed briefly here, but we note that findings might differ because of the different methods or framing used (including the choice of comparator scenarios presented) and axioms governing the analysis. However, in the absence of accompanying qualitative insights, there is no way of knowing why a particular preference has been expressed and why findings are not replicated between similar studies. Hence, an important supplement to this growing literature, to inform these and other research questions, is in-depth, qualitative and mixed-method studies exploring what it is about life-extending treatments that members of the public might value differently from other competing uses of the health budget.

This chapter introduces Q methodology as a structured approach to eliciting and describing societal values, combining qualitative and quantitative techniques to study subjectivity. Q methodology is not an economics-based method (the focus of this book), but it is an effective means of investigating societal perspectives, which we have used to address health economic research questions in a number of different studies, most recently examining societal views on the value of life extension for people with terminal illnesses [12]. The chapter is structured in four sections. First, we outline the basics of Q methodology and the types of research questions that Q lends itself to, highlighting the use of Q methodology in health research, as a tool for exploring shared perspectives and for systematically describing societal viewpoints. The second section outlines the main stages involved in conducting a Q study. The third section describes the application of Q in a recent study of societal perspectives on the value of life extension for people with terminal illnesses. Finally, in the discussion we address the potential application of Q within a broader mixed-method research paradigm and the development of policies that better incorporate societal views and values.

10.2 Understanding Q

First described by the British physicist and psychologist William Stephenson [13], Q methodology permits the systematic study of 'subjectivity' (matters relating to opinion, values and beliefs). Q combines qualitative and quantitative techniques to identify and describe shared views around a given topic. It comprises a set of techniques most commonly described in terms of two main features: the means of data collection (a card sort) and factor analysis to identify underlying patterns of similarity between individuals' card sorts. Each of these is explained in more detail in what follows.

The central purpose of Q methodology is to reveal the structure and form of subjectivity on any given topic, such that shared views can be identified, interpreted and described. Subjectivity alludes to the communication of one's own point of view [14], but most Q studies are concerned with *shared* perspectives, i.e. those features of subjectivity that connect individuals. Three questions underlie every Q study – '(1) What is the range of communicated ideas in a particular discourse? (2) What are the prevalent variations in it? (3) How do these variations logically relate to each other?' [[15], p. 20]. Examples of health-related research questions to which Q has been applied include understandings of chronic pain [16]; lay perceptions of mental health [17]; health-related quality of life [18]; the ethics of end-of-life decision-making [19]; the attitudes of young people to their health lifestyle [20]; economic rationality, health and lifestyle choices in people with diabetes [21]; understandings of Down's syndrome [22] and, the subject of this chapter, societal perspectives on life-extending treatments for patients with terminal illness [12].

10.3 Conducting a Q Study: In Five Steps

A Q study generally follows a sequence of five steps, some of which will be iterative and linked and so the application of these steps is not a simple linear process. The first step involves the selection of a sample of statements to represent the range of communicated ideas in relation to the topic of study. Next, participants are selected and guided through a card sorting process in which they rank order the statements (e.g. from most agree to most disagree) as per a condition of instruction. A correlation matrix is then calculated, representing the similarity between each participant's card sort and all others. 'By-person' factor analysis is used to identify underlying dimensions in the data, connecting similar Q sorts and distinguishing dissimilar sorts. Finally, the resulting factors are interpreted to produce rich and detailed descriptions of shared perspectives on the topic of study.

10.3.1 Step 1: The Q set

The first stage of any Q study is the derivation of a set of statements that represents the 'concourse'. The concourse refers to all communication, arguments, beliefs and conversational possibilities on the topic of interest. Statements can be gathered from primary sources such as interviews and group discussions and/or secondary sources such as media reports, editorials, online discussions and literature. The gathering of statements is, at the outset, a process of identifying any and all expressions of opinion related to the research question, seeking out the range of different perspectives and retaining the original language used by those expressing the opinions. The initial set of statements identified in this way is often substantial but typically includes a good deal of repetition and overlap and must be condensed into a smaller selection of statements – termed the Q set – which can be sorted by respondents. Researchers might use either a structured or unstructured approach to developing a Q set, but either way the key principles are to make sure that the statements are representative of the concourse, that there is a balance across the statements so that one particular issue within a concourse is not overrepresented within the final Q set and that respondents will agree with some statements and disagree with others [23]. The number of items in a Q set varies between studies; it can be between 20 and 100 statements [24] but is most commonly 30–50 statements.

10.3.2   Step 2: Selecting Participants in Q Studies

Participants are selected who are likely to have strong views on the topic in question and whose views are likely to differ from other participants. For example, a Q study focussed on an organisational unit such as a university department would involve people who have different roles, responsibilities and power within that department and those who may have spoken on the topic in question in different ways and in different contexts. One might also identify people with different employment back-grounds or experiences, different disciplinary training or those with domestic versus international education, depending on the nature of the research question. As views begin to emerge, researchers may identify additional sampling variables or indi-viduals whose perspectives are different and important. This approach has much in common with qualitative sampling techniques and differs from statistical power-based sampling strategies used in quantitative studies. The emphasis in Q is on identifying the viewpoints that exist rather than identifying the proportion of a pop-ulation that belongs to one viewpoint versus another; therefore, it is not necessary to have large participant samples. Purposive sampling thus allows for the selection of information-rich cases and individuals who are likely to strengthen or challenge emerging theory. A sufficiently large sample is one in which enough participants are included in order to establish the existence of different, shared perspectives that can be described distinctly. Although the preferred number of participants cannot be firmly established until data are collected, a sample of 40–60 participants is usually adequate [14]. As a general rule, the more factors that eventually emerge, the larger the number of participants required to provide good factor definition.

10.3.3   Step 3: The Q Sort

Q sorting is the main data collection technique used in Q studies and requires par-ticipants to rank-order statements within the Q set. The researcher will usually introduce the topic of study and then guide the respondent through the sorting of the set of statements according to a condition of instruction such as:

Most disagree   Most agree

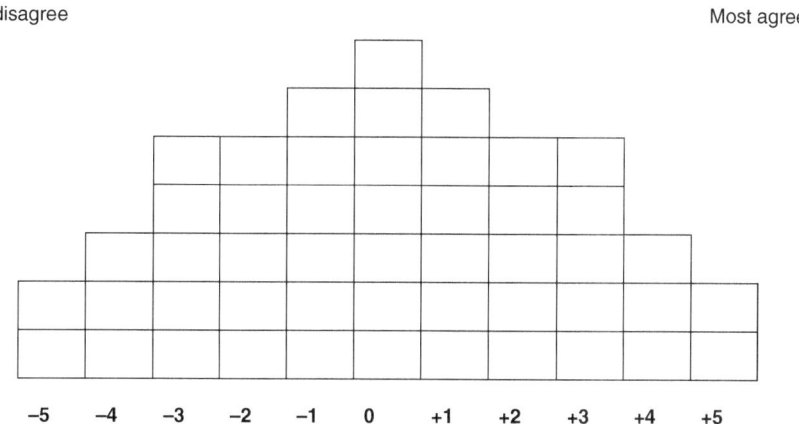

          −5   −4   −3   −2   −1   0   +1   +2   +3   +4   +5

Fig. 10.1 Q grid

*Sort the items from to those with which you most agree to those with which you
most disagree.*

Q statements are printed onto cards and respondents are initially asked to read
and sort these cards into three rough piles, for example, 'agree', 'disagree' and
'neutral'. The Q sort then follows, using a grid marked with a scale, for example,
from −5 to +5 and the number of cards permitted in each 'pile' or 'column' indicated. An example of a sorting grid is shown in Fig. 10.1. This example shows a
typical Q grid, quasi-normal in shape, with only a few statements permitted in the
strong disagree/agree columns and more in the centre of the grid.

Respondents are guided through the positioning of the cards into each space on
the grid. In this example two cards would be placed in the −5/+5 columns, three
cards in the +4/−4 columns, four cards in the +3/−3 columns and so on. From the
initial rough 'agree' card pile, respondents are asked to select two cards that they
most strongly agree with and place them in the +5 column. Next, selecting from the
'disagree' card pile, respondents are asked to select two cards they *most strongly*
disagree with and place them in the −5 column. This process is repeated from the
outside of the grid working inwards towards the centre until all cards have been
placed. The positioning of cards is recorded by the researcher and these rankings are
the basis of the subsequent factor analysis. Usually, a brief interview or open-ended
questionnaire is administered after the Q sort so the respondent might further elabo-
rate on rank ordering of their cards. This qualitative data is used to aid interpretation
of the factors that emerge from the analysis (explained in more detail in the next
section).[1]

---

[1]Q sorts can also be conducted online and usually online procedures are designed to mimic, as
closely as possible, the manual sorting process, given the restrictions of screen size and so on.
Many Q methodologists would still prefer face-to-face Q sort interviews, if it is practical to do so,
for several reasons including the ability of respondents to view all materials together (a completed
Q sort can be difficult to present legibly on a computer screen) and the opportunity for interaction
and explanation afforded by in-person Q sort interviews.

Importantly, although the range and number of statements are determined prior to respondents sorting them (as described in Step 1), the respondent is in control of where each statement is placed, thereby determining the significance of each item in relation to all other items in the set. The shape of the Q grid is designed to help the respondent sort the statement cards into a rank order. The quasi-normal or pyramid shape of the grid used in most Q studies reflects an expectation that individual respondents will feel strongly about a subset of statements and less strongly about a larger subset. It is worth noting, however, that whilst it is the convention amongst Q methodologists to use a grid shaped in this way, it is not a requirement of the method. The shape can be altered for the sorters' convenience as needed, and the use of differently shaped grids has not been shown to substantially alter the resulting factors (see Brown [25] p. 288–289 and Cottle and McKeown [26]). The centre of the grid represents a point of neutrality where statements do not matter to sorters, but the shape of the sorting grid can be rectangle rather than pyramid shaped if there is reason for doing so. Equally if respondents find it very hard to place statements within the grid they are presented with, then the sorter should be allowed to place more statements in some columns and fewer in others, and analysis can accommodate individual Q sorts that take a different shape – although our experience is that almost all respondents manage to place statements onto the standard grid without difficulty.

The resulting distribution of items reflects the sorters attributed meaning of the scale rather than representing an index of predefined meaning as is the case with traditional rating scales where items are usually scored serially and independently of each other. The Q sorting process arguably yields richer subjective data than conventional rating scales, and the interpretation of Q sorts includes the positioning of groups of statements together and in relation to each other.

10.3.4 Step 4: Factor Analysis

Factor analysis consists of a number of statistical techniques that enable the simplification of complex datasets by identifying underlying dimensions based on the correlations between larger numbers of variables [27]. It has been used extensively, notably in psychometrics, to reduce a large number of test scores to a smaller number of factors that are more readily interpreted. *By-person* factor analysis, employed in Q methodology, is based on the correlations between participants, correlating each Q sort with every other Q sort. Patterns (factors) can be identified by drawing a 'statistical line' through the data, connecting similar Q sorts and setting them apart from other Q sorts. Each of the resulting factors represents the viewpoint shared by of a group of respondents with similar Q sorts.

Every respondent's Q sort is associated, to a greater or lesser degree, with each factor identified. Some respondents will be highly associated with one factor and correlated negatively with the other factors. Others will be 'mixed' across the factors, meaning that they have something in common with more than one perspective.

The degree to which each participants' Q sort is (dis)similar to each factor is indicated by their 'factor loadings', which are correlation coefficients, taking a value between −1 and +1 [28]. Those Q sorts which *define* a factor – i.e. 'pure' Q sorts that are only significantly correlated with one factor and not significantly associated with other factors – are used in the construction of the 'factor array'. The factor array is a composite Q sort, calculated for each factor, as a weighted average of the scores (i.e. −5 to +5) given to each item by all of the defining Q sorts for that factor [29]. Since defining Q sorts are only associated with one factor, different participants' Q sorts will contribute to each of the factor arrays, illustrated in Fig. 10.2. A factor array is laid out, for each factor, using the original sorting grid by placing each item in the spaces on the grid as an aid to interpretation [30]. For further explanation of factor analysis and Q terminology, see Brown [14] or Watts and Stenner [23]. Specialist software (PQMethod) is available to conduct the factor analysis required for Q [31].

10.3.5   Step 5: Factor Interpretation

The factor array (i.e. composite Q sort for each factor) is the main focus of interpretation. The objective of interpretation is to produce rich descriptions of each shared perspective (factor) on the topic of study. In doing so the specific features which

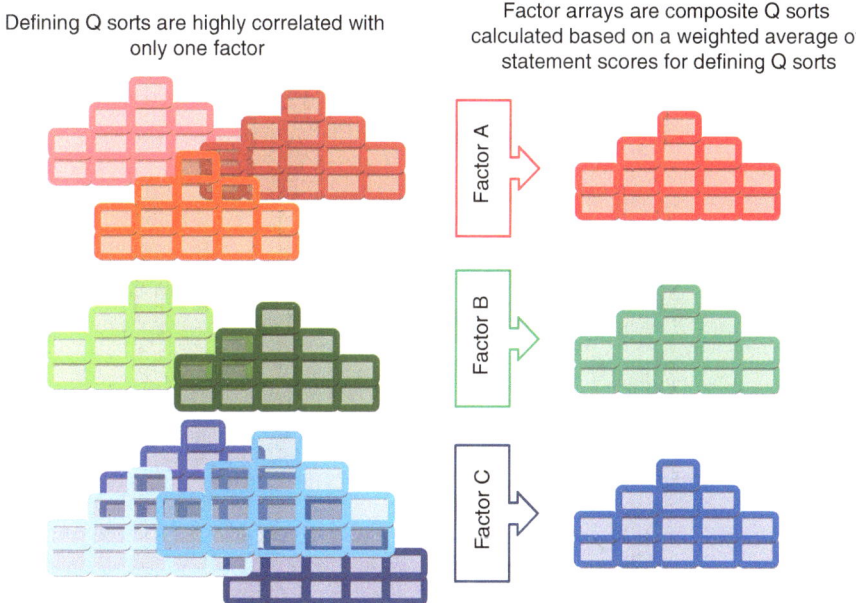

Fig. 10.2 Factor arrays

delineate and bind the factors are identified and 'whole perspectives' described by examination of the composite Q sorts together with the post-Q sort interviews of exemplary (defining) respondents. A typical starting point would be examination of the statements placed at the positive and negative poles of each factor (most agree and most disagree) as these are the statements that people who are associated with a factor feel most strongly about. Neutral items, ranked in the centre of the distribution, may also be informative when comparing their placement in other factors. Items which distinguish or represent consensus views between factors also contribute towards the interpretation and description of the perspectives represented by each factor. The final step is to attach a descriptive label to each factor.[2]

10.4   Q and the Value of Life Extension at the End of Life

Having described the conduct of a Q study in general terms, we turn to a specific example of the use of Q methods to study the nature of societal perspectives in relation to the relative value of life extensions for people with terminal illnesses (see www.gcu.ac.uk/endoflife for details of the project). What follows is a brief summary of the Q study, which is reported in detail elsewhere [12]. Statements were sourced from newspaper and popular media articles, records of a public consultation conducted by NICE as a precursor to the introduction of their supplementary guidance for the assessment of end-of-life technologies [32, 33] qualitative interviews with key informants and focus groups with members of the general public. This resulted in over 200 statements of belief or value related to the research question which were then assessed for coverage and balance to form a 49-statement Q set to be ranked by respondents. A purposive sample of 59 respondents was selected because of their different experiences or expertise in the 'end of life' whether in a professional or personal capacity. This included individuals and groups connected, but not limited, to academia, the pharmaceutical industry, charities and patient groups, lobby groups, religious groups, clinicians and people with experience of terminal illnesses (e.g. bereaved family members). Analysis of their Q sorts along with accompanying qualitative data led to the identification of three factors or shared perspectives.[3]

  The first factor offers a utilitarian, system-level perspective which emphasises that a publicly funded healthcare service, operating within a limited budget, must aim to maximise health benefits overall for the population in order to best serve the interest of society. Treatments yielding the greatest health improvements in relation to cost should be prioritised as they would offer good value for money, and all patient groups must be considered equally deserving of treatment. According to this

---

[2] It is worth noting that the process of interpretation tends to be iterative with factor extraction and rotation, and several attempts at interpretation of different solutions will be required prior to settling on a satisfactory solution.

[3] This purposive sample was supplemented by a larger general population sample of 250 respondents who also completed the Q sort, but analysis did not generate any additional perspectives.

perspective, life-extending treatments would not be a cost-effective use of resources, and any health gains for terminally ill patients should not be treated as a special case as doing so would devalue the health of all other patients.

The second factor places the individual at the centre of a decision and is grounded in right-based arguments. In this view human life is precious and cost considerations should not determine treatment provision. Rather, individual patient choice should be the prime decision-making criteria, and treatments must be provided if a patient desires it as everyone contributes to the funding of a public healthcare system. Accordingly, the denial of life-extending treatments is considered to be morally wrong as it does not account for the substantial non-health benefits these treatments might have for patients or their families, such as giving them time to prepare for death, put their affairs in order or say goodbye.

The third factor has elements in common with the first (value for money) and second (patient choice) factor but represents a distinct perspective worthy of separate description. Although the importance of achieving value for money with respect to limited resources is recognised, decisions must also incorporate the value that patients and their families attach to life extension at the end of life, including the non-health benefits which are presently not captured in cost-effectiveness analyses. There is also additional importance placed on treatment-related quality of life for the patient and the 'quality of death'. For this factor, health gains in the form of life extension for people with terminal illness may be more valued than health gains for patients with nonterminal conditions – in certain cases. However, this is not unconditional and there must be significant benefits from treatment because the economic principles of efficiency and opportunity cost are crucial for factor 3. Factor 3 is similar to factor 1 in the importance of achieving value for money in NHS spending, but benefits are more broadly conceived than in factor 1 and there is not the same emphasis on maximising health for the population.

10.5   Discussion

The three factors described above highlight the plurality of views surrounding this topic and also reveal that key philosophical positions pertaining to the just allocation of resources (e.g. utilitarianism, egalitarianism) have a basis in public opinion. However, whilst these factors might be a reasonable description of the positions existing amongst the public, the perspectives themselves cannot be directly translated into policy for ethical and pragmatic reasons. The study described here has generated evidence of the nature of views that exist on the topic, but one might reasonably ask how prevalent these views are in a population, or demand a critical assessment or ethical analysis of the accounts presented before incorporating public perspectives into policy.

In a second phase of work, following this Q study, the research team designed and administered a survey assessing the distribution of these views within society in a larger population sample. Analysis of these findings is ongoing but preliminary results suggest that there is no single majority view. Further research is required to develop such survey methods but there is intuitive appeal in a phased approach combining an initial, exploratory Q study with a subsequent quantitative phase, as a means of satisfying the dual objectives of *understanding* individual or societal perspectives and *measuring* the extent to which the different societal viewpoints identified are held in society. Our work also goes some way to critically examining the three factors, but more work is needed to develop and apply Q techniques in empirical ethics research, combining social science methods with ethical analysis at all stages of the research process [34].

The recent surge in interest and demand for mixed methods research in multidisciplinary fields has prompted a shift in the focus of methodological debates, moving away from conflicts questioning the validity of quantitative versus qualitative methods towards innovative strategies that complement and combine evidence from both methodologies and enhancing the potential for explanation. There is intrinsic appeal in the use of Q for the purposes of methodological triangulation, especially in environments where qualitative methods are regarded with scepticism due to the absence of mathematical techniques and tools [30, 35]. The structuring of data as factors offers different ways of 'seeing' the data and presenting a simplified structure for understanding complex subjective data, *'Only subjective opinions are at issue in Q, and although they are typically unprovable, they can nonetheless be shown to have structure and form, and it is the task of Q technique to render this form manifest for purposes of observation and study'* [[36], p. 58].

One of the appealing features of Q methodology is the ability to transform (relatively unbounded) subjective data into an interpretable form with relatively little researcher bias – at least in the process of generating the data – though clearly the development of the Q set and selection of factor solution is influenced, in part, by the analyst (however careful and exhaustive the methods used to develop the Q set and interpret alternative factor solutions). That said, although the statements depend on a framework specified by the researcher, the rank ordering of those statements is entirely self-referent and controlled by the participant [30]. It is arguably more transparent than the development of themes and coding structures derived through qualitative analyses. Q analysis also generates numeric information (e.g. factor loadings representing individuals' association with different points of view) that can be used to complement other quantitative measures. Such quantitative measures may be useful in conjunction with preference elicitation techniques, or other survey methods, to provide a deeper understanding of individual choices, values and preferences [30, 37]. Combining Q survey questions with willingness to pay or person trade-off questions in studies of societal preferences and end-of-life treatments, such as those used by Pinto-Prades et al. [6], could be a means of understanding the differences in findings between preference elicitation studies noted in the introduction to this chapter.

10.6 Conclusions

Q methodology is comprised of a set of techniques that are useful in the study of societal perspectives. It offers transparency and demonstrable rigour (in terms of repeatability and an 'audit trail') that can be difficult to demonstrate using 'pure' qualitative approaches yet maintains the rich contextual and reflexive qualities associated with qualitative research. The rich accounts represented by Q factors have the potential to inform the design of larger, more quantitative surveys and preference studies as well as aid in the accurate interpretation of their results. With respect to end-of-life research, we have identified three different societal perspectives on the topic, not previously explored in other empirical studies, which serve to highlight some of the normative tensions which must be resolved if we are to develop policy which reflects the views and values of society.

References

1. NICE (2009) Technology appraisal guidance 178: Bevacizumab (first-line), sorafenib (first- and second-line), sunitinib (second-line) and temsirolimus (first-line) for the treatment of advanced and/or metastatic renal cell carcinoma. National Institute for Health and Clinical Excellence, London
2. NICE (2010) Technology appraisal guidance 189: sorafenib for the treatment of advanced hepatocellular carcinoma. National Institute for Health and Clinical Excellence, London
3. NICE (2011) Technology appraisal guidance 219: everolimus for the second-line treatment of advanced renal cell carcinoma. National Institute for Health and Clinical Excellence, London
4. NICE (2013) Guide to the methods of technology appraisal 2013. NICE, London
5. Linley WG, Hughes DA (2013) Societal views on NICE, cancer drugs fund and value-based pricing criteria for prioritising medicines: a cross-sectional survey of 4118 adults in Great Britain. Health Econ Policy Law 22:948–964
6. Pinto-Prades JL, Sánchez-Martínez FI, Corbacho B, Baker R (2014) Valuing QALYS at the end of life. Soc Sci Med 113:5–14
7. Rowen D, Brazier J, Mukuria C, Keetharuth A, Risa Hole A, Tsuchiya A, Whyte S, Shackley P (2015) Eliciting Societal Preferences for Weighting QALYs for Burden of Illness and End of Life. Medical Decision Making 2016;210–222
8. Shah KK, Tsuchiya A, Wailoo AJ (2015) Valuing health at the end of life: A stated preference discrete choice experiment. Soc Sci Med 124:48–56
9. Shah KK, Tsuchiya A, Wailoo AJ (2013) Valuing health at the end of life: an empirical study of public preferences. Eur J Health Econ 15(4):389–399
10. Olsen JA (2013) Priority preferences: "End of Life" does not matter, but total life does. Value Health 16:1063–1066
11. Pennington M, Baker R, Brouwer W, Mason H, Hansen DG, Robinson A, Donaldson C, The EuroVaQ Team (2013) Comparing WTP values of different types of QALY gain elicited from the General Public. Health Econ 24(3):280–293
12. McHugh N, Baker R, Mason H, Williamson L, van Exel J, Deogaonkar R, Collins M, Donaldson C (2015) Extending Life for People with a Terminal Illness: A Moral Right and an Expensive Death? Exploring Societal Perspectives. BMC Medical Ethics 16(1):14
13. Stephenson W (1935) Correlating persons instead of tests. Character Pers 4:17–24
14. Brown S (1980) Political subjectivity. Applications of Q methodology in political science. Yale University Press, New Haven
15. Stricklin M (1999) Chaos: knowledge and death of a cliché. Prepared for the symposium circulo de debates sobre o mundo contemporâneo. Universidade Federal do Piauí, Teresina
16. Eccleston C, Willams ACD, Stainton Rogers W (1997) Patients' and professionals' understandings of the causes of chronic pain: blame, responsibility and identity protection. Soc Sci Med 45:699–709
17. Herron S (2000) Lay perspectives of mental health: a Q method study. J Contemp Health 8:25–33

18. Stenner PHD, Cooper D, Skevington SM (2003) Putting the Q into quality of life; the identification of subjective constructions of health-related quality of life using Q methodology. Soc Sci Med 57:2161–2172
19. Wong W, Eiser A, Mrteck R, Heckerling PS (2004) By-person factor analysis in clinical ethical decision making: Q methodology in end-of-life care decisions. Am J Bioeth 4:W8–W22
20. van Exel J, DE Graaf G, Brouwer WBF (2006) "Everyone dies, so you might as well have fun!" Attitudes of Dutch youths about their health lifestyle. Soc Sci Med 63:2628–2639
21. Baker R (2006) Economic rationality and health and lifestyle choices for people with diabetes. Soc Sci Med 63:2341–2353
22. Bryant LD, Green JM, Hewison J (2006) Understandings of Down's syndrome: a Q methodological investigation. Soc Sci Med 63:1188–1200
23. Watts S, Stenner P (2012) Doing Q methodological research – theory method and interpretation. Sage, London
24. Barbosa JC, Willoughby P, Rosenberger CA, Mrtek RG (1998) Statistical methodology: VII. Q-Methodology, a structural analytic approach to medical subjectivity. Acad Emerg Med 5:1032–1040
25. Brown SR (1980) Political subjectivity. Yale University Press, New Haven
26. Cottle CE, Mckeown BF (1980) The forced-free distinction in Q technique: a note on unused categories in the Q sort continuum. Operant Subjectivity 3:58–63
27. Kline P (1994) An easy guide to factor analysis. Press (Padstow) Ltd, Cornwall
28. Brown SR (1993) A primer on Q methodology. Operant Subjectivity 16:91–138
29. McKeown B, Thomas D (1988) Q methodology. Sage, Newbury Park
30. Baker R, Thompson C, Mannion R (2006) Q methodology in health economics. J Health Serv Res Policy 11:38–45
31. Schmolck P, Atkinson J (2002) PQMethod software and manual 2.11
32. NICE (2008) Appraising end of life medicine, Consultation document. National Institute for Health and Clinical Excellence, London
33. NICE (2009) Appraising life-extending, end of life treatments. National Institute for Health and Clinical Excellence, London
34. Frith L (2012) Symbiotic empirical ethics: a practical methodology. Bioethics 26:198–206
35. Coast J (1999) The appropriate uses of qualitative methods in health economics. Health Econ 8:345–353
36. Brown SR (1986) Q technique and method: principles and procedures. In: Berry WD, Lewis-Beck MS (eds) New tools for social scientists: advances and applications in research methods. Sage, Beverly Hills
37. Baker R, van Exel NJA, Mason H, Stricklin M (2010) Connecting Q & surveys: a test of three methods to explore factor membership in a large sample. Operant Subjectivity 34:38–58

Part IV
End of Life Care and Society

Chapter 11
Does Society Place Special Value on End of Life Treatments?

Koonal Shah

11.1 Introduction: Simple QALY Maximisation

Economic evaluation is used to estimate the efficiency of health-care interventions and subsequently to inform decisions about whether those interventions should be reimbursed. A common approach is to measure the health benefits of a given intervention in terms of quality-adjusted life years (QALYs), a generic measure of health that combines quality of life and length of life in a single index number. The cost-effectiveness of the intervention can be expressed by calculating its cost per QALY gained. Decisions about whether to reimburse the intervention can then be guided by comparing the cost-effectiveness of that intervention to the cost-effectiveness of other interventions or to some threshold value that reflects displaced activities (for a general introduction, see Drummond et al. [1]).

   If it is assumed that the principal objective of health care is to maximise population health using available resources [2] and that the QALY is an acceptable measure of health benefit, it follows that health-care resources should be prioritised so as to maximise the total number of QALYs gained. This "QALY maximisation" rule [3] entails distributive neutrality – that is, it does not incorporate concerns for how the benefits are distributed across individuals. All QALY gains are therefore deemed to be of equal social value, regardless of to whom they accrue or the circumstances in which they are gained – this is the "a QALY is a QALY" principle. The National Institute for Health and Care Excellence (NICE), the organisation responsible for providing advice on the cost-effective use of health-care resources in England and Wales, formally documents this principle in the reference case defined in its method

K. Shah
Office of Health Economics, London, UK

School of Health and Related Research, University of Sheffield, Sheffield, UK
e-mail: KShah@ohe.org

© Springer International Publishing Switzerland 2016   155
J. Round (ed.), *Care at the End of Life: An Economic Perspective*,
DOI 10.1007/978-3-319-28267-1_11

guide: "an additional QALY should receive the same weight regardless of any other characteristics of the people receiving the health benefit" ([4], section 5.4.1).[1]

However, maximising health may not be the only purpose of health care. For example, the UK National Health Service (NHS) also has equity objectives such as seeking to "improve the health of the poorest fastest" [5]. There is nothing that requires QALYs to be used only in a maximising context [6]. Indeed, NICE recognises that the "a QALY is a QALY" approach can conflict with people's considered moral convictions and consequently uses a flexible approach whereby its appraisal committees (independent committees responsible for formulating NICE guidance) are expected to make judgements about what is appropriate and acceptable for society (social value judgements) in order to decide whether there is a case for departing from the reference case position for reasons of equity or fairness [7].

A number of studies have examined whether the social value of a QALY varies according to how the QALYs are distributed, the characteristics of the patients receiving the QALYs or the characteristics of the health effect itself (for a review, see Dolan et al. [3]). Typically these studies have surveyed members of the general public, whose preferences may be considered to be representative of the overall views of society. NICE's position on social value judgements is that its recommendations should embody values that are generally held by the population that the NHS serves [8].

11.2   Severity of Illness as a Priority-Setting Criterion

There is a growing body of empirical evidence that members of the general public are willing to sacrifice aggregate health gains in order to direct resources towards those who are worst off in terms of the severity of their condition [9]. This implies that the social value of a QALY accruing to a severely ill patient is greater than that of a QALY accruing to a patient who is not severely ill. However, severity is typically described in terms of current quality of life rather than expected length of life or proximity to death. Most empirical studies in the health economics literature do not make it clear how duration is to be considered (though there have been a number of recent additions to the literature that *do* examine length of life explicitly – see below). Hence, it is unclear whether society values a QALY accruing to patients with shorter life expectancy more highly than a QALY accruing to patients with longer life expectancy and whether it considers "end of life" patients – those whose life expectancy is extremely short – to be worthy of special consideration.

---

[1] It should be added, however, that NICE does make allowances for other criteria, such as the innovative nature of the technology, to be taken into consideration – see NICE [4], section 6.3.3.

Table 11.1 Summary of selected empirical studies

Study	Country	Sample size	Sample type	Method	Mode of administration	End of life comparison	Findings relevant to end of life
Abel Olsen [10]	NOR	503	Public	Pairwise choice tasks	Web-based survey	LE gains ranging from 1 month to 3 years for patients (of different ages) with LE without treatment ranging from 1 to 10 years	No or limited evidence consistent with a premium for life-extending end of life treatments
Baker et al. [11]	UK	40	Public	Ranking exercise	Focus group	3-month LE gain for patients with 6–8-month LE without treatment vs. QOL gain for patients with non-EOL condition	Evidence consistent with a premium for life-extending end of life treatments
Linley and Hughes [12]	UK	4,118	Public	Budget allocation	Web-based survey	6-month LE gain for patients with 18-month LE without treatment vs. 6-month LE gain for patients with 60-month LE without treatment	No or limited evidence consistent with of a premium for life-extending end of life treatments
Pennington et al. [13]	Multiple	17,657	Public	Willingness to pay	Web-based survey	LE gain for patients with terminal illness vs. LE gain for patients at the end of their natural life expectancy vs. various scenarios involving QOL gains (all gains equivalent to 1 QALY)	Evidence consistent with a premium for life-extending end of life treatments
Pinto Prades et al. [14]	SPA	813	Public	Willingness to pay, person trade-off	Computer-assisted personal interview	6-or 18-month LE gain for patients with 3-month LE without treatment vs. 50 % QOL gain for patients with 6- or 18-month LE without treatment vs. 50 % QOL gain lasting 6 or 18 months for non-EOL patients	Evidence consistent with a premium for end of life treatments, but QOL-improving end of life treatments were valued more highly than life-extending end of life treatments

(continued)

Table 11.1 (continued)

Study	Country	Sample size	Sample type	Method	Mode of administration	End of life comparison	Findings relevant to end of life
Rowen et al. [15]	UK	3,669	Public	Discrete choice experiment	Web-based survey	LE gains ranging from 0 months to 60 years for patients with LE without treatment ranging from 3 months to 60 years	Evidence consistent with a premium for life-extending end of life treatments, but responses to the follow-up attitudinal questions cast doubt on this finding
Shah et al. [16]	UK	50	Public	Pairwise choice tasks	Face-to-face interview	6-month LE gain for patients with 1-year LE without treatment vs. 6-month LE gain for patients with 10-year LE without treatment	Some evidence consistent with a premium for end of life treatments, but QOL-improving end of life treatments were valued more highly than life-extending end of life treatments
Shah et al. [17]	UK	3,969	Public	Discrete choice experiment	Web-based survey	LE gains ranging from 0 months to 12 months for patients with LE without treatment ranging from 3 months to 5 years	No or limited evidence consistent with a premium for life-extending end of life treatments
Skedgel et al. [18]	CAN	656	Public, decision makers	Discrete choice experiment	Web-based survey	1-year, 5-year or 10-year LE gain for patients with 1-month, 5-year or 10-year LE without treatment	No or limited evidence consistent with a premium for life-extending end of life treatments

LE life expectancy, *QOL* quality of life

11.3   The Rest of This Chapter

This remainder of this chapter is set out as follows. First I will describe the policy context in the UK, focusing on the way in which NICE appraises life-extending end of life treatments. I will then summarise a selection of recent UK and non-UK studies examining priority-setting preferences regarding end of life treatments, before noting some of the discussion points arising from the evidence. Finally, I will set out some recommendations for future research.

11.4   The Situation in the UK

In January 2009, NICE issued supplementary advice to its appraisal committees to be taken into account when appraising life-extending end of life treatments [19]. This advice constitutes an explicit departure from the reference case "a QALY is a QALY" position described above. It indicates that if certain criteria are met, it may be appropriate to recommend the use of treatments for terminal illness that offer an extension to life even if their base-case cost-effectiveness estimates exceed the range normally considered acceptable. Some aspects of the supplementary advice were revised following a 5-week public consultation exercise [20]. The revised criteria [21], enshrined in NICE's method guide [4], are set out below; if met, the appraisal committee is asked to consider the impact of giving greater weight to the treatment gains achieved in the later stages of disease:

1. The treatment is indicated for patients with short life expectancy (normally less than 24 months).
2. The treatment offers an extension to life compared to current NHS treatment (normally at least three additional months).
3. The treatment is licensed, or otherwise indicated, for small patient populations (normally less than 7,000 patients).

Rawlins et al. [22] suggest that this supplementary policy reflects a recognition by NICE that the general public places special value on life-extending treatments for end of life patients, as long as the life extension is of a reasonable quality. However, NICE's public consultation [20] revealed concerns that there is little scientific evidence to support the premise that society wishes to give higher priority to end of life treatments than to other types of treatments. If this is *not* the case, and there is in fact no additional social value generated by extending the lives of patients with very short life expectancy, then giving higher priority to end of life treatments than to other types of treatments would mean that non-end of life patients could suffer unfairly if cost-effective treatments for their conditions are being displaced in favour of relatively cost-ineffective end of life treatments [23].

There are a few cases of NICE recommending life-extending end of life treatments that would not normally be considered cost-effective that predate the issuing of the supplementary guidance [24]. Subsequently, between January 2009 (when the supplementary advice was issued) and April 2011, NICE published technology appraisals of 70 individual technologies. Twenty-three of these technologies were considered under the end of life criteria as they were associated with patients with short life expectancy (i.e. less than 24 months). Of these technologies, 13 were considered to fulfil the criteria, and 8 of those were then recommended for use in the NHS [25]. In some cases – such as the appraisal of pemetrexed for the treatment of non-small cell lung cancer – the most plausible estimate of cost-effectiveness (£47,000 per QALY gained) was considerably greater than the range normally considered acceptable.

In Scotland, the Scottish Medicines Consortium (SMC) uses cost-effectiveness information when assessing new medicines, with other factors taken into consideration when the cost per QALY for a given medicine is relatively high. Following a parliamentary review, the Health and Sport Committee called on the SMC to revise its appraisal methods to take better account of orphan, ultra-orphan and end of life treatments. The Cabinet Secretary has directed the SMC "to apply different approaches in the evaluation of these medicines, including a rapid review of the wider aspects of value and QALYs in order to increase access to patients to these medicines" ([26], p. 5).

11.5   Review of the Empirical Evidence

There have been calls for research on whether society supports placing a premium on end of life treatments [27], and NICE itself has highlighted the need for exploration of the issues ([20], section 2.7). This section summarises a selection of recent research on society's preferences regarding end of life treatments (Table 11.1).

11.5.1   Studies Undertaken in the UK

Linley and Hughes [12] conducted a large-scale study of the preferences of 4,118 members of the general public in Great Britain regarding a variety of prioritisation criteria, including the so-called end of life premium. Respondents were asked how they would prefer NHS money to be spent when faced with a choice between treating one patient group with a life expectancy of 18 months and another patient group with a life expectancy of 60 months. The results suggest, all else being equal, that the end of life premium is not supported, with about two-thirds of respondents opting not to allocate more resources to the group with shorter life expectancy. When respondents were advised that the treatment for the non-end of life patients offered a life extension that was twice as large as that offered by the treatment for the end of life patients, there was a slight shift towards choosing the former group. The most popular choice, however, was to allocate an equal amount of funding to both groups.

In a study funded by the UK Department of Health, Rowen et al. [15] conducted a large-scale discrete choice experiment (DCE) ($N = 3,669$) which sought to elicit preferences to support QALY weights for use in the proposed value-based assessment scheme [28]. Respondents were asked to choose between alternatives that differed in terms of life expectancy (with and without treatment) and quality of life (with and without treatment). Each respondent was randomly allocated to one of four study versions, each of which presented a different level of life expectancy in the absence of disease (i.e. burden of illness) throughout the choice tasks. The authors reported robust and consistent support for an end of life premium, with respondents preferring to treat patients with shorter life expectancy without treatment. The results also indicated some support for giving priority to patients with relatively high levels of burden of illness, though the authors warn that on theoretical grounds end of life and burden of illness should not be used together, either in regressions or to weight QALY gains, as the two factors overlap conceptually (because end of life patients have high levels of survival-related burden, leading to collinearity).

Rowen et al. also included some follow-up attitudinal questions in which respondents were presented with various statements about how the NHS should make prioritisation decisions and were asked which they agreed with most. The responses to these questions cast some doubt on the strength of the DCE results, with, for example, only 12 % of respondents agreeing that "the NHS should give priority to extending the life of patients expected to die soon" (whereas 88 % of respondents agreed that priority should be given to those who will gain the largest benefits from treatment).

Shah et al. conducted two studies examining public preferences regarding end of life treatments. The first [16] was a small-scale study in which 50 respondents answered six questions asking them to choose which of two hypothetical patients they would prefer to treat, assuming that the health service has enough funds to treat one but not both of them. They reported some evidence of support for giving priority to the end of life patients – the majority of respondents chose to give a 6-month life extension to the patient with 1 year left to live without treatment rather than to the patient with 10 years left to live without treatment – but noted that a non-trivial minority of respondents expressed the opposite preference. They also observed preference for quality of life improvements over life extensions for end of life patients.

The authors' second study [17] was a large-scale DCE ($N = 3,969$) undertaken as part of a web-based survey. They used a similar study design and the same attributes as Rowen et al. [15], but focused on attribute levels that were close to the cut-offs implied by NICE's criteria for defining life-extending end of life treatments. In contrast to their previous study, this second study found little evidence that respondents on average were willing to sacrifice aggregate health gains in order to give priority to the treatment of end of life patients. The choices made about which patient to treat were dominated by the sizes of the health gains achievable from treatment. Most respondents chose to treat the end of life patient only when the benefits of treating that patient (in terms of QALYs gained) were similar to or greater than the benefits of treating the non-end of life patient. In another departure from the findings of their earlier study, the authors reported that life-extending treatments were valued more highly than quality of life-improving treatments that offer similar gains in terms of QALYs. The results of both studies suggest that people's preferences regarding the treatment of end of life patients may be driven by concerns about those patients' ability to "prepare for death" rather than the amount of time they have left to live per se.

In a small-scale exploratory study ($N=40$), Baker et al. [11] found that the majority of general public respondents in Scotland expressed preference for a treatment that offers a 3-month life extension to a relatively small number (five) of terminally ill cancer patients by a short duration over a treatment that offers an (unquantified) improvement in quality of life for a relatively large number (100) of patients with a non-life-threatening condition.

11.5.2   Studies Undertaken Outside of the UK

In a study of the preferences of members of the general public in Norway, Abel Olsen [10] found little evidence of support for giving higher priority to end of life treatments, with the majority of respondents choosing to prioritise the patient whose gains from treatment (life extensions) were largest. He reported that respondents were less interested in reducing inequalities in prospective health than in reducing inequalities in total lifetime health. He therefore concluded that "fair innings trumps the end of life argument", referring to the fact that a clear majority of respondents chose to reduce total lifetime inequalities despite a tenfold difference in proximity to death (p. 1065).

Pinto Prades et al. [14] used willingness-to-pay and person trade-off tasks to examine the preferences of 813 members of the general public in Spain. Respondents were asked to compare scenarios involving life-extending end of life treatments (with no quality of life improvement), palliative/quality of life-improving end of life treatments (with no life extension) and treatments offering temporary quality of life improvements for non-end of life patients. The scenarios were designed such that the gains offered by the competing treatment options were equal sized in QALY terms. The authors found that QALYs gained at the end of life were valued more highly than those gained from alleviating temporary health conditions and that quality of life-improving end of life treatments were valued more highly than life-extending end of life treatments. They also noted that the sample was divided into two groups – one group appeared not to place much value on 6-month (or even 18-month) life extensions for end of life treatments, whilst the other group was willing to pay substantially more for such treatments than for treatments offering temporary quality of life gains.

Skedgel et al. [18] conducted a DCE using a sample of the Canadian general public ($N=612$) and health-care decision makers ($N=44$). Although the overall direction of preferences observed in their study was largely consistent with their expectations based on the existing empirical ethics literature, the authors reported evidence of an overall aversion to treating patients with the shortest life expectancy (1 month) relative to those with longer life expectancies (5 and 10 years), all else being equal.

As part of a large-scale pan-European study ($N = 17,657$) seeking to develop methods for determining the monetary value of a QALY, Pennington et al. [13] presented respondents with a range of hypothetical scenarios each involving a gain of one QALY and sought their willingness to pay for that gain. They found that across countries the median values for life-extending QALYs were larger than those for quality of life-improving QALYs. The authors also reported evidence of a premium for end of life QALYs (i.e. life extension when facing imminent, premature death, as opposed to life extension at the end of one's natural life expectancy). However, they acknowledge that it is difficult to interpret willingness to pay valuations made by individuals facing the prospect of imminent death because the opportunity costs in those circumstances are low or nonexistent.

11.6   Selected Discussion Points

Since NICE issued its supplementary end of life policy in 2009, a number of researchers have attempted to use stated preference methods to examine whether society wishes to give higher priority to life-extending end of life treatments than to other types of treatments. The existing evidence is mixed, with some studies reporting strong evidence and others reporting little or no evidence of support for an end of life premium. Conflicting results have been reported even by studies that used very similar samples, study designs and methodologies to each other [15, 17]. Framing effects are likely to have driven some of the findings, as demonstrated by the observation by Rowen et al. [15] that many respondents in their study expressed support for prioritising life-extending end of life treatments in the DCE tasks but then gave responses to the attitudinal questions that suggested that they did not believe that the NHS should give priority to such treatments. A potential concern is that respondents being presented with complex DCE tasks do not always fully understand what is being asked of them. For example, they may have given responses that corresponded to the patient(s) they would prefer to be in the position of themselves rather than to the patient(s) they considered to be more deserving of treatment. A drawback of web-based surveys is that they offer limited opportunities for instructing and debriefing respondents, which makes it difficult to know for certain the extent to which the choice data truly reflect the respondents' beliefs and preferences (or whether the respondents interpreted and answered the questions as the researcher had intended them to).

The evidence is also mixed with regard to whether society considers life-extending or quality of life-improving end of life treatments to be more important. Pinto Prades et al. [14] and Shah et al. [16] both reported that when asked to choose between giving equal-sized (in QALY terms) life extensions and quality of life improvements to patients with short life expectancy, the majority of respondents in their respective studies preferred the quality of life improvements. By contrast, Rowen et al. [15] and Shah et al. [17] both reported regression analyses that suggested that life-extending treatments were valued more highly than quality of life-improving treatments overall. It is noteworthy that the current NICE policy involves giving greater weight to life-extending but not to quality of life-improving treatments for those at the end of life.

In empirical ethics research, it is often reported that there are sharp splits in public opinion with respondents dividing themselves into multiple subgroups with strongly opposing attitudes [29] – something that may be missed when reporting average values, therefore making it difficult to understand what the "overall" view of society is. Some of the studies mentioned above note that their respondents fell into two distinct groups – one that supported an end of life premium and another that did not (e.g. Pinto Prades [14]). However, few researchers have been able to demonstrate the types of sociodemographic and other background characteristics that predict whether a given respondent is likely to belong to one or another of these subgroups. Shah et al. [17] found that some respondents appeared to support a QALY-maximisation type objective, whilst other respondents always chose to prioritise the treatment of the patient with shorter life expectancy without treatment (though the majority seemed to advocate a mixture of the two approaches). They noted that membership of these subgroups was not particularly well predicted by any of the observable characteristics that they had collected information about. They also found the excluding from the sample respondents with experience of close friends or family members with terminal illness, or respondents with responsibility for children, did not have a major impact on the results. There may be characteristics that are more difficult to observe (such as cultural values) which are driving respondents' choices when faced with trade-offs involving end of life scenarios.

11.7   Future Research Agenda

Given the conflicting results reported to date, the question of whether society wishes to give higher priority to end of life treatments than to other types of treatments cannot yet be answered satisfactorily. The studies reviewed in this chapter have highlighted a number of issues that may warrant further investigation as we seek to improve our understanding of public preferences.

First, when asking respondents to complete abstract choice tasks (particularly in web-based surveys, which, as mentioned above, offer limited opportunity for interaction and feedback), it would be useful to understand the extent to which they agree with researchers' interpretation of their choices. A useful addition to future stated preference studies, particularly those administered in an unsupervised setting, would be to design follow-up questions which can be used to check whether respondents agree with the policy implications of their responses to the choice tasks.

Second, the majority of the studies described in this chapter required general public respondents to complete choice tasks (involving hypothetical scenarios) whilst adopting a societal or "caring for others" perspective. This is in contrast to standard welfare economic approaches, which are based on individuals' preferences for themselves. It would be interesting to compare end of life-related preferences elicited under a range of perspectives and to understand whether preferences for oneself correspond to preferences for others or whether public preferences correspond to the preferences of end of life patients and their family members.

Third, it has been found that people's preferences regarding the prioritisation of end of life treatments may be driven by concerns about the suddenness of the patients' disease onset, how long they have known about their prognosis and how much time they have to prepare for death. However, the evidence collected thus far is tempered by a number of caveats, so further, more robust investigation of preferences regarding "preparedness" is recommended.

Finally, given that we often observe two or more distinct groups with conflicting views – both within and across study samples – future research should investigate how best to aggregate and summarise elicited preferences in order to express the overall view of society.

Acknowledgements I am grateful for the contributions of Aki Tsuchiya and Allan Wailoo, who provided comments on draft versions of this book chapter. I would also like to thank Rachel Baker, Mark Pennington, Jose Luis Pinto Prades and Chris Skedgel for their suggestions and clarifications.

References

1. Drummond MF, Sculpher MJ, Torrance GW, O'Brien BJ, Stoddart GL (2005) Methods for the economic evaluation of healthcare programmes. Oxford University Press, Oxford
2. Culyer AJ (1997) Maximising the health of the whole community. In: New B (ed) Rationing: talk and action in health care. BMJ/King's Fund, London
3. Dolan P, Shaw R, Tsuchiya A, Williams A (2005) QALY maximisation and people's preferences: a methodological review of the literature. Health Econ 14:197–208
4. NICE (2013) Guide to the methods of technology appraisal 2013. National Institute for Health and Care Excellence, London
5. Department of Health (2003) Tackling health inequalities: a programme for action. Department of Health, London
6. Williams A (1996) QALYs and ethics: a health economist's perspective. Soc Sci Med 43(12):1795–1804
7. NICE (2008) Social value judgements: principles for the development of NICE guidance, 2nd edn. National Institute for Health and Care Excellence, London
8. Rawlins MD, Culyer AJ (2004) National Institute for Clinical Excellence and its value judgments. BMJ 329:224–227
9. Shah KK (2009) Severity of illness and priority setting in healthcare: a review of the literature. Health Policy 93:77–84
10. Abel Olsen J (2013) Priority preferences: "end of life" does not matter, but total life does. Value Health 16(6):1063–1066
11. Baker R, McHugh N, Mason H, Currie G, Donaldson C (2011) Valuing end of life technologies, investigating the existence of a 'cancer premium' and methodological questions for

health economics virtuous. Paper presented at the Health Economists' Study Group meeting, Bangor, 29 June–1 July 2011

12. Linley WG, Hughes DA (2013) Societal views on NICE, cancer drugs fund and value-based pricing criteria for prioritising medicines: a cross-sectional survey of 4118 adults in Great Britain. Health Econ 22(8):948–964

13. Pennington M, Baker R, Brouwer W, Mason H, Donaldson C, The EuroVaQ Team (2015) Comparing WTP values of different types of QALY gain elicited from the general public. Health Econ 24(3):280–293

14. Pinto-Prades JL, Sanchez-Martinez FI, Corbacho B, Baker R (2014) Valuing QALYs at the end of life. Soc Sci Med 113:5–14

15. Rowen D, Brazier J, Mukuria C, Keetharuth A, Risa Hole A, Tsuchiya A, Whyte S, Shackley P (2014) Update: eliciting societal preferences for weighting QALYs according to burden of illness, size of gain and end of life. EEPRU Research Report. Universities of Sheffield and York

16. Shah KK, Tsuchiya A, Wailoo AJ (2014) Valuing health at the end of life: an empirical study of public preferences. Eur J Health Econ 15:389–399

17. Shah K, Tsuchiya A, Wailoo A (2015) Valuing health at the end of life: a stated preference discrete choice experiment. Soc Sci Med 124:48–56

18. Skedgel C, Wailoo A, Akehurst R (2015) Societal preferences for distributive justice in the allocation of healthcare resources: a latent class discrete choice experiment. Med Decis Making 35:94–105

19. NICE (2009) Appraising life-extending, end of life treatments. National Institute for Health and Care Excellence, London

20. NICE (2009) End of life treatments: summary response to consultation. National Institute for Health and Care Excellence, London

21. NICE (2009) Appraising life-extending, end of life treatments. Revised in July 2009. National Institute for Health and Care Excellence, London

22. Rawlins M, Barnett D, Stevens A (2010) Pharmacoeconomics: NICE's approach to decision-making. Br J Clin Pharmacol 70(3):346–349

23. Collins M, Latimer N (2013) NICE's end of life decision making scheme: impact on population health. BMJ 346:f1363

24. Shah KK, Cookson R, Culyer AJ, Littlejohns P (2013) NICE's social value judgements about equity in health and health care. Health Econ Policy Law 8(2):145–165

25. Trowman R, Chung H, Longson C, Littlejohns P, Clark P (2011) The National Institute for Health and Clinical Excellence and its role in assessing the value of new cancer treatments in England and Wales. Clin Cancer Res 17:4930–4935

26. Scottish Government (2013) Response to the Health and Sport Committee inquiry into access to new medicines. Available via: http://www.scottish.parliament.uk/S4_HealthandSportCommittee/Inquiries/Scottish_Government_Response_-_Access_into_New_Medicines.pdf. Accessed 6 Aug 2015

27. Green C (2011) Looking for the 'values' to inform value-based pricing: a review of the empirical ethics (equity) evidence! Paper presented at the Health Economists' Study Group meeting, Bangor, 29 June–1 July 2011

28. NICE (2014) Value based assessment of health technologies. National Institute for Health and Care Excellence, London

29. Schwappach DLB (2002) Resource allocation, social values and the QALY: a review of the debate and empirical evidence. Health Expect 5:210–222

Chapter 12
What About Informal Carers and Families?

Claire Hulme, Fiona Carmichael, and David Meads

12.1 Background

Care for people at the end of life is complex; it includes management of pain and other symptoms and the provision of psychological, social, spiritual and practical support [1]. Changing demographics mean that people are living longer and there is an increase in the number of older people who are frail and living with co-morbidities. Caring for this group requires the involvement of a wide range of health and social care professions with the aim to support people approaching the end of their life to live as well as possible until they die. The financial costs to the health and social care sectors are high. This is partly explained by the use of hospital beds as many people are admitted as inpatients as they approach death [2, 3]. Over the last century, there was a trend in many countries towards an increase in deaths in hospital whilst fewer people died at home [4]. Though this trend is slowing or reversing in many countries, including Canada, the USA and more recently the UK [4], most people still die in hospital. In the UK in 2007, over half of patients with cancer died in NHS hospitals, 17 % in hospices and 5 % in nursing homes [5]. These figures are often used to illustrate the impact on, or cost to, the health-care sector of end-of-life care. However, they belie the fact that over the final 6 months of life, the majority of time is spent at home and that most people prefer to die at home [1, 6, 7]. Whilst the third sector provides assistance with care in the home, family and friends take a central role in providing support whether the patient is at home or

C. Hulme (✉) • D. Meads
Academic Unit of Health Economics, Leeds Institute of Health Sciences,
University of Leeds, Leeds, UK
e-mail: c.t.hulme@leeds.ac.uk

F. Carmichael
Department of Management, Birmingham Business School,
University of Birmingham, Birmingham, UK

© Springer International Publishing Switzerland 2016
J. Round (ed.), *Care at the End of Life: An Economic Perspective*,
DOI 10.1007/978-3-319-28267-1_12

elsewhere [8]. Indeed, family and friends are the main providers of both long-term and end-of-life care [9].

Friends and family who provide this type of support or care are known as informal carers. Although individuals often don't recognise themselves as carers, they are people who look after a relative or friend who needs support because of age, physical or learning disability or illness, including mental illness [10, 11]. Estimates of the number of individuals who provide informal care vary from country to country. For example, in the USA, it has been posited that there are around 70 million informal carers making up 29 % of the adult population, whilst in the UK, there are around 5.8 million informal carers representing around one tenth of the total population [12, 13].

The people who provide informal care span gender, age and ethnicity; in the UK, as in many other countries, the older generation supplies a disproportionate amount of informal care with over 16 % of those aged >65 years providing some form of care [14], and there is a small but growing body of literature aimed at understanding the caring contribution of older people [15–19]. However, the peak age for becoming an informal carer is between 45 and 64 years of age [20], and, as in many other countries, women are more likely than men to provide unpaid care [21, 22] although this has become less weighted in recent years [14]. Among people of working age, the economically inactive are most likely to be carers although in the UK around three million workers also provide informal care [23].

In general terms, the scope of informal care is wide ranging, including personal care, monitoring medication and practical tasks such as shopping and household chores as well as emotional support [11, 14]. This practical and emotional support is echoed in end-of-life care with family and friends also providing nursing care and administering medication [9]. Additionally, as the person they care for approaches the end of life, the informal carer will often take a lead role in coordinating, chasing and communicating with the professionals involved in the care [24]. The time given to care also tends to increase as the health of the cared-for deteriorates and the closer they are to death [25]. Informal care has been found to be a significant substitute for formal long-term care [26]. Whilst estimates for the economic value of informal care vary considerably, the scale of the contribution to the economy is agreed to be considerable. For example, Carers UK estimate the value of informal care to be £119 billion per annum which is greater than NHS spending; in the USA, AARP Public Policy estimates place informal carers' contribution at $450 billion per annum [12, 27].

The estimates and figures above provide a revealing insight into the economic costs of informal care. In this chapter focus lies on the financial implications to individuals and their families of supporting a family member or friend at the end of life. Whilst in general terms the financial implications of informal care are well documented, they are less so within the context of end-of-life care [28] and as such we draw on both sets of literature. It is also important to note that defining end of life is complicated; there may be no clear-cut point for an individual patient as to when end-of-life care begins [1]. Thus, the duration and therefore impact of the illness is often much longer and the impact of any long-term condition is wide ranging, potentially affecting the income and increasing risk of poverty [29, 30].

The chapter is structured into three sections: Sect. 12.2 describes out of pocket expenses, Sect. 12.3 discusses work-related implications (changes to employment) and Sect. 12.4 concludes with discussion of the impact of financial costs and government policies aimed to provide financial support for informal carers.

12.2   Out of Pocket Expenses

Family or friends often incur out of pocket expenses as a result of providing informal care. These expenses span a range of items including day to day costs due to conditions and/or symptoms such as travel and parking expenses for hospital visits; treatment costs including the cost of medication or diet and one large one-off costs such as the need to move house to be closer to the person being cared for in order to be on hand to provide support or home modification. Gardiner et al. [28] in their recent review of the financial impact of palliative and end-of-life care found a wide variety of out of pocket expenses to the informal carer. These included medical equipment, prescription and non-prescription drugs, nursing home expenses, private care home, travel expenses and childcare costs. The authors report that these expenses varied across country and health system and that some carers sold assets or took out loans to meet these expenses. Health-care systems also play a part – countries with comprehensive public funding reported less out of pocket medication, physician and home care costs [28]. This is borne out by evidence from the UK, which provides more comprehensive public funding than, say, the USA, in which travel costs, rather than medication, are one of the most frequently cited out of pocket costs.

A recent study from New Zealand considered the financial costs faced by family and caregivers within a palliative care context [31]. Their findings concurred with Gardiner's inasmuch as parking and transport costs and medical treatment were identified, but also included medical costs for the carer, for example, physiotherapy for back injury from lifting or costs relating to treatment for anxiety, depression and insomnia. This also highlights the potential for the negative impact of caring on carers' health [32]. Carers as a group suffer disproportionately from ill health and lower well-being [33]. More intensive caring roles, caring roles in which the care recipient is strongly related to the carer and transitions into caring roles, have been associated with lower levels of well-being [34–37]. Schulz et al. [38] found that a lack of choice in becoming an informal caregiver among carers of older people was associated with greater emotional stress, physical strain and negative health effects.

Gott et al. [31] also highlight the cost of food of the person they cared for. Food has been identified in previous studies and an important expense (see, e.g. [39]). However, Gott et al. seek to explain this further in the end of life context inasmuch as carers had a sense of urgency about meeting the person's needs, regardless of cost, as death approached. This was for a number of reasons, for example, carers may buy special food to satisfy the cultural preferences of the dying individual or source luxury items to 'tempt' their family member to eat when appetite was poor [31].

Other increased or additional household costs might include higher heating and laundry bills [27, 31].

Out of pocket expenses represent an unequal burden with those in the lowest income distributions spending the highest proportion of their income [40]. In their study of medical expenditures at the end of life, McGarry and Schoeni report average out of pocket medical expenses in the final 2 years of life equal to 30 % of annual income, but for those in the bottom quarter of the income distribution, this increases to 70 %. For those in this latter group, this is likely to represent a severe financial strain; for those families and individuals experiencing financial hardship as a result of caring for someone at the end of their life, there may also be implications for the medical services the person being cared for uses. The *insurance effect* suggests intensive services may be utilised in the last week of life despite a small chance of benefit as the cost is borne by the insurer rather than as an out of pocket expense by the family [41].

12.3   Employment Costs

It is well documented that in caring for a relative or friend who needs support because of age, physical or learning disability or illness, the individual is likely to impact on the carers' paid employment [42]. This may be through giving up paid work to care or reducing hours of paid employment, and if the carer has given up work, subsequently returning to employment can be difficult. Employment decisions are affected by a number of factors including *the duration of a caring episode, financial considerations, the needs of the person they care for, carers' beliefs about the compatibility of informal care and paid work and employers' willingness to accommodate carers' needs* [16, p 3]. These factors are no less relevant for individuals caring at the end of life; indeed, as mentioned earlier, the duration an individual has been providing care and therefore the impact is often much longer than the definition that end-of-life care implies. Carers providing support for an individual at the end of life report having given up work, reduced hours of work or having used annual leave or sick leave to cope with demands of caregiving [28, 43]. In the UK a survey of 3,400 carers found that 83 % report a negative impact of caring on their physical health and 87 % on their mental health with 37 % of carers aged 18–64 ceasing work because of their caring responsibilities [32].

However, the decision to give up work is not an easy one since it can put the carer and their family under considerable financial pressure [44]. Additionally for those carers not in paid work, their caring responsibilities can mean a cut in their benefit entitlement as they cannot actively look for work [31]. For some low-paid workers, a rise in wages or increase in hours may mean a cut in benefits leaving them no better off [44]. Whilst self-employment can allow greater flexibility, it also means there are typically no paid leave provisions [31]. Gott et al. describe one self-employed participant in their study whose *income halved when caring for his wife who had to leave her full-time job, leaving him with the 'balancing act' of trying to work, care for two children and care for her. After her death, he was forced to sell the family home and buy a smaller, more affordable property* [31, p 4]. The increasing trend towards individuals' desire to die at home can also incur a financial cost to carers who have to give up work to provide full-time care. This may be exacerbated by official policy that encourages people to die in their place of choice if sufficient formal support is not made available.

There is a strong belief among informal carers themselves that their caring responsibilities affect employment. Carers face considerable constraints on their time and there is a significant time investment required by any carer of a patient at end of life [28]. Previous studies have quantified this time investment by either quantifying caregiver time or quantifying the proportion of total care costs met by informal caregivers [28]. However, Gardiner and colleagues [28] report that estimates vary widely across countries and are also highly dependent on the method used – for example, the human capital approach in which estimates use gross earnings or the friction cost method where production lost depends on the time needed for organisations to restore the initial production level [45].

Not only do carers face constraints on their time, but those who remain in paid work also have particular needs that employers are sometimes unwilling or unable to meet. These difficulties lead some carers to give up paid work completely and make it impossible for others to return to employment after a period of time outside the labour market. Carers who want to take on paid work have therefore needed to adopt various strategies in order do so. These include working part-time, changing jobs and working for particular employers who embrace carer-friendly practices.

Some people may have a choice about whether to care, but other people, perhaps those who are less wealthy or who have no siblings or other close relatives with whom to share their caring responsibilities or those who feel a strong obligation or duty to care, will have less choice as the alternatives will be limited. Gendered norms of responsibility can also mean that the pressure to undertake care is even stronger for women. Furthermore, the time and effort involved in informal care and the strategies adopted by carers in order to make it easier for them to combine work and care are likely to lead to an erosion of a caregiver's human capital and consequently restrict their employment opportunities still further. This amounts to a gradual, drip-drip effect that weakens carers' longer-term employment prospects and ultimately their labour market attachment. This trend is likely to become more difficult to reverse the longer the duration of an individual caring episode. When a long caring episode does end, some carers can find themselves stranded without a job and without any state support. Older female carers in particular may find it difficult to return to employment when their caring episode ends because of gendered ageism in employment [44].

12.4   Overall Impact and the Role of Government Support

Informal care has myriad financial implications for the carer and their family. It can affect employment, earnings and expenditure in multiple ways: there may be a substitution effect whereby the time commitment leads the carer to substitute unpaid for paid work (worsening their financial situation); the extra financial expenditure associated with informal care may lead to increased hours of employment (the income effect); there may be a respite effect whereby the desire for a break from the emotional demands of caring can lead to increased hours of employment; and an earnings effect in which the demands of caring restrict hours of employment and therefore limits job opportunities, for example, to jobs with more flexible hours which are typically located in part-time employment where average earnings are lower [46].

Caring is often most intense at the end of life with a high burden placed on the caregiver. In addition carers may have multiple roles including paid employment or other family responsibilities [43]. Gardiner et al. [29] highlight life changes that are often required due to cost of illness. These include moving house, delayed medical care for other family members and changes to working hours. They go on to say that this can lead to inability to function normally, increased worry, difficulties coping, family conflict and caregiver strain. The financial costs of caring therefore outlast the period of care resulting in severe long-term financial hardship including debt or in extreme cases even bankruptcy [31, 47].

There is also evidence that the financial costs of informal care are not borne equally. Carers are more likely to be women [48] and financial strain has a greater impact on those in lower socioeconomic groups and for ethnic minorities [28], although financial hardship associated with age is less clear cut [28].

It is clear that the financial impacts are set in the context of family and other support networks, for the carer as well as the person being cared for. Gott et al. [31] propose a framework that takes into account how costs operate at a number of levels: personal, interpersonal, sociocultural and structural (Fig. 12.1).

The outer circle, the structural dimension, includes government policies (employment, health care, social services); moving towards the centre, the sociocultural includes social norms and views, community and neighbourhood supports; the personal includes income and employment, economic resources, values and motivation to care; the interpersonal includes relationships with the care receiver, links with other carers, other care needs and assertiveness in dealing with the system. In their study they conclude that in the palliative care context, for the carer, meeting needs was prioritised over costs and that support from statutory services and access to financial support were limited.

There has been a move towards supporting carers at end of life. In the UK the End of Life Care Strategy recognises the *physical, psychological, social, financial and spiritual consequences* of supporting someone who is nearing end of life [1, p 107]. In terms of financial help, there is a Carer's Allowance to help look after someone with substantial caring needs – albeit this is a generic grant for which anyone aged over 16 years and spending at least 35 h a week caring can apply (though access is limited by earnings and hours of employment). In addition the person being cared for can apply for a personal health budget which can be used to pay for a wide range of items and services, including social care, therapies, personal care and equipment [49]. Other countries have instigated programmes whereby the carer receives money to purchase formal services or pay the caregiver in kind (Austria, France, Germany) [43]. However, the amount of these benefits is typically

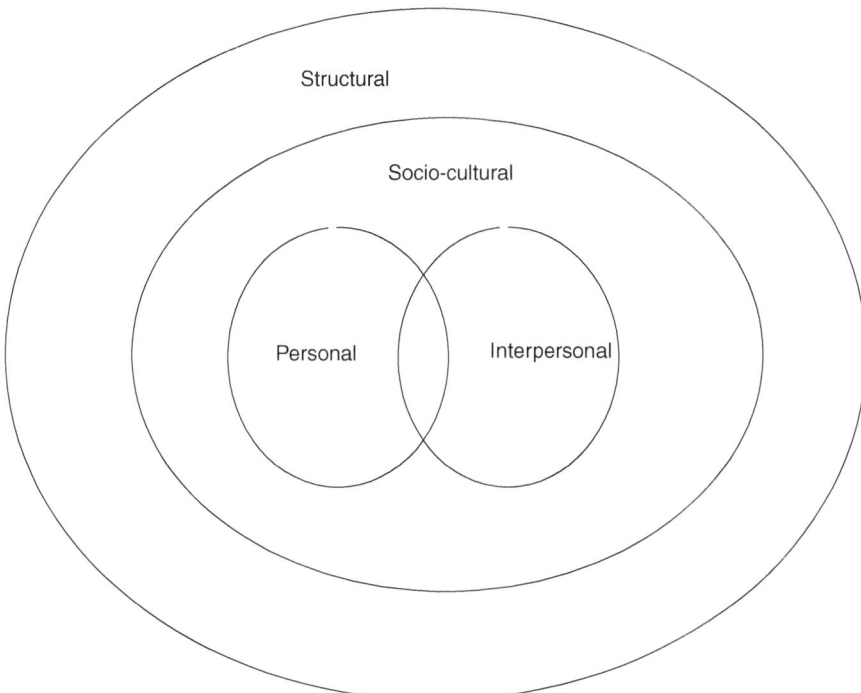

Fig. 12.1 Framework of dimensions that influence financial costs of care (Adapted from Gott et al. [31])

small representing less than 30 % of the average wage, and it can lead to the creation of informal markets which in Austria and, to an extent, Germany has led to a reliance on undocumented migrant carers [50]. In many countries, like the UK, payment of benefits is often dependent on provision of full-time care which limits paid or full-time employment (e.g. Ireland, Norway, Slovenia) [50].

Although few policies focus on specifically for individuals caring for someone at end of life, in Canada, employed carers caring for someone at end of life can apply for the Compassionate Care Benefit. The benefit is delivered through Employment Insurance and allows paid leave from work whilst maintaining job security [43]. However, as Gardiner et al. suggest [28], *ongoing assessment of the financial impact on family caregivers may enable earlier intervention and provision of support and prevent carer breakdown. Early interventions could include financial planning as part of a palliative care package of services, to aid family caregivers in planning and managing finances, and accessing sources of financial support* (p 388). Whilst government support is moving in the right direction in these respects, there needs to be greater recognition of the costs (financial and other) faced by family caregivers at the end of life.

In summary, informal carers are a large, and often hidden, population. As a group they span gender, age and ethnicity. The scope of informal care is wide ranging, including personal care, monitoring medication and practical tasks such as shopping and household chores as well as emotional support [10, 11]. This is echoed in end-of-life care with family and friends also providing nursing care and administering medication [9]. The financial costs of caring for a person at end of life include out of pocket costs or expenses. The scale and nature of out of pocket costs incurred by caregivers varies widely; they include transport costs, food, moving house and delayed medical care for other family members. The impact on employment may include having to give up work, reduce hours of work or use of annual leave or sick leave to cope with demands of caregiving, and if the carer has given up work, subsequently returning to employment can be difficult [28, 43].

The impact of these costs depends in part on the nature of the health-care system with countries with comprehensive public funding reporting less out of pocket expenditure on medication, physician and home care [28]. There is also evidence that the financial costs of informal care are not borne equally. Carers are more likely to be women [48], and financial strain has a greater impact on those in lower socioeconomic groups and for ethnic minorities [28]. In addition, the financial costs of caring can often outlast the period of care resulting in severe long-term financial hardship including debt or in extreme cases even bankruptcy [31, 47].

Despite the evidence illustrating the financial costs, and potentially devastating impact of providing informal care at end of life (and more widely), there still appears to be limited access to financial support for carers. Whilst there is increased recognition within government policies of the contribution of informal carers, financial support often comes with a trade-off in terms of restrictions on employment [50].

References

1. Department of Health (2008) End of life care strategy promoting high quality care for all adults at the end of life. Department of Health, London, https://www.gov.uk/government/uploads/system/uploads/attachment_data/file/136431/End_of_life_strategy.pdf. Accessed 28 Nov 2014
2. Costantini M, Higginson IJ, Boni L, Orengo MA, Garrone E, Henriquet F, Bruzzi P (2003) Effect of a palliative home care team on hospital admissions among patients with advanced cancer. Palliat Med 17(4):315–321
3. Jordhøy MS, Fayers P, Saltnes T, Ahlner-Elmqvist M, Jannert M, Kaasa S (2000) A palliative-care intervention and death at home: a cluster randomised trial. Lancet 356(9233):888–893
4. Higginson I, Sarmento VP, Calanzani N, Benalia H, Gomes B (2013) Dying at home – is it better: a narrative appraisal of the state of the science. Palliat Med 0(0):1–7. doi:10.1177/0269216313487940
5. National Audit Office (2008) End of life care. The Stationery Office, Norwich, Available on line: http://www.nao.org.uk/wp-content/uploads/2008/11/07081043.pdf
6. Gomes B, Calanzani N, Gysels M, Hall S, Higginson IJ (2013) Heterogeneity and changes in preferences for dying at home: a systematic review. Palliat Care 12:7. doi:10.1186/1472-684X-12-7
7. Higginson IJ, Sen-Gupta GJA (2000) Place of care in advanced cancer: a qualitative systematic literature review of patient preferences. J Palliat Med 3:287–300

8. Candy B, Jones L, Drake R, Leurent B, King M (2011) Interventions for supporting informal caregivers of patients in the terminal phase of a disease. Cochrane Database Syst Rev (6):CD007617. doi:10.1002/14651858.CD007617.pub2
9. Wolff JL, Dy SM, Frick KD, Kasper JD (2007) End of life care. Findings from a national survey of informal caregivers. Arch Intern Med 167(1):40–46. doi:10.1001/archinte.167.1.40
10. Department of Health (2005) Caring about carers: government information for carers. Available online at: www.carers.gov.uk/
11. Macmillan Cancer Support (2011) Understanding the UK's carers of people with cancer – a report by Ipsos Mori for Macmillan Cancer Support. http://www.macmillan.org.uk/Documents/Cancerinfo/Ifsomeoneelsehascancer/More_than_a_million.pdf. Accessed 28 Nov 2014
12. National Alliance for Caregiving and AARP (2009) Caregiving in the U.S. National Alliance for Caregiving, Washington, DC
13. White C (2011) Census analysis: unpaid care in England and Wales, 2011 and comparison with 2001. http://www.ons.gov.uk/ons/dcp171766_300039.pdf. Accessed 28 Nov 2014
14. Beesley L (2006) Wanless social care review: informal care in England. Kings Fund, London, http://www.kingsfund.org.uk/sites/files/kf/informal-care-england-wanless-background-paper-lucinda-beesley2006.pdf. Accessed 28 Nov 2014
15. Buckner LJ, Yeandle SM (2007) Valuing carers: calculating the value of unpaid care, research report prepared for Carers UK. Carers UK, London
16. Carmichael F, Ercolani MG (2014) Overlooked and undervalued: the caring contribution of older people. Int J Soc Econ 41(5):397–419
17. Dahlberg L, Demack S, Bambra C (2007) Age and gender of informal carers: a population-based study in the UK. Health Soc Care Commun 5:439–445
18. McGarry J, Arthur A (2001) Informal caring in late life: a qualitative study of the experiences of older carers. J Adv Nurs 33:182–189
19. Vlachantoni A (2010) The demographic characteristics and economic activity patterns of carers over 50: evidence from the English Longitudinal Study of Ageing. Popul Trends 141:1–23
20. Arksey H, Kemp P, Glendinning C, Kotchetkova I, Tozer R (2005) Department for work and pensions, research report 290. Department for Work and Pensions, Research Report 290, Her Majesty's Stationery Office, Norwich
21. Eaton SC (2005) Eldercare in the United States: inadequate, inequitable, but not a lost cause. Fem Econ 11(2):37–51
22. Lázaro N, Moltó M-L, Sanchez R (2004) Paid employment and unpaid caring work in Spain. Appl Econ 36(9):977–986
23. Yeandle S, Bennett C, Buckner L, Shipton L, Suokas A (2006) Who cares wins: the social and business benefits of supporting working carers. Report to Carers UK. Centre for Social Inclusion, Sheffield Hallam University: Sheffield
24. National Council for Palliative Care (2013) Who cares? Support for carers of people approaching end of life. http://www.ncpc.org.uk/sites/default/files/Who_Cares_Conference_Report.pdf. Accessed 28 Nov 2014
25. Dumont S, Jacobs P, Turcotte V, Anderson D, Harel F (2010) Measurement challenges of informal caregiving: a novel measurement method applied to a cohort of palliative care patients. Soc Sci Med 71:1890–1895
26. Van Houtven CH, Norton EC (2004) Informal care and health care use of older adults. J Health Econ 23(6):1159–1180
27. Carers UK (2014) Facts about carers. http://www.carersuk.org/for-professionals/policy/policy-library/facts-about-carers-2014. Accessed 1 Apr 2015
28. Gardiner C, Brereton L, Frey R, Wilkinson-Meyers L, Gott M (2014) Exploring the financial impact of caring for family members receiving palliative and end of life care: a systematic review of the literature. Palliat Med 28(5):375–390
29. Department of Health (2013) 2010 to 2015 government policy: long term health conditions. https://www.gov.uk/government/policies/improving-quality-of-life-for-people-withlong-term-conditions. Accessed 23 Sept 2013

30. Joseph Rowntree Foundation (2007) Long-term ill health, poverty and ethnicity. http://www. jrf.org.uk/sites/files/jrf/1995-health-ethnicity-poverty.pdf. Accessed 23 Sept 2013
31. Gott M, Allen R, Moeke-Maxwell T, Gardiner C, Robinson J (2015) No matter what the cost: a qualitative study of the financial costs faced by family and whānau caregivers within a pallia- tive care context. Palliat Med 2015 June. 29(6):518–528. pii: 0269216315569337. [Epub ahead of print]
32. Carers UK (2012) In sickness and in health. http://www.carersuk.org/36-for-professionals/ report/128-in-sickness-and-in-health. Accessed 28 Nov 2014
33. ONS (2013) 2011 census analysis: unpaid care in England and Wales, 2011 and comparison with 2001. http://www.ons.gov.uk/ons/rel/census/2011-census-analysis/provision-of-unpaid- care-in-england-and-wales – 2011/art-provision-of-unpaid-care.html
34. Dolan P, Peasgood T, White M (2008) Do we really know what makes us happy? A review of the economics literature on the factors associated with subjective well-being. J Econ Psychol 29:94–122
35. Hirst M (2005) Carer distress: a prospective, population-based study. Soc Sci Med 61:697–708
36. Marks N, Lambert J, Choi H (2002) Transitions to caregiving, gender and psychological well- being: a prospective US national study. J Marriage Fam 64:657–667
37. Van Den Berg B, Ferrer-I-Carbonell A (2007) Monetary valuation of informal care: the well- being valuation method. Health Econ 16:1227–1244
38. Schulz R, Beach S, Cook T, Martire L, Tomlinson J, Monin J (2012) Predictors and conse- quences of perceived lack of choice in becoming an informal caregiver. Aging Ment Health 16:712–721
39. Macmillan (2013) Cancer's hidden price tag: revealing the costs behind the illness. http:// www.macmillan.org.uk/Documents/GetInvolved/Campaigns/Costofcancer/ TheCostofCancercampaignreport.pdf. Accessed 28 Nov 2014
40. McGarry K, Schoeni RF (2005) Widow(er) poverty and out-of-pocket medical expenditures near the end of life. J Gerontol B Psychol Sci Soc Sci 60(3):S160–S168
41. Tucker Seeley RD, Abel GA, Uni H, Prigerson H (2015) Financial hardship and the intensity of medical care received near death. Psychooncology 24(5):572–578. doi:10.1002/pon.3624
42. Lilly MB, Laporte A, Coyte PC (2007) Labor market work and home care's unpaid caregivers: a systematic review of labor force participation rates, predictors of labor market withdrawal, and hours of work. Milbank Q 85(4):641–690
43. Williams AM, Wang L, Kitchen P (2015) Impacts of caregiving and sources of support: a comparison of end of life care and non-end of life caregivers in Canada. Health Soc Care Commun. doi:10.1111/hsc.12205
44. Carmichael F, Hulme C, Sheppard S (2008) Work – life imbalance: informal care and paid employment in the UK. Fem Econ 14(2):3–35. doi:10.1080/13545700701881005
45. Drummond MF, Sculpher MJ, Torrance GW, O'Brien BJ, Stoddart GL (2005) Methods for the economic evaluation of health care programmes. Oxford University Press, Oxford
46. Anderson G, Carmichael F, Connell G, Hulme C, Sheppard S (2005) Informal care and unequal opportunities in the formal care market. University of Salford, Salford
47. Payne S, Grande G (2013) Towards better support for family carers: a richer understanding. Palliat Med 27(7):570–580
48. Carmichael F, Charles S (2003) The opportunity cost of informal care: does gender matter? J Health Econ 22:781–803
49. Department of Health (2010) End of life care planning with people who have a personal health budget. Discussion paper September 2010. http://www.personalhealthbudgets.england.nhs. uk/_library/Resources/Personalhealthbudgets/EOLC_discussion_paper_Sep_10.pdf. Accessed 1 Mar 2015
50. Hoffmann F, Rodriques R (2010) Informal carers: who takes care of them? European Centre. Policy Brief April 2010. European Centre for Social Welfare Policy and Research, Vienna

Chapter 13
Measuring and Valuing Health-Related Quality of Life in Children with Terminal and Life-Limiting Illness

Katherine Stevens and Jeff Round

13.1   Introduction

The concept of quality of life is necessarily vague. The meaning of the term is often dependent on the user and the population or individual under consideration [1]. The concept of quality of life has been central to discussions of western philosophy and politics for thousands of years and is central to the decision-making process of individuals and societies today. Many have tried to define it and measure it, though no consensus view on what it means or how it should be assessed has emerged. Often in economic evaluations of health-care interventions, it is restricted to mean health-related quality of life, though even this leaves a yawning chasm from which significant debate arises. This is no different when researchers turn their attention to measuring and valuing the quality of life of children or those at the end of life (as seen elsewhere in this volume).

That children are not just little adults is often either ignored or not considered important by researchers. But there exist important differences between children and adults that affect the ways in which we must understand and measure health-related quality of life. These include important physical and cognitive differences between children and adults, differences in the types and severity of illnesses that affect children and methodological and ethical issues related to conducting research in children. The physical and cognitive differences between children and adults and between different age groups within the child population are reflected in a number of areas. These include issues related to understanding which domains of life

K. Stevens (✉)
School of Health and Related Research, The University of Sheffield, Regent Court, Sheffield, UK
e-mail: k.stevens@sheffield.ac.uk

J. Round
Lecturer in Health Economics, School of Social and Community Medicine,
University of Bristol, Canynge Hall, Bristol, UK

© Springer International Publishing Switzerland 2016
J. Round (ed.), *Care at the End of Life: An Economic Perspective*,
DOI 10.1007/978-3-319-28267-1_13

children consider to be important [2], the physiological and mental development of children from birth to adulthood [3] and the social context in which children find themselves in relation to age-centred social roles, including aspects of life related to dependence and autonomy [4].

Aristotle may have argued that death was a preferable outcome for an adult than a reversion to the life of a child [5], but it is clear that at present, the prevailing outlook on the role of children in society is not so unkind. Great attention is now beginning to be paid to the unique methodological concerns faced by researchers when measuring the quality of life of child populations [4, 6–8]. A common approach in the past has been to use measures of quality of life developed for use in adults in a population of children. Though it is possible that this may be appropriate in a minority of cases, best practice would dictate that measures that are to be used in any population, including populations of children, should be developed and tested in line with the established standards of measurement science [9].

In this chapter we provide an overview of the difficulties in measuring and valuing paediatric quality of life, with a particular emphasis on doing so in populations of children with terminal or life-limiting illnesses. We raise a number of questions we believe researchers should ask themselves when deciding how to measure quality of life for the purposes of economic evaluation. In particular, we discuss what domains of health should be measured, who should undertake the measurement and using which instrument.

13.2   What Should Be Measured?

A first key issue in paediatric outcome measurement and valuation is what should be measured. An instrument used for measuring health-related quality of life should contain dimensions that are relevant to the purpose of the specific evaluation being undertaken. For health-care resource allocation decision making concerning paediatric populations, the dimensions should be relevant to the health of children and measure the impact of health problems on children's health-related quality of life. While it is possible to measure a near-limitless number of dimensions of life, they must still bear a direct relevance to the health of the individuals. Those dimensions that are related to other (still important) areas are perhaps not appropriate within a measure focused on health. While we might consider within health dimensions relating to physical and social functioning or mental well-being, other dimensions based on housing or income (such as having enough food, clothes or toys) are less directly relevant; these dimensions are unlikely to be directly or significantly affected by health-care resource allocation decisions.

It is also important that the dimensions are pertinent and of relevance to the population being studied. Several adult preference-based measures have existed for a number of years, such as the EQ-5D [10] and the SF-6D [11]; however, their application in a paediatric population is questionable. They may contain dimensions that are not relevant to children (such as work) and also may not contain dimensions that are pertinent in children's lives, for example, school or particular activities. There has been a growing recognition that children have their own unique views and a right to express them in matters affecting them [12]. This is of particular importance in health where the ways in which health conditions affect children may not necessarily be the ways that parents and/or health-care professionals believe.

A particular difficulty is ensuring that the dimensions are relevant to children of all ages. Definitions of who is a child typically cover an age range from birth to 17 years. Within this span, there is a huge range of developmental differences and stages of a child's life where particular dimensions may or may not be relevant. The age group in which this is perhaps most an issue is in children under 5 years of age. By the time children reach school age (around 5 years), most of the largest developmental stages have occurred. For example, most children over 5 years of age can walk and talk and are capable of providing some information about how they are feeling. This is not necessarily the case in the under-5 age group whose abilities vary greatly both across and within age bands. This raises particular difficulties for measuring health-related quality of life, where changes arising from normal natural development may confound measurement scales. For example, if you are measuring mobility, then a child's ability to walk might be a good item in a measure. However, a child who is still crawling would score poorly on such an item, due to their particular development stage, not due to a problem with mobility. Given the natural differences in ages at which developmental milestones occur, even a well-designed measure could be afflicted by such confounding, highlighting the importance of ensuring that instruments and outcome measures reflect the population being studied.

When thinking about end-of-life care and children who have terminal illnesses, there may also be additional dimensions of health-related quality of life that are relevant (and perhaps some which may no longer be relevant). Johnston in this volume provides an overview of the debate surrounding the appropriateness of the current economic evaluation framework in end-of-life care, including the measurement and valuation of quality-of-life outcomes. Little research has been undertaken to evaluate the use of health-related quality-of-life instruments specifically in paediatric palliative care populations. A review of studies that included HRQoL data collection found that the most commonly used instrument was the Paediatric Quality of Life 4.0 Generic Score Scales (PedsQL) [13]. The authors went on to assess this instrument in a paediatric palliative care population and found that it lacked valid psychometric properties. In particular, they found that the PedsQL lacked construct validity, suggesting that the instrument did not measure domains of life important to the paediatric palliative care population. We are not aware of any studies that assess the suitability of preference-based generic measures of HRQoL in paediatric palliative care populations.

13.2.1 Existing Preference-Based Measure of General HRQoL

Existing generic preference-based measures for children have all taken different approaches to determining what should be measured. The Quality of Well-Being (QWB) was developed to measure health outcomes for both adults and children. It draws its items mainly from an existing US Health Interview Survey, a Social

Security Administration Survey and several rehabilitation scales and ongoing community surveys [14].

The Health Utilities Index 2, the first preference-based measure developed specifically for use in a paediatric population, generated its dimensions by conducting a large review of existing paediatric measures and pooling candidate attributes together [15]. They then undertook research with child and parent dyads to rank the attributes and thus determine which were most important. This led to the development of an instrument for generic use with six dimensions – sensation, mobility, emotion, cognition, self-care and pain. The original descriptive system also includes a fertility dimension as it was developed for use in oncology where preservation of future fertility was considered to be important. By assuming fertility to be normal, the measure can be used as a generic instrument.

The 16D and 17D were developed for adolescents (12–15 years [16]) and children (8–11 years [17]), respectively, from the original instrument developed for adults, the 15D. Many of the dimensions from the adult measure were kept and some additional ones added.

The EQ-5DY has been developed in more recent years and has also been adapted from the adult version, the EQ-5D, which has been widely used and validated [18]. It was developed by a collaborative task force formed from teams from several countries. The task force considered evidence from studies where the adult EQ-5D had been used in younger populations and also considered results from previous qualitative assessments. This evidence was then used to alter the instructions, dimension descriptions and wording of response levels where it was felt necessary [19]. The concepts of the dimensions were kept the same. This means that a key assumption with the EQ-5DY is that the dimensions of the adult measure are also those which are relevant for children. This is an important assumption and one which is acknowledged by the EQ-5DY team, who state that further work may be necessary to confirm these dimensions [20].

The AQoL-6D is a preference-based measure for adolescents and was adapted from an adult preference-based measure, the AQoL8D. Research was undertaken with adolescents to test the semantics and language and the dimensions were reduced accordingly [21]. It is not advised for use in younger children as the domains are specific to adolescents.

The Adolescent Health Utility Measure (AHUM) [22] was developed to measure the impact of chronic conditions on adolescents. In developing this measure, attributes were selected by considering those covered by common adult generic preference-based measures, specifically the EQ-5D and SF-6D. In addition, the developers undertook a review focusing on the impact of childhood conditions and also interviewed children and caregivers with Hunter syndrome due to its wide-ranging impact on health-related quality of life. Interestingly, an attribute on anxiety or emotional impact was intentionally omitted as it was felt that any emotional impact of a health state being valued would already be captured in the process of valuation.

The most recently developed measure, the Child Health Utility 9D (CHU9D), was developed exclusively with children [7]. The dimensions were developed through a series of interviews with children with a wide range of health conditions. These interviews were used to develop dimensions and levels, and the measure subsequently underwent testing in both general and clinical settings [23]. While originally developed with children age 7–11 years, the measure has since been validated in an adolescent population.

Table 13.1 compares the existing generic paediatric preference-based measures in terms of their coverage of dimensions of health-related quality of life. In choosing a suitable preference-based outcome measure for children at the end of life, researchers could opt for one of the existing measures outlined in this table, bearing in mind that these were not designed for specific use in end-of-life populations. While it is possible that they are suitable, it may also be the case that there are important aspects of health that are particularly important to children who are terminally ill but that are not captured by these measures.

There are a number of ethical issues that must be considered when undertaking studies of children, and researchers must be wary of these when selecting a measure of quality of life. In some areas of research, for example, medicine and psychology, there are formal codes of ethics governing what sort of research may or may not be undertaken in children and what constitutes informed consent (General Medical Council, 2006; British Psychological Society, 2006). Such codes affect what information researchers can collect from children and how they may obtain it. The presence of such ethical codes in some disciplines raises a risk that information that is obtained in a way that may be considered unethical or that is obtained without having first been granted the necessary ethical approval, as sometimes occurs (Royal Liverpool Children's Inquiry, 2001), may not be considered legitimate, regardless of whether there is a formal code of conduct in the researchers' own field.

To take one instrument as an example, the CHU9D has not (yet) been specifically validated in an end-of-life population. In its original development phase, a series of interviews was undertaken with children with a wide range of health problems. A decision was taken not to include terminally ill children or those who were permanently in hospital as it was felt that it was not ethical to interview these children who were 7–11 years old about how their health affected their lives. Instead children in schools were recruited. For similar reasons, the CHU9D was not tested in an oncology ward when tested in a clinical setting as it was felt not to be appropriate in such a vulnerable population. The consequences of this approach are that researchers remain unclear about what matters to children with terminal or life-limiting illnesses.

13.3 Who Should Measure and Value Quality of Life in Children?

Another important issue to consider in outcome measurement in children is who should provide the information about their health-related quality of life. There has been a growing recognition that children have their own unique views and a right to

Table 13.1 Domains captured in existing generic preference-based measures of HRQoL for children

CHU9D	HUI2	AQoL 6D	EQ 5D Y	16D	17D	QWB	AHUM
Worried	Emotion	Mental health	Feeling worried, sad or unhappy	Anxiety	Mental function	14 mental health symptoms and behaviours	
Sad					Depression		
Annoyed				Depression	Distress		
Tired				Vitality	Vitality		
Pain	Pain	Pain	Having pain or discomfort	Discomfort and symptoms	Discomfort and symptoms	25 acute physical symptoms	Pain
Sleep				Sleeping	Sleeping		
Daily routine	Self-care	Independent living	Looking after myself	Eating Excretion	Eating Excretion	Social and self care activity	Selfcare
Schoolwork	Cognition		Doing usual activities	School and hobbies	School and hobbies		
				Concentration			
				Learning and memory			
Joining in activities	Mobility		Mobility (walking about)	Mobility	Mobility	Mobility	Mobility
			Doing usual activities			Physical activity	Perceptions of strenuous activities

Sensation	Senses	Vision	Vision		Self-image
	Relationships	Hearing	Hearing		Health perceptions
	Coping	Speech	Speech		
		Friends	Friends		
		Physical appearance	Physical appearance		
		Breathing	Breathing		
				19 chronic symptoms/problems	

express them in matters affecting them [12] (R3). It is also increasingly recognised in clinical trials and health service research more generally that descriptions of the experience of a health state should be elicited from the patients themselves in order to reflect the actual experience of the disease and its treatment [12, 24]. Therefore, there are strong arguments that if they are able, then ideally measurement of health should come directly from children rather than from a proxy, whether this is a parent, health-care professional or someone else. This would require a measure that is reliable and valid for children to self-complete. If children were not able to complete a measure themselves, then it could be interviewer administered, which would still give children the ability to provide information on their health themselves. Getting a measurement of a child's health indirectly, such as through parent/proxy completion, brings with it a risk of bias. For example, there is evidence that the subjective domains in particular child self-reported outcomes and proxy reported outcomes differ [25]. Clearly in some cases, the use of proxies is unavoidable – younger children or those who are very ill will not be able to self-report and so there is no option but to use a proxy report. The CHU9D has been validated for self-completion by children from age 7 years and the EQ-5DY from 8 years. The HUI2 is recommended for self-completion from 13 years.

13.3.1   Who Should Value It?

For a measure to be used to calculate quality-adjusted life years (QALYs), utilities (or preference weights) must exist for each of the health states defined by the descriptive system. On the QALY scale, these preference weights range from 1 (full health) to 0 (equivalent to dead) and can also include negative weights, indicating a health state is judged to be worse than dead. The issue of who should provide these preference weights has been widely debated in the literature, particularly with reference to whether they should be provided by the general population or by patients [26].

There are well-rehearsed arguments that in a publicly funded health-care system, the general public, as rational and informed individuals, should be the ones who provide the preference weights, as they are the ones who potentially bear the opportunity cost of any resource allocation decision. At the core of this argument is that health states obtained from groups of patients with experience of the illness impose opportunity costs on unidentified groups without experience of that illness (but with experience of other illnesses or of future illnesses). The identifiable patient group is given a voice but those who bear the cost of the decisions are not. It would be difficult to accept this as an equitable way of allocating scarce resources (see McCabe et al., Chap. 9, in this volume, for a more detailed discussion of this argument).

Whether preference weights should be obtained from children is a normative issue. Arguments against include that children are not taxpayers and so do not have a financial stake in the distribution of public resources and are not as yet fully rational and informed individuals – after all, many limits are placed on the involvement of children in public life on grounds of age, such as voting, joining the military or the age at which a child is criminally liable for their actions. However, we accept responses from the general population even where respondents are not taxpayers (students, the retired, those not in work for a wide range of reasons) so it would be difficult to exclude children on these grounds. And as Flynn and colleagues argue elsewhere in this volume (Chap. 5), rationality as an assumption in decision making is being increasingly challenged by empirical evidence. The argument in favour of children providing the values includes that children should have a right to have their views heard in matters affecting them, in particular with regard to important issues such as health care [6]. It is important to note that the objection about the equity of giving one group a greater say in distribution of resources would still apply here – we would no more accept child-specific responses than responses from any other group defined solely by age on the grounds of age alone.

If it were accepted that values should be obtained from children, there are two main barriers to doing so. Firstly, the valuation tasks typically used to elicit the preference weights (standard gamble and time trade-off) are cognitively complex. Children, especially younger children, may struggle with understanding the questions asked. In fact there is evidence showing that some adults have difficulty with the questions [27]. Recently, research by Ratcliffe and Stevens has shown promise for the use of ordinal methods in obtaining adolescent preference weights [28], and an adolescent valuation tariff for the CHU9D has now been developed [6]. This is a growing area of future research. Secondly, there are ethical issues with asking children to think about questions that include either a risk of death or trading off a number of life years. It is felt that it is not appropriate to ask children (and in particular younger children) these questions.

13.3.2 Is a QALY to a Child Worth More Than a QALY to an Adult?

The current view of the National Institute for Health and Care Excellence (NICE) is that a QALY is of equal weight regardless of who receives it [29]. Therefore, no distinction is made by age. Some people may argue that a QALY is worth more to a child and therefore should be given a higher weight, and there is some evidence that some in society place a greater weight on health gains accrued by children relative to older people. A review by Dolan and colleagues [30] revealed an incredibly complex range of preferences for health gains by age. Some empirical studies found that people valued health gains for children more highly than gains for the elderly, while others found no preference by age. One study examined whether there was an age preference within a child population and found that health gains for an 8 year old were valued more highly than gains for a 2 year old [31]. There is additional evidence from both the revealed preference and stated preference literature, which seems to indicate an inverted-U-shaped relation between age and the value placed on health gain [32]. Gains accruing to those between the ages of 10 and 40 were rated more highly than gains for those under 10 or over 40 [32]. This is also consistent with the relationship observed between age and the value of a statistical life identified in labour market studies.

From this evidence, it is clear that weighting health gains according to age would be controversial for policy and decision makers. Some decision-making bodies acknowledge that they do think about weighting criteria for different age groups; however, this is not typically done explicitly or through formal methods. While NICE guidelines on technology appraisal processes indicate that there should be no preference for QALYs gained in different age groups, elsewhere in the same document, it is stated that utility values can be adjusted according to age, though no detail is given on the circumstance of when this would be appropriate or how it should be done. This confusion reflects a current challenge in the research community about whether or how QALYs should be weighted across different categories of individuals, including by age, in order to address concerns of equity in resource allocation decisions.

Even were it agreed that equity weights, including for age, should be applied, there are numerous difficulties that arise in trying to develop such weights. Wailoo et al. [33] highlight many of these challenges. Of the problems raised, one with particular relevance to children is the selection of the appropriate time horizon for analysis and weighting. The question is whether additional weight should be given to health gain just during the years of childhood, or should all potential future health gain be weighted according to what happened during childhood? The second challenge is that patient populations are heterogeneous. Where equity weights are considered according to a single characteristic (age, disability, etc.), how should weights be distributed across patients who have more than one of the characteristics of interest?

One such additional characteristic is the end-of-life criteria applied by NICE since 2009. Under these criteria, treatments are assessed against a less-stringent cost-effectiveness threshold than other treatments, if they meet certain conditions. These are (i) that the treatment is indicated for patients with a short life expectancy, normally less than 24 months; (ii) there is sufficient evidence to indicate that the treatment offers an extension to life, normally of at least an additional 3 months, compared to current NHS treatment; and (iii) the treatment is licensed or otherwise indicated, for small patient populations. The de facto effect of these criteria is to apply an equity weight to a particular characteristic of a patient population. In this case that characteristic can be summarised as proximity to death.

There are important methodological issues raised in a situation where there is a conjoint distributional problem – in this case, both an age weighting interacting with an end-of-life weighting. Health economists have paid little attention to the methodological challenges associated with employing equity weights when applied individually. To our knowledge no consideration has been given to the joint application of such weights. The most immediate solution to the problem would be to apply each weight individually in sequence. This in turn gives rise to the problem of what order to consider the weights. Do we consider age first and then apply end-of-life criteria or vice versa?

Table 13.2 An example of a two-characteristic equity-state ranking

	End of life	
Age	Yes	No
0–5	1	3
6–18	2	4
Adult	5	6

A more sophisticated approach would be to estimate joint distributions of preference across a range of equity considerations, generating a series of equity profiles. Patient groups could then be categorised according to an equity profile, with preference given according to a global profile ranking. A two-characteristic (age and end of life) example of how such a profile might look is given in Table 13.2. In this scenario, each of the six possible equity states is ranked according to preference, with the youngest end-of-life patients being given the greatest weight and adult non-end-of-life patients the lowest. With a joint distribution established, the problem is then no different than applying a single equity weight. Such a system raises difficulties of its own in terms of the number of possible equity states and the challenges of ranking them, though these are not on the face of it any different to those faced when defining and ranking health states.

There is also a challenge here about how to consider the displacement implications of adoption decision and the implications for valuing benefits foregone. Recent work using programme budgeting data for the English NHS has sought to estimate economic values for the cost-effectiveness threshold that reflect the displacement implications of adoption decisions and the magnitude of the health forgone [34]. However, this framework is not compatible with individual or group-based equity weights, or indeed any other system of weighting, which depends on characteristics other than patient programme budgeting categories predicated on primary clinical diagnosis. Further research is required to establish the impacts on both efficiency and equity objectives in the presence of equity weighted adoption decisions.

13.4 Which Instrument to Use in Indirect Utility Measurement?

Until relatively recently, research in the area of child and adolescent utility was fairly limited. Instead, outcome measurement and valuation was typically done using an adult measure as there was a lack of indirect utility measures available for children. Now, however, there is a choice, including amongst others, the Health Utilities Index 2 (HUI2), the Child Health Utility 9D (CHU9D), the EQ5DY and the AQoL6D. These all differ in terms of their development methods, ages that they are suitable for, dimensions that they cover, valuation methods and whose values they use. A comparison of some of these features is presented in Table 13.3. A more detailed comparison of these features can be found in the review by Chen and Ratcliffe [35].

Table 13.3 Summary of generic preference-based paediatric health-related quality-of-life measures

Instrument	How was the content generated?	Who completes it?	Valuation methods	Whose values?
CHU9D	Interviews with children	Child or proxy	Standard gamble	UK adult general population
			Best worst scaling	Australian adolescents
HUI2	Literature review followed by views of parent/child	Child or proxy	VAS and standard gamble	Parents (Canada)
			Statistical inference	Adult general population (UK)
AQoL 6D	Adaptation of adult instrument	Adolescent	Time trade-off	Adolescent (Australian)
EQ 5D Y	Adaptation of adult instrument	Child	To be determined	To be determined
16D	Adaptation of adult instrument	Self assessed/interview administered/proxy assessed	Rating scale	Adolescent
17D	Adaptation of adult instrument	Interview administered/proxy assessed	Rating scale	Adult
QWB	Review of health surveys	Interview administered/proxy assessed	Rating scale	Adult
AHUM	Review of existing common adult generic preference-based measures and interviews with children and caregivers with Hunter syndrome	Self-assess	Time trade-off	Adult

13.4.1 Continuity into Adulthood

One issue that has not been resolved is how you deal with measuring outcomes in children and continuing this measurement as they go forward into adulthood. Some interventions in adolescents, for example, may well have health benefits that extend long into adulthood, and we would want to measure these. As child measures may not be applicable in adulthood, one option is to use adult measures after a certain age. However, these will contain different dimensions of health and will have usually different valuation methods. This may make it difficult to compare QALYs gained from an intervention when measured by different instruments. One solution is that you measure what is pertinent and relevant to the individual at their particular life stage using an appropriate instrument. When choosing instruments, the researcher should then consider the valuation methods used and whether the resulting preference weights have the same anchors (i.e. the 0–1 QALY scale). Given the current understanding of quality-of-life measurement, this is likely to give the most comparable and robust results.

However, using different instruments may change what the health-care payer is buying – is a QALY derived from the use of one instrument the same as a QALY derived from the use of an alternative instrument? A number of studies have compared the results of studies measuring outcomes using both the EQ-5D and SF-6D, and it has been found that concurrence between these measures is variable [36, 37]. The closer the domains match between instruments, the greater the likelihood that the health being valued is similar. In the case of the EQ-5DY and EQ-5D, the two instruments cover the same domains, with only the language having changed. While the language used may influence values at the margin, it may be that the degree of divergence is acceptable, as on the face of things what is being measured is broadly the same. But the greater the divergence in the measurement tools, the greater the possible divergence in the underpinning conceptualisation of the utility assigned to a health state. It isn't clear whether a QALY is a QALY if measured using a different tool. But given that many illnesses experienced by adolescents may be chronic or otherwise long lasting, this question deserves further investigation.

Determining which measure to choose is likely to depend on a number of factors. These include:

- The geographical study setting
- The age range of the participants
- The valuation methods
- The range of dimensions covered relevant to the study population
- Whether the measure has been previously validated in a particular clinical population or setting
- Whether the measure aligns to what is recommended by national decision-making bodies

However, the majority of the decision-making bodies around the world do not contain explicit guidelines on what measure to use. For example, the latest guidance from the National Institute for Health and Care Excellence (NICE) in 2013 recommends that the EQ-5D be used for adults, whereas for children it recommends that "consideration should be given to alternative standardised and validated preference-based measures of health-related quality of life that have been designed specifically for use in children" [17] but does not state a measure.

13.4.2 Measuring and Valuing Quality of Life in Children at the End of Life

It is difficult to decide the best approach for measuring and valuing quality of life in children; it is even more difficult to do so when those children are at the end of life. Earlier in this volume (Chap. 2), Johnston raises points of how quality-of-life measurement at the end of life is complicated in ways not seen in other populations, for example, by the way people may view the value of time when approaching the end of life. Elsewhere, Coast and colleagues identify a range of challenges to the analytical framework and commonly used outcome measures when valuing care at the end of life (Chap. 7). In a recent paper, Round and colleagues argue that outcomes based on functioning or capability may not be appropriate for some end-of-life patients and how we might go beyond subjective self-reporting of health to valuing utility derived from the processes of caring [38]. Perhaps the only agreed aspect of measuring outcomes at the end of life is that doing so is difficult and that there are challenges not faced when measuring outcomes in other populations. These challenges apply when thinking about how to measure the quality of life of children at the end of life. But in addition to these, we must consider the issues raised above with respect to measuring HRQoL in children more broadly.

13.5   Conclusion

There is little evidence, either conceptual or empirical, to guide researchers on how to measure outcomes for children at the end of life. In this chapter we have outlined some of the specific difficulties that relate to measuring and valuing outcomes for child populations. Throughout this volume, others have described in detail the serious challenges faced in measuring and valuing outcomes for those at the end of life. Measuring and valuing outcomes for children at the end of life is thus self-evidently difficult!

An added challenge when working with children is that in many cases, these young people will live for considerable lengths of time with life-limiting conditions prior to (a typically premature) death. Some conditions, such as Duchenne's muscular dystrophy, may be present for long periods of a person's life. They have poor prognoses and high care needs, and much of that care is palliative in nature, focusing on symptom management and comfort care rather than curative treatment. Again, there is no agreed way of assessing outcomes of care for this population, despite the high level of care need and concomitant resource requirements.

It is clichéd to come to the end of a journal article or book chapter and state that further research is needed; in this case we believe it is an obvious necessary statement to make. It is difficult to think of a more vulnerable population than children with life-limiting illnesses, especially those near to dying. The care we provide these patients affects not only the individual patient but impacts more widely on families and communities. In this chapter we have highlighted many of the shortcomings in economic evaluation methodology when assessing interventions aimed at children. It is important that in future research when considering how we improve methodology for children, we pay close attention to those most vulnerable.

References

1. Bowling A (2009) Measuring disease: a review of disease-specific quality of life measurement scales, 2nd edn. Open University Press, Buckingham
2. Stevens K (2009) Developing a descriptive system for a new preference-based measure of health-related quality of life for children. Qual Life Res 18(8):1105–1113
3. Harris M, Butterworth G (2002) Developmental psychology: a student's handbook. Taylor & Francis Ltd, New York
4. Matza LS, Swensen AR, Flood EM, Secnik K, Leidy NK (2004) Assessment of health-related quality of life in children: a review of conceptual, methodological, and regulatory issues. Value Health 7(1):79–92
5. Aristotle (1982) Eudemian ethics. In: Woods M (ed) Aristotle's eudemian ethics. Clarendon Press, Oxford, pp EE 1214b30–EE 1214b36
6. Ratcliffe J, Flynn T, Terlich F, Stevens K, Brazier J, Sawyer M (2012) Developing adolescent-specific health state values for economic evaluation: an application of profile case best-worst scaling to the Child Health Utility 9D. Pharmacoeconomics 30(8):713–727
7. Stevens KJ (2010) Working with children to develop dimensions for a preference-based, generic, pediatric, health-related quality-of-life measure. Qual Health Res 20(3):340–351
8. Petrou S (2003) Methodological issues raised by preference-based approaches to measuring the health status of children. Health Econ 12(8):697–702
9. Landgraf J, Abetz L (1996) Measuring health outcomes in pediatric populations: issues in psychometrics and applications. In: Spiker B (ed) Quality of life in pharmacoeconomics and clinical trials, 2nd edn. Lippincott-Raven, Philadelphia, pp 793–802
10. Dolan P (1997) Modeling valuations for EuroQol health states. Med Care 35(11):1095–1108
11. Brazier J, Roberts J, Deverill M (2002) The estimation of a preference-based measure of health from the SF-36. J Health Econ 21(2):271–292
12. United Nations Childrens Fund FACT SHEET: a summary of the rights under the convention on the rights of the child. 19-5-2014. United Nations. 23-6-2015. Ref Type: Online Source
13. Huang IC, Shenkman EA, Madden VL, Vadaparampil S, Quinn G, Knapp CA (2010) Measuring quality of life in pediatric palliative care: challenges and potential solutions. Palliat Med 24(2):175–182
14. Kaplan RM, Anderson JP (1988) The quality of well-being scale: rationale for a single quality of life index. In: Walker S, Rosse R (eds) Quality of life: assessment and application. MTP Press, London, pp 51–77
15. Cadman D, Goldsmith C, Torrance G, Boyle M, Furlong W (1986) Development of a health status index for Ontario children. McMaster University, Hamilton
16. Apajasalo M, Sintonen H, Holmberg C, Sinkkonen J, Aalberg V, Pihko H et al (1996) Quality of life in early adolescence: a sixteen-dimensional health-related measure (16D). Qual Life Res 5(2):205–211
17. Apajasalo M, Rautonen J, Holmberg C, Sinkkonen J, Aalberg V, Pihko H et al (1996) Quality of life in pre-adolescence: a 17-dimensional health-related measure (17D). Qual Life Res 5(6):532–538
18. Brooks R (1996) EuroQol: the current state of play. Health Policy 37(1):53–72
19. Wille N, Badia X, Bonsel G, Burstrom K, Cavrini G, Devlin N et al (2010) Development of the EQ-5D-Y: a child-friendly version of the EQ-5D. Qual Life Res 19(6):875–886
20. Ravens-Sieberer U, Wille N, Badia X, Bonsel G, Burstrom K, Cavrini G et al (2010) Feasibility, reliability, and validity of the EQ-5D-Y: results from a multinational study. Qual Life Res 19(6):887–897

21. Moodie M, Richardson J, Rankin B, Iezzi A, Sinha K (2010) Predicting time trade-off health state valuations of adolescents in four Pacific countries using the Assessment of Quality-of-Life (AQoL-6D) instrument. Value Health 13(8):1014–1027
22. Beusterien KM, Yeung JE, Pang F, Brazier J (2012) Development of the multi-attribute Adolescent Health Utility Measure (AHUM). Health Qual Life Outcomes 10:102
23. Stevens K (2011) Assessing the performance of a new generic measure of health-related quality of life for children and refining it for use in health state valuation. Appl Health Econ Health Policy 9(3):157–169
24. McColl E (2005) Developing questionnaires. In: Fayers P, Hays R (eds) Assessing quality of life in clinical trials, 2nd edn. Oxford University Press, Oxford, pp 9–23
25. Eiser C, Morse R (2001) Quality-of-life measures in chronic diseases of childhood. Health Technol Assess 5(4):1–157
26. Brazier J, Ratcliffe J, Salomon J, Tsuchiya A (2007) Measuring and valuing health benefits for economic evaluation, 1st edn. Oxford University Press, Oxford
27. Dobrez DG, Calhoun EA (2004) Testing subject comprehension of utility questionnaires. Qual Life Res 13(2):369–376
28. Ratcliffe J, Couzner L, Flynn T, Sawyer M, Stevens K, Brazier J et al (2011) Valuing child health utility 9D health states with a young adolescent sample: a feasibility study to compare best-worst scaling discrete-choice experiment, standard gamble and time trade-off methods. Appl Health Econ Health Policy 9(1):15–27
29. National Institute for Health and Care Excellence (2013) Guide to the methods of technology appraisal. National Institute for Health and Clinical Excellence, London
30. Dolan P, Shaw R, Tsuchiya A, Williams A (2005) QALY maximisation and people's preferences: a methodological review of the literature. Health Econ 14(2):197–208
31. Lewis PA, Charny M (1989) Which of two individuals do you treat when only their ages are different and you can't treat both? J Med Ethics 15(1):28–34
32. Baker R, Bateman I, Donaldson C, Jones-Lee M, Lancsar E, Loomes G, Mason H, Odejar M, Pinto Prades JL, Robinson A, Ryan M, Shackley P, Smith R, Sugden R, Wildman J (2010) Weighting and valuing quality-adjusted life-years using stated preference methods: preliminary results from the Social Value of a QALY Project. Health Technol Assess 14(27). doi: http://dx.doi.org/10.3310/hta14270
33. Wailoo A, Tsuchiya A, McCabe C (2009) Weighting must wait: incorporating equity concerns into cost-effectiveness analysis may take longer than expected. Pharmacoeconomics 27(12):983–989
34. Karl C, Steve M, Marta S, Nigel R, Eldon S, Sebastian H, Nancy D, Peter CS, Mark S (2015) Methods for the estimation of the National Institute for Health and Care Excellence cost-effectiveness threshold Health Technology Assessment, No. 19.14, Southampton (UK): NIHR Journals Library
35. Chen G, Ratcliffe J (2015) A review of the development and application of generic multi-attribute utility instruments for paediatric populations. Pharmacoeconomics 33:1013–1028
36. van Stel HF, Buskens E (2006) Comparison of the SF-6D and the EQ-5D in patients with coronary heart disease. Health Qual Life Outcomes 4:20
37. McCrone P, Patel A, Knapp M, Schene A, Koeter M, Amaddeo F et al (2009) A comparison of SF-6D and EQ-5D utility scores in a study of patients with schizophrenia. J Ment Health Policy Econ 12(1):27–31
38. Round J, Sampson EL, Jones L (2013) A framework for understanding quality of life in individuals without capacity. Qual Life Res 23:477–484

Chapter 14
Living Up to a Good Death: Complexities and Constraints in End of Life Choices

Jeff Round and Henry Llewellyn

14.1 Introduction

The concept of choice has gained favour with politicians and policymakers over the past two decades as a means of driving down costs, driving improvements in healthcare and empowering patients in decisions about their care. It is a concept equally taken up by patients and families and now appears to have secured its place as a moral imperative in the public imagination. In the UK NHS, as with other high-income healthcare systems, choice has become a key principle guiding the way that healthcare is organised and delivered, a principle clearly seen in healthcare policies such as the recent white papers *Liberating the NHS: No decision about me, without me* [1] and *Building on the best: choice, responsiveness and equity in the NHS* [2].

Recently, attempts have been made to apply the logic of choice to the context of care at the end-of-life [3]. The *End of life care strategy: Promoting high quality care for all adults at the end of life* [4], for example, emphasises the need to understand patients' preferences and facilitate their choices as they approach the end of life, with a particular focus on where they die. This was furthered in 2014 by a UK government-endorsed independent commission for the purposes of advising on "how to expand choice to improve end-of-life care for adults" [5]. The terms of reference for the review [6] illustrate how choice is seen by policymakers, where it exists not to provide options per se but as a key means of achieving a "good death". Yet, what is

J. Round (✉)
Lecturer in Health Economics, School of Social and Community Medicine,
University of Bristol, Canynge Hall, Bristol, UK
e-mail: j.round@ucl.ac.uk

H. Llewellyn
Marie Curie Palliative Care Research Department, UCL Division of Psychiatry, University
College London, London W1T 7NF, UK

© Springer International Publishing Switzerland 2016
J. Round (ed.), *Care at the End of Life: An Economic Perspective*,
DOI 10.1007/978-3-319-28267-1_14

meant by a good death is unclear and what has been heavily debated within academic literature is, within end-of-life care policy, "treated as a relatively unproblematic ideal and goal" [7, p. 79]. Here, a good death is set around key elements where the dying person dies free of pain and symptoms, in familiar surroundings and in the company of close family. Moreover, principles such as dignity, respect and autonomy are highly valued, principles themselves connected with discourses of choice.

These policy initiatives represent one small albeit visible locus in which the ideal of choice is sketched out and made productive. They sit within a much larger landscape wherein such enterprises as lobby groups, charities and policy think tanks as well as diverse academic communities drive forward to increase the possibilities for patients to decide on their own care and treatment. Within this broader landscape, the idea of choice exists in diverse accounts complicating its application and having important implications for the type and quality of care people receive, how and where they receive it and how they, and those close to them, feel satisfied with that care.

In this chapter, we explore two central accounts of choice: the *market version of choice* and the *civic version of choice*. We introduce the ideas that underpin each version and discuss the ways in which patients are implicated and defined in relation to them. We then discuss how each version becomes complicated in the context of the end of life, taking the ideal of a "good death" (Fig. 14.1) as our central point of reference. Our aim is to outline tensions in the choice agenda and to highlight the complexities inherent in the application of choice to care at the end-of-life.

What does it mean to have a good death?

What it means to have a good death is not something with a simple immutable answer. The notion of a good death changes over time and is dependent on prevailing societal constructs and mores. In the middle ages in Europe a good death (at least for the literate and affluent) might have been communal, religious and one that took place at home, guided perhaps by the *ars moriendi*. The aim was to settle matters in the current life and to free the soul for entry into the afterlife. Death now is more typically private, clinical and secular and is likely to take place in a hospital or other facility where people have access to medical care.

Today in countries with advanced systems of medical practice the process of dying bears little resemblance to the death of the middle ages. Spiritually, less attention is paid to freeing the soul and more to the idea of death as the last great journey, a notion popularised by Kübler-Ross in the 1960s and quickly accepted into the mainstream. The form this journey takes can vary, but the ultimate consequence is that the aim of the dying person should be achieve some form of personal growth, be it spiritual, existential or in personal relationships.

Although there is little obvious connection between the concepts of the good death of the present age and that of the middle ages, perhaps what links them is the notion of taking control over the process of dying. We cannot avoid death, but we can decide how we will approach it. We can free the soul, we can fight battles, we can grow. We have choice – we can die in the place of our choosing and, for some, at the moment of our choosing. Perhaps the societal ideal of good death is to accept that we cannot defeat death but to believe that we can take control of it, to subvert it.

Fig. 14.1 What is a good death?

14.2   Economics: Market Failure and Choice

14.2.1   Market Failure in Healthcare

The conditions necessary for perfect competition to prevail are rarely present in the market for healthcare [8]. In healthcare, markets are characterised by information asymmetry (including between patients and providers as well as that arising from the irreducible uncertainty that is the nature of many illnesses), lack of competition between providers, the presence of public goods and the existence of externalities [8]. Even where markets do exist and function otherwise well, they may still fail to deliver outcomes that satisfy societal objectives other than economic efficiency. Of particular concern with healthcare is where markets fail to achieve objectives relating to equitable access and provision of care across areas such as age, ethnicity, other socio-economic factors and diagnosis. As a result, it is common for governments to act to achieve equity-related goals through high levels of intervention in the market. This leads to a highly regulated market place and thus the power of markets to deliver efficient outcomes is curtailed. Achieving a balance between efficiency and equity goals drives much of health policy.

Achieving efficiency objectives subject to equity constraints (and vice versa) therefore requires further government involvement in healthcare. Bevan and Fasolo [9] provide an overview of the different governance arrangements that might be applied to public systems in order to meet societal aims. They class these as altruism, hierarchy and targets, reputation and choice and competition [9]. In the UK, some manner of each of these variations has been applied with the NHS since its inception.

In the English NHS, all of these governance frameworks have at some time been implemented. The dominant governance approach from the inception of the NHS has been *altruism*, an approach reliant on professional motivations and no external incentives. Bevan [10] argues that this approach led to a system where failures were tolerated and successes ignored. In recent decades focus has switched to methods emphasising external incentives, such as *hierarchy and targets*, provider *reputation* and, most recently, the *choice and competition*-based quasi-market mechanism (for a more detailed overview of the history of NHS governance approaches, see Bevan and Faloso [9]). This competition-based system generates incentives for both consumers and providers of healthcare. It involves more choice for patients over when and where to be cared for and payments to providers based on patient episodes of care. From the perspective of the patient, the quasi-market is believed to lead to benefits through the exercise of choice, giving them greater control over their healthcare and allowing them to determine what aspects of the experience matter most [11]. For providers this quasi market approach encourages them to improve care quality, thereby attracting more patients and more income. To this end, the provision of choice has thus itself become an objective of the English healthcare system – that patients have a choice has come to be seen as a benefit in and of itself [6, 12].

End-of-life care is in this sense no different from any other healthcare market and the choice agenda has influenced end-of-life and palliative care. Patients and the public are routinely questioned as to their preferred places of care and death [13], GP practices are eligible for payment through the quality outcomes framework if they record patients' preferred place of care on palliative care registers [14] and research frequently compares preferred versus actual place of death [13, 15]. This is a natural progression within a policy agenda that prioritises patient choice as a means of improving outcomes. Yet some have questioned the role choice should play in end-of-life care. Can choice over care provision at the end of life be meaningful? Does the economist's assumption of the rational consumer with consistent, stable preferences hold in healthcare, especially at the end of life? What happens to those who lack capacity to express a choice and is choice as a lever of improvement sufficient to ensure that the care they receive will be of high quality irrespective of where it happens? How can choice account for differences in preferences between those providing care, those receiving care and the friends and family of the care recipient?

14.2.2   Homo Economicus

At the core of textbook economic theory is the idea of the individual as a rational, utility maximising agent with preferences, known as expected utility theory. This rational being ranks and then chooses between the available set of goods to consume. As such, the starting point for the classically trained economist when thinking about how people make choices is to consider the rational individual seeking to maximise their utility [8]. The rational individual is one that is assumed to know what they want and will, subject to constraints, act in such a way as to achieve that.

Underlying this idea of preferences are the assumptions of completeness and transitivity.[1] Any set of preferences must be complete in such that when faced with a series of alternatives, the individual must have an opinion on which they prefer. Where there are two alternatives, a and b, the individual should be able to specify whether they prefer a or b or are indifferent between them. The second assumption about transitivity follows from this. The rational individual's preferences must be transitive, such that if the individual prefers a to b, and b to c, they must then prefer a to c. Given these two assumptions, it follows that the rational individual when making a choice will rank all of the available alternatives in a way that satisfies the transitive property and then choose that alternative that will maximise their utility, subject to constraints (such as budget).

So if it is assumed that the patient is a rational agent making utility maximising choices about health and healthcare, then it can be argued that the levers of choice

---

[1]Completeness requires that all possible options are ranked according to preferences between them. Transitivity is the principle that if option a is preferred to b, and b is preferred to c, then a must be preferred to c.

and markets can be used to improve health and healthcare provision. Giving patients greater choice in which goods to consume will lead them to choose those consumption bundles that maximise their utility. Subjecting providers to patient choice will require them to deliver the goods of interest to the patient. This approach puts the patient as consumer at the centre of healthcare decision-making. This is the *choice and competition* approach as described by Bevan and Fasolo [9]. It is argued (most notably by Le Grand [16]) that this approach can harness both altruistic and selfish motives of providers and should be the primary policy lever of governments to improve public services.

Yet accepting the primacy of the *choice* model has significant implications. It requires that in the context of healthcare patients can be rational agents. Recent theoretical and empirical evidence challenges this assumption. This is the subject of Sect. 14.3.

14.3   Deconstructing Homo Economicus

It is increasingly the case that expected utility theory and the idea of the rational agent are being challenged, both in theory and by empirical evidence. Two of the most notable critiques come from outside the realm of economics. The first of these is from a philosophical perspective and is typified by Hausman [17] and the challenges he presents to economists about the way they conceptualise preferences, self-interest and choice. The second is exemplified by Kahneman (e.g. see Thinking Fast and Slow [18]) and focuses on the psychology of decision-making. The earlier work of Kahneman and Tversky [19] led to the development of prospect theory and provided early evidence of the way people actually make choices and how this conflicted with expected utility theory. Over time continued empirical evidence has been generated to illustrate how individuals do not always conform to the assumptions of rationality made about them by economists.

Hausman's [17] critique of the rational agent focuses on the assumed link between preferences, choices and self-interest. In the classical model, as described above, the agent ranks all options and chooses the one that maximises utility subject to constraints. From this process it is argued we learn about people's preferences in one of two ways (Sen, as described by Hausman [17]). The first is that options are ranked according to the expected benefit in terms of the individual's self-interest. The second is that preferences are revealed through choices. Hausman critiques both of these views, and these critiques have important implications for thinking about patient choice at the end of life.

Hausman's first critique focuses on the link between preferences and self-interest or what he calls "expected advantage ranking". Hausman, in discussing Sen's views, describes the standard view of preferences as expected advantage ranking as synonymous with the individual being better off (i.e. having greater utility). In this view a person prefers x to y because they believe they will be better off from x. But as Hausman highlights, a person's preferences may be dependent on many factors that do not directly relate to their own wellbeing. If so, then this view of preferences does not hold. That this is the case in end-of-life decision-making is evident. For example, when discussing place of death, patients often consider the impact of their preferred place to die on their family as well on themselves [3]. We discuss this further in the section citizenship. Clearly for some individuals, preferences are influenced by factors other than their own wellbeing, suggesting merit in the Hausman critique of preferences as self-interest.

In his second critique, Hausman turns to the idea that choices can reveal preferences. In this view, utility maximisation and choice are synonymous and give rise to revealed preference theory. Hausman argues against the idea that choices can define preferences. At the core of this critique is that preferences can only be defined by choices when considered alongside beliefs. That is, it is not possible to say that a person who chooses x over y prefers x unless we understand their beliefs about x and y. In end-of-life care, a person may choose to die in hospital because of a fear of unmanaged pain, whereas their preference would be to die at home. If the patient is made aware of the options available to manage pain at home, they may choose differently to better reflect their preferences. A public policy that assumes that choices reflect preferences – without accounting for beliefs – will potentially lead to suboptimal outcomes. Patients in the current model are placed in a position of having to make choices owing to a set of assumptions about rationality, utility and preferences that may not hold. In addition, they will often be making choices from a position of low information (given the acknowledged information asymmetry that characterises healthcare markets). That these choices are frequently interpreted as preferences in turn distorts the information feedback loop to policymakers, who may see the making of a choice as a positive outcome in itself, given that choice is assumed to reflect preference.

While Hausman focuses on the conceptual links between preferences, choice and welfare, others, notably Kahneman and Tversky, have empirically tested assumptions about rationality and found them wanting [20]. The work of Kahneman and Tversky that led to prospect theory [19, 20] characterises choice as a decision between expected losses and expected gains rather than final assets (or outcomes). In their early experiments, they found that people consistently misestimate the expected gains and losses from decisions and treat decisions in ways that lead to inconsistent preferences, dependent on how the choice is presented [19, 21]. This work has been replicated by others (e.g. see Abdellaoui et al. [22] or Story et al. [23]) and refined so that we now understand in much greater detail the role of heuristics and loss aversion in decision-making. Again, this can be seen in end-of-life care decision-making. Recording the preferred place of death has become an indicator of care quality [14], and many have argued for the opportunity for more patients to die in their preferred location, typically at home [24]. However, it has been found that preferred place of death changes with age, a useful proxy for proximity to death [25, 26]. This may reflect changes in time preference for different outcomes or a greater aversion to losses associated with death occurring in a particular place. Story and colleagues [23] have recently found that people are unlikely to exhibit fully consistent decision-making over time, though stable preferences are an assumption of expected utility theory.

Hausman's critiques of how economists frame preferences in the context of decision-making are highly relevant in healthcare and in end-of-life care. To successfully place the patient as consumer at the core of how health is directed and "done" requires dependence on assumptions about rationality and preferences that arguably do not hold. It is also evident from the empirical work of Kahneman and others that even where we assume rationality, people are poor predictors of the expected advantage of an outcome. Casting patients in the role of consumer in order to drive improvements in the system is dependent on the assumptions about rationality holding. Yet, given the evidence, how can we then assume that patients are capable of making rational decisions in their best interests? On the other hand, despite empirical evidence and arguments against patients as rational consumers, the autonomy of the individual in healthcare decision-making is a key foundation of ethical treatment [27]. From the perspective of the patient at the end of life, it can be agreed that they have a right to be given autonomy over what happens to them and that includes the freedom to make mistakes when choice is viewed through the lens of the utility maximising rational framework. It is clear that patient choice has value beyond the policy context of service improvement. Choice can also be seen as a core part of what constitutes autonomy and how we engage with others in society. In the next section, we discuss an alternative way of framing patients as choosers but not necessarily as economic agents.

14.4   The Civic Version of Choice

The civic version of choice works in different ways to that of the market and conjures different figures for patients. Rather than *consumers*, patients are conceptualised as *citizens* [28]. This section introduces two accounts of citizenship that play on the categories of rights and duties in different ways. After introducing a model of citizenship in which patients are bound to health professionals through particular contracts, we introduce a different way in which citizenship might work. Here, we discuss how the work of choice might be to produce the goal of healthy populations yet how this goal is complicated in the context of the end of life.

14.4.1   The Emancipated Patient

While consumers are foremost defined in relation to markets, citizens are defined in relation to nation-states [28–30]. They are the units of the body politic-given rights and duties through legal diktats. It is through these rights and duties that citizens are supposed to carry the nations of liberal democracies and hence govern themselves. As well as regulating affairs between the people and state, citizenship implies the governance of the affairs between people. This is done through the application of civic laws that frame the relations between people as contracts. These contracts embed a particular configuration of rights and duties to which different parties are bound to respect.

Many countries with highly developed healthcare systems have enshrined sets of "patient laws" that position patients and health professionals as citizens in relation to each other [28]. When a patient seeks out or is referred to a doctor and is brought into contact with them in the context of the clinic, he or she implicitly enters a contract with them. The doctor, by agreeing to help the patient, does similarly. This obliges them each to act according to certain duties and bestows upon them certain rights [28]. Central to the agreement, and underpinning the logic of choice according to the civic version, is the right of the patient to have jurisdiction over interventions into his or her body and life [31]. Health professionals must allow patients to decide what happens to their bodies in the course of the diagnostic and treatment process. In order for patients to do this, health professionals must provide them with "the facts" about the various interventions and record patients' decisions in the form of "consent". As for patients, they must tell the truth and be open with everything that is relevant to their disease, and once a course of action is decided upon, they are expected to adhere to this.

While the market version of choice has been presented as a means towards public service reform, the civic version of choice might be described as a means towards ending medical "paternalism" [31, 32]. Paternalism, characterised by the idea that the "doctor know best", was said to produce patients as passive and unquestioning recipients of care who are subjugated to the will of the doctor. Since its portrayal by the sociologist Talcott Parsons in the mid-twentieth century [33], this asymmetry of power has been approached with much mistrust. It is in this context then that civic laws and codes of conduct attempt to reconfigure the relations between patients and health professionals and imagine an emancipated position for the patient as citizen [28].

14.4.2   The Responsible Citizen

The civic version of choice is, however, not only about celebrating autonomy and self-determination. It is about responsibility [34, 35]. And it is not only about taking responsibility for oneself but also about taking responsibility for oneself in the context of society. In this way, the civic version of choice does not necessarily argue for individual choice as a simple principle [31]. For a nation-state to function properly, it must be healthy, and since citizens are, through the metaphor of the body politic, the units of nation-states, the implication is that they must be healthy too. This idea resonates with observations that chronic illness is increasingly viewed as culpability in the face of known risks and how it is becoming less acceptable to enter and remain in a physically incapacitated state [35]. The patient is reconfigured as taking responsibility for his or her condition and, given information about risk and so on, they should choose to engage in healthy thoughts and behaviours [35]. So in contrast to the paternalism and passivity described by Parsons [33], where the patient was said to occupy a state of "sanctioned deviance" and responsible only for access-ing medical competence and cooperating with medical professionals, patients in the civic version of choice are made responsible in new and different ways.

These new types of responsibility are clearly embedded in policy programmes of health promotion that aim to construct and maintain healthy populations [35]. Such programmes aim by and large to instantiate a condition of self-appraisal and reflex-ivity about health and illness within individuals that turns on the idea of health behaviours [34, 36]. As part of this, programmes aim to condition choices towards activities deemed healthy and away from those deemed unhealthy. Built into these subtle shifts is a language of risk and individual susceptibility that is informed by the science of epidemiology [35, 37, 38]. This works alongside a certain moral qual-ity to health and illness as issues of responsibility and agency are distributed in particular ways along causal pathways [36]. Choice is therefore reconstituted away from simply an individual concern to one that concerns populations, as individuals are to make "responsible choices".

Health has therefore become a moral concern constituting the "affirmation of the life lived virtuously" [39, p. 359]. The healthy person is, in effect, symbolic of the ideal neoliberal citizen, autonomous, active and responsible, while those who devi-ate from this are made morally culpable [35]. In this way, bodies and lives, instead of being the jurisdiction of patients and hence under their control, must be subju-gated according to a set of moral parameters that is determined by the body politic [28]. But what does it mean to be a responsible citizen at the end of life when the goal of health is no longer possible? And what responsible choices should citizens at the end of life make? At the heart of these questions is the issue of what it means to die well.

14.4.3 Citizenship at the End of Life

Dying well has been a cultural preoccupation for centuries with the *ars moriendi* ("The Art of Dying") among the earliest and most famous guides to dying and death in a Western literary tradition. Written in the early fifteenth century, the tract was intended to bring comfort and practical instruction to the dying man and his family according to the Christian precepts of the late Middle Ages. Among these precepts are exhortations that the dying make peace with their maker, avoid temptations like despair, impatience and avarice and approach death without fear. In the Middle Ages, these exhortations underpinned what it meant to die responsibly.

Yet the "ars moriendi" of the Middle Ages is very different to the "good death" of modern societies [40]. While it was religion that undergirded earlier instruction, it is perhaps medicine that sets the frame in modern times, and whereas death was assumed to come quickly to people through infectious and unmanageable disease, we now live in a time when we are struggling to learn how to die from degenerative diseases and old age [40]. It is in modern care practices that the question of how to die is bound up with practical questions and an ever-expanding list of choices about where we should die, what technologies should be available and used, what should be taken away and, for cultures where euthanasia is an option, exactly *when* to die. In the modern world, patients at the end of life are called upon to design their own deaths, whether viewed as consumers or citizens.

However, the practices and technologies we deploy in designing our deaths appear to evolve faster than the moral frameworks guiding their use [41, 42]. This is reflected by a cultural ambiguity in which social norms around dying and the application of technologies are so fragmented as to become meaningless and nonexistent. We want deaths that are natural yet to know that we have tried everything. We want to be heroic and fight death yet graceful in our acceptance that the time has come. Such ambiguity is compounded by a rhetoric that we, as individuals, should author our own scripts for dying as we do for living [40]. The responsible citizen at the end of life is therefore located betwixt and between multiple and conflicting narratives about what it means to die well; we die amid this cultural ambiguity.

In summary, patients according the civic version of choice are made autonomous, defined in relation to the state and bound to health professionals by sets of patient laws. However, their emancipation into citizens implies new responsibilities for health and an underlying logic for patients to make the right choices in accord with what is publicly configured as the moral standard. These standards have been constructed and recently used in programmes that attempt to fashion healthy populations. Citizenship, then, makes patients individuals in the image of the population and takes its shape in relation to the nature of the state [30, 43]. It therefore represents both an impetus to act and a constraint upon acting [44], generating the paradox of the "patient chooser": agents who are free to choose but systems that work upon them to guide their choices towards prescribed ends. However, what patients, as citizens, internalise about the choices they should make at the end of life is increasingly vacuous and contradictory. Whether this is liberating or frightening, an opportunity or itself a constraint remains to be seen.

14.5   Living Up to a Good Death

Choice is a complex phenomenon and the previous sections have introduced two versions of choice and a number of contexts that turn on and shape what choice means. Two main figures of the patient have been introduced: the patient as consumer who, rational and informed, makes choices according to preference, as ascribed by the conditions of the market, and the patient as citizen who has rights and duties that are ascribed through civic laws and social norms. It has also been introduced how these versions of choice position patients as instruments of change that allow either the reform of services or the maintenance of a healthy population.

The models of choice as presented here make the patient, whether consumer or citizen, responsible for their own health and thus responsible for the quality of their own death and by proxy for living up to the ideal of a good death. In the market framework, the patient who is ill or dies a poor death (however defined) because they failed to make choices has thus failed to exercise their rights as a consumer. In the patient as a citizen view, the patient who falls ill is considered responsible if they have failed to conform to the norms or diktats urging them to live a healthy life or to die in a socially sanctioned fashion. A further complication here is the ambiguity that surrounds these norms, whether to die a "natural" death accepting that now is our time or to fight death through the application of an ever-expanding list of technologies. So dying is at once constrained by norms yet made ambiguous by the continual fragmentation of these norms. While this might appear to set a structure in which "anything goes", in practice, some forms of dying are made acceptable and others unacceptable. This belies the social contexts in which choices are made, contexts that appear to be absent from choice policy where instead decisions are presented as the private concerns of the individual [3, 28].

Within the NHS, much policy is conceived within a framework of the patient as consumer [45]. The thinking goes that if market conditions can be recreated in a non-market setting, then this will drive up standards [11] (and in some cases choice has been shown to improve outcomes [46]). But within this market patients are constrained by the choices that are made available to them by the institutions providing the service. For example, many treatments are only approved for access if they demonstrate cost-effectiveness. While this is an appropriate way to allocate scarce resources and achieve societal objectives in healthcare, it is inconsistent with the idea of the patient as consumer exercising choice. Choices are limited in other ways. Patients may choose a particular hospital or service, but they may not choose a specific clinician [45]. If the quality of clinical practice varies within a service, then choice here is in some sense meaningless – if the purpose of introducing choice was justified for clinical performance reasons, restricting choice of clinician prevents this.

Improvements in clinical performance are not the only justification for the introduction of choice in care. The dying patient may also be offered a choice of where to die for more patient-centred reasons, such as the chance to have the death they want near to family or free from pain. Again here we see the contradictory influences of different models of choice at work. The burden of providing a good death is shifted from those providing care to those receiving it. If a patient fails to exercise choice over where or how to die, they have failed as consumers and citizens to exercise their autonomy. If they do make a choice but then do not receive the care they might need, they can be said to have chosen poorly.

In essence, whatever the model of choice implemented, the result is the restriction of that choice to a series of options presented as if a menu to the patient. The patient is free to choose, so long as they choose from the given menu. At the end of life, the patient as citizen might choose to die fighting or to die accepting death and in both cases surrounded by loved ones. But what seems unacceptable is to die scared, alone and in denial, for this would offend socially sanctioned responses to dying. Things are little different for the patient as consumer who must choose how and where to die well in advance of the event, irrespective of the fact that until the time comes, they will be unaware of what the experience is like. If, during their last days and weeks, a person decides they have chosen poorly what they are unfortunate for, unlike goods in most other markets, there is no second chance to get it right in end-of-life care.

References

1. Department of Health (2012) Liberating the NHS: no decision about me, without me – further consultation on proposals to secure shared decision-making
2. Lawrence Z (2004) Building on the best – choice, responsiveness and equity in the NHS. Health Expect 7(2):176–179
3. Borgstrom E, Walter T (2015) Choice and compassion at the end of life: a critical analysis of recent English policy discourse. Soc Sci Med 136:99–105
4. Department of Health (2008) End of life care strategy: promoting high quality care for all adults at the end of life
5. HM Government (2014) Choice in end of life care: independent review. 7-8-2015. Ref Type: Online Source
6. HM Government (2015) Draft terms of reference for the review to consider a national choice offer for end of life care to support people's preferences about how and where to have good end of life care. 7-8-2015. Ref Type: Online Source
7. Borgstrom E (2014) Planning for death? An ethnographic study of English end-of-life care. University of Cambridge, Cambridge
8. Morris S, Devlin NJ, Parkin D (2007) Economic analysis in health care, 1st edn. John Wiley and Sons, Ltd, Chichester
9. Bevan G, Fasolo B (2013) Models of governance of public services: empirical and behavioural analysis of 'econs' and 'humans'. In: Oliver A (ed) Behavioural public policy. Cambridge University Press, Cambridge, pp 38–62
10. Bevan G (2010) Approaches and impacts of different systems of assessing hospital performance. J Comp Pol Anal 12(2):33–56
11. NHS England (2013) Putting patients first: the NHS England business plan for 2013/14–2015/16
12. NHS Choices (2015) Personal health budgets. 26-1-2015. 7-8-2015. Ref Type: Online Source
13. MarieCurieCancerCare(2011)Preferencesforplaceofdeath.Availablefrom:http://www.mariecurie. org.uk/en-gb/press-media/news-comment/marie-curie-welcomes-palliative-care-funding-review/
14. Royal College of General Practitioners (2006) Palliative care and the GMS contract quality and outcomes framework (QOF). 1-3-2006. 21-2-2013. Ref Type: Pamphlet
15. Higginson IJ, Astin P, Dolan S (1998) Where do cancer patients die? Ten-year trends in the place of death of cancer patients in England. Palliat Med 12(5):353–363
16. Le Grand, Julian (2003) Motivation, agency, and public policy: of knights and knaves, pawns and queens. Oxford University Press, Oxford, UK
17. Hausman, Daniel M. (2012) Preference, value, choice and welfare. Cambridge University Press, New York
18. Kahneman, Daniel (2011) Thinking, Fast and Slow. Allen Lane, London
19. Kahneman D, Tversky A (1979) Prospect theory – analysis of decision under risk. Econometrica 47(2):263–291
20. Tversky A, Kahneman D (1981) The framing of decisions and the psychology of choice. Science 211(4481):453–458
21. Tversky A, Kahneman D (1992) Advances in prospect-theory – cumulative representation of uncertainty. J Risk Uncertain 5(4):297–323
22. Abdellaoui M, Bleichrodt H, L'Haridon O (2008) A tractable method to measure utility and loss aversion under prospect theory. J Risk Uncertain 36(3):245–266
23. Story GW, Vlaev I, Dayan P, Seymour B, Darzi A, Dolan RJ (2015) Anticipation and Choice Heuristics in the Dynamic Consumption of Pain Relief. PLoS Comput Biol 11(3):e1004030. doi:10.1371/journal.pcbi.1004030
24. Gomes B, McCrone P, Hall S, Koffman J, Higginson IJ (2010) Variations in the quality and costs of end-of-life care, preferences and palliative outcomes for cancer patients by place of death: the QUALYCARE study. BMC Cancer 10:400

25. Munday D, Petrova M, Dale J (2009) Exploring preferences for place of death with terminally ill patients: qualitative study of experiences of general practitioners and community nurses in England. BMJ 339:b2391
26. Higginson IJ, Sen-Gupta GJ (2000) Place of care in advanced cancer: a qualitative systematic literature review of patient preferences. J Palliat Med 3(3):287–300
27. Gillon R (2003) Ethics needs principles – four can encompass the rest – and respect for autonomy should be "first among equals". J Med Ethics 29(5):307–312
28. Mol A (2008) The logic of care: health and the problem of patient choice. Routledge, London
29. Marshall TH (1992) Citizenship and social class. Pluto, London
30. Turner BS (1989) Aging, status politics and sociological-theory. Br J Sociol 40(4):588–606
31. Mol A (2002) The body multiple: ontology in medical practice. Duke University Press, London
32. Coulter A (2002) The autonomous patient: ending paternalism in medical care. TSO/The Nuffield Trust, Norwich
33. Parsons T (1951) The social system. Collier-Macmillan, London
34. Armstrong D (2014) Actors, patients and agency: a recent history. Sociol Health Illn 36(2):163–174
35. Galvin R (2002) Disturbing notions of chronic illness and individual responsibility: towards a genealogy of morals. Health 6(2):107–137
36. Cohn S (2014) From health behaviours to health practices: an introduction. Sociol Health Illn 36(2):157–162
37. Castel R (1991) From dangerousness to risk. In: Burchell R (ed) The foucault effect. Harvester Wheatsheaf, Hemel Hempstead
38. Lupton D (1995) The imperative of health: public health and the regulated body. Sage, London
39. Leichter HM (1997) In: Rozin P, Brandt A (eds) Lifestyle correctness and the new secular morality. Routledge, New York
40. Walter T (2003) Historical and cultural variants on the good death. BMJ 327(7408):218–220
41. Kaufman SR (2005) And a time to die: Ho American hospitals shape the end of life. Simon and Schuster, London
42. Kaufman SR (2000) In the shadow of "death with dignity": medicine and cultural quandaries of the vegetative state. Am Anthropol 102(1):69–83
43. Mann M (1987) Ruling-class strategies and citizenship. Sociol J Br Sociol Assoc 21(3):339–354
44. Burchell D (2002) Ancient citizenship and its inheritors. In: Isin E, Turner B (eds) Handbook of citizenship studies. Sage, London
45. Department of Health (2014) 2014/15 choice framework. Department of Health
46. Cooper Z, Gibbons S, Jones S, McGuire A (2011) Does hospital competition save lives? Evidence from the English Nhs patient choice reforms. Econ J 121(554):F228–F260